Interpreting at the First Frankfurt Auschwitz Trial

BLOOMSBURY ADVANCES IN TRANSLATION SERIES

Series Editor:
Jeremy Munday, Centre for Translation Studies, University of Leeds, UK

Bloomsbury Advances in Translation publishes cutting-edge research in the fields of translation studies. This field has grown in importance in the modern, globalized world, with international translation between languages a daily occurrence. Research into the practices, processes and theory of translation is essential and this series aims to showcase the best in international academic and professional output.

A full list of titles in the series can be found at:
www.bloomsbury.com/series/bloomsbury-advances-in-translation

Titles in the series include:

Celebrity Translation in British Theatre, Robert Stock
Collaborative Translation, edited by Anthony Cordingley and Céline Frigau Manning
Community Translation, Mustapha Taibi and Uldis Ozolins
Corpus-Based Translation Studies, edited by Alet Kruger, Kim Wallmach and Jeremy Munday
Extending the Scope of Corpus-Based Translation Studies, edited by Sylviane Granger and Marie-Aude Lefer
Genetic Translation Studies, edited by Ariadne Nunes, Joana Moura and Marta Pacheco Pinto
Global Trends in Translator and Interpreter Training, edited by Séverine Hubscher-Davidson and Michał Borodo
Institutional Translation for International Governance, Fernando Prieto Ramos
Intercultural Crisis Communication, edited by Federico M. Federici and Christophe Declercq
Islamic State in Translation, Balsam Mustafa
Music, Text and Translation, edited by Helen Julia Minors
The Pragmatic Translator, Massimiliano Morini
Quality in Professional Translation, Joanna Drugan
Retranslation, Sharon Deane-Cox

Sociologies of Poetry Translation, Jacob Blakesley
Systemic Functional Linguistics and Translation Studies, edited by Mira Kim, Jeremy Munday and Zhenhua Wang
Theatre Translation, Massimiliano Morini
Translation, Interpreting and Technological Change, edited by Marion Winters, Sharon Deane-Cox and Ursula Böser
Translating for Singing, Ronnie Apter and Mark Herman
Translating Holocaust Lives, edited by Jean Boase-Beier, Peter Davies, Andrea Hammel and Marion Winters
Translating the Poetry of the Holocaust, Jean Boase-Beier
Translating in Town, edited by Lieven D'hulst and Kaisa Koskinen
Translation and Interpreting as Social Interaction, edited by Claire Y. Shih and Caiwen Wang
Translation Solutions for Many Languages, Anthony Pym
Telling the Story of Translation, Judith Woodsworth
Vladimir Nabokov as an Author-Translator, Julie Loison-Charles
Walter Benjamin and Cultural Translation, Birgit Haberpeuntner
What Is Cultural Translation? Sarah Maitland

Interpreting at the First Frankfurt Auschwitz Trial

How is a Witness Heard?

Peter Davies

BLOOMSBURY ACADEMIC
LONDON • NEW YORK • OXFORD • NEW DELHI • SYDNEY

BLOOMSBURY ACADEMIC
Bloomsbury Publishing Plc, 50 Bedford Square, London, WC1B 3DP, UK
Bloomsbury Publishing Inc, 1385 Broadway, New York, NY 10018, USA
Bloomsbury Publishing Ireland, 29 Earlsfort Terrace, Dublin 2, D02 AY28, Ireland

BLOOMSBURY, BLOOMSBURY ACADEMIC and the Diana logo are trademarks of Bloomsbury Publishing Plc

First published in Great Britain 2025

Cover design: Jade Barnett

A catalogue record for this book is available from the British Library.

Library of Congress Cataloging-in-Publication Data
Names: Davies, Peter, author.
Title: Interpreting at the first Frankfurt Auschwitz Trial : how is a witness heard? / Peter Davies.
Description: London ; New York : Bloomsbury Academic, 2025. | Series: Bloomsbury advances in translation | Includes bibliographical references and index. | Summary: "Exploring the work of interpreters and translators at the First Frankfurt Auschwitz Trial, this book asks vital questions about how victims of genocide can make their voices heard in legal systems, and the processes by which the testimony of Holocaust survivors has entered the public record. The author discusses interpreters' professional practice and ethical self-understanding in the unequal linguistic and institutional structures of the courtroom, showing how interpreting and translation affected the way victims' voices were heard. He explores the contribution of interpreting and translation to the developing memory of the Holocaust in the 1960s and to the public image of the survivor-witness"– Provided by publisher.
Identifiers: LCCN 2024050816 (print) | LCCN 2024050817 (ebook) |
ISBN 9781350469648 (hardback) | ISBN 9781350469686 (paperback) |
ISBN 9781350469662 (epub) | ISBN 9781350469655 (ebook)
Subjects: LCSH: Auschwitz Trial, Frankfurt am Main, Germany, 1963–1965. | Trials (Genocide)–Germany–Frankfurt am Main. | Holocaust survivors–Legal status, laws, etc.–Germany. | Jehovah's Witnesses–Nazi persecution. | Preliminary examinations (Criminal procedure)–Germany–History. |
Auschwitz (Concentration camp) | Holocaust, Jewish (1939–1945)–History–Sources.
Classification: LCC KK73.5.A98 D38 2025 (print) | LCC KK73.5.A98 (ebook)
| DDC 345.43/0238–dc23/eng/20241105
LC record available at https://lccn.loc.gov/2024050816
LC ebook record available at https://lccn.loc.gov/2024050817

ISBN: HB: 978-1-3504-6964-8
ePDF: 978-1-3504-6965-5
eBook: 978-1-3504-6966-2

Series: Bloomsbury Advances in Translation

Typeset by Newgen KnowledgeWorks Pvt. Ltd., Chennai, India

For product safety related questions contact
productsafety@bloomsbury.com.

To find out more about our authors and books visit www.bloomsbury.com
and sign up for our newsletters.

Contents

Acknowledgments

Much of the initial research and discussion for this project was carried out during the Covid-19 pandemic, meaning that everybody who contributed, read, discussed, critiqued, and supported what I was doing went an extra mile at a time when their own lives were turned upside down. They could have found a dozen good reasons not to help, but they did anyway, and that means everything.

First of all, I am indebted to the Leverhulme Trust, whose generous support with a Major Research Fellowship made this work possible. I would also like to extend my gratitude to Sybille Steinbacher of the Fritz Bauer Institute, who donated time and support for the project from the start and has given me the opportunity to discuss and develop the work at the institute. The institute's resources, especially the digitized recordings and already prepared transcriptions, made an otherwise impossible task doable.

I have also benefitted enormously from a collaboration with colleagues from the institute, in particular Katharina Stengel and Sara Berger, who have given me new perspectives and opened new doors. I also thank the institute's archivist, Johannes Beermann-Schön.

I've bent the ears of numerous colleagues at Edinburgh University about the project over the years, but there are a few that need special mention. My fellow adventurers in Translation Studies have always helped me see what is important, and Charlotte Bosseaux and Hephzibah Israel took time to read and improve my initial application so that it asked the right questions. The same goes for Greg Walker, who helped me knock it into shape when it needed it, and Laura Tomlinson, who made everything work.

Special thanks go to people who took time to read and comment on my work, which is a generous use of a limited resource: I mention here in particular Hannah Holtschneider, who has been an important interlocutor for many years. I'm also indebted to Roma Sendyka and Magda Heydel for helping me see the Polish perspective of this translation complex more clearly. I have had invaluable language advice from Beata Kohlbek and Eva Goletz: Dziękuję bardzo!

A project like this would be nothing without archivists: I am especially grateful to the cheerfully *zuvorkommend* archivists of the Hessisches Hauptstaatsarchiv in Wiesbaden and also to Elise Bath of the International Tracing Service, Alon

Tauber of the Zentralarchiv zur Erforschung der Geschichte der Juden in Deutschland, and Heike Drummer of the Frankfurt Jewish Museum. I am also grateful to the Nederlands Instituut voor Beeld en Geluid for access to archive material.

Ian Foster and Beate Müller wrote vital references for the project, which set me on this journey. Helen Finch, Dorota Głowacka, and Anna Hájková have been unfailingly supportive, and I'm grateful to many others for conversations and opportunities, including Kathrin Stoll, Jenny Watson, Andrea Rudorff, Dominic Williams, Christoph Thonfeld, Sheila Jelen, Anabel Carballo Mesa, plus Julia Przybytek for some important references, and Sherry Simon for my first trip to Montreal.

Note on Translations and Sources

I have translated sources into English in cases where the precise qualities of language are not important for the discussion. Otherwise, I leave the text in the original and provide a guideline English translation below: this applies mostly to the words of the survivor-witnesses and to the interpreted exchanges in court.

References to the recorded courtroom exchanges are made in the main text, with the date and the time in the recording in minutes. With the name of the witness, this enables a reader to locate the digitized recording of the testimony in the freely available online resource curated by the Fritz Bauer Institute, Frankfurt am Main: https://www.auschwitz-prozess.de/. The testimonies are listed by date and name of the witness and are easily accessible and searchable in order to find the testimony and the moment being discussed.

Each testimony has a transcript, which is also searchable, but I have made my own for the purposes of this study. My transcriptions often differ from those provided on the website, so it will not always be possible to use text searches.

My major archive resource has been the trial archive, held at the Hessisches Hauptstaatsarchiv, Wiesbaden (HHStAW). The archive of the First Frankfurt Auschwitz Trial itself, within the archive of the Frankfurt Prosecutor's Office (HHStAW Abt. 461 LG Frankfurt a. M., 4 Ks 2/63, 37638/1–456), has UNESCO status and is digitized and freely available online through the portal of the HHStAW. To conform with the in-text referencing system, I have abbreviated references to this specific archive in the text to series/piece, item, for example, 37638/19, 18150; where there are page numbers within the item, I give them as p., and where there is no item (Blatt) number I use the abbreviation o. Bl. (ohne Blatt). On occasion, where there are important documents without item number, as in the *Kostenbände* (records of expenses) for the trial (found in 37638/190-211), I have given the page number of the digitized version of the document. For material from other archives, I give the reference in full.

Abbreviations

BDÜ	Bundesverband der Dolmetscher und Übersetzer e.V. (Federal Association of Interpreters and Translators)
IAC	International Auschwitz Committee
StPO	Strafprozessordnung (Code of Criminal Procedure)
WJC	World Jewish Congress
ZuSEG	Gesetz über die Entschädigung von Zeugen und Sachverständigen (law concerning the remuneration of witnesses and expert witnesses)

Introduction: The Trial

On March 4, 1965, in a courtroom in Frankfurt during what has become known as the First Frankfurt Auschwitz Trial, the survivor George Preston (born Grisza Priszkulnik in Rivne in 1914) confronts the former prisoner functionary Emil Bednarek and, seemingly losing control of himself, begins to shout. Identifying him as a man who had brutally beaten the inmates in his block at the slightest provocation, but comparing his memory with the rather ordinary looking man sitting among the accused, Preston declares in a loud voice in English that he knows him but "oh, he got fat … Yes, sir, he got greatly fat." He also for a brief moment challenges the court's authority, declaring a desire for vengeance: "I wish I could have my justice to you … I wish I could do justice under a different law" (4.3.1965, 93'). The courtroom, for a moment, becomes a stage for a clash between different conceptions of truth, justice, power, and permitted language.

After the Presiding Judge Hans Hofmeyer calls on him to take his seat again, Preston apologizes for his words, and the testimony concludes soon afterward. The witness's outburst interrupts the ritualistic order of the questioning, threatening not only the accused but also the authority of the judge, who has to intervene to restore order. Preston challenges a set of conventions about what kinds of speech are permitted in this courtroom, and his apology (at least, to judge by his tone of voice) seems to be meant only as a formality so that the court can return to its work and restore the interactional order.

This dramatic moment causes problems for another individual in the room: Franz Schuh, the German–English interpreter. Preston has used a moment of transition between different modes of communication in court—going from the formal structure of question and answer, where he is seated, to a ritual of identification, where the witness stands and approaches the defendants—for his own purposes. The interpreter has a different role in each of these frameworks, but Preston's improvisation produces a situation that has no established patterns.

Schuh loses his concentration, interpreting only small snippets of what is being said and seeming to laugh at one point.

On further listening, it becomes clear that Preston has by no means lost control: he knows what he is doing, taking advantage of the change in communicative frame to pursue his own ends with a sense for the dramatic. He does not shout wildly but makes short, clear, loud, simple statements, pausing after each one: apparently waiting for the interpreter to work, exploiting the rhythms of consecutive interpreting, in order to increase the impact of his own words. Thus, the presence of the interpreter contributes to structuring the communication, even when he is unable to work. Franz Schuh is a direct participant, affecting the interaction, but what he lacks is the authority to restore order himself when things break down: only the intervention of the judge can achieve this.

On the recording of the incident, we hear Preston in the background, at some distance from the microphone on the witnesses' table, while Schuh's struggles are very close to us as listeners: the way the source is structured at this moment of confusion draws attention away from the witness and his outburst and toward the interpreter. We as listeners are aware of him in a way that the listeners in the courtroom may also not be, as they are presumably concentrating on what Preston is shouting. The source therefore gives us access to aspects of the testimony situation that are often disregarded, namely the vital role of the interpreter, not only in making testimony understood but also in shaping how the stories are told. This is a striking moment of failure, which makes things visible that often go unnoticed, but we also need to ask: what is happening when things appear to be going well? What can we hear now that was not heard at the time? How are the testimonies of Holocaust survivors in court shaped by the work of interpreters? Who were the people who did this work, and how did they approach their tasks?

Coming only a few years after the trial of Adolf Eichmann in Jerusalem, this scene may have reminded spectators of similar moments when Holocaust survivors confronted and denounced a perpetrator in open court, breaking for a moment the established rules of communication. In the Jerusalem court, as at Nuremberg, Tokyo, and many other subsequent post-genocide tribunals, where simultaneous interpreting was used, participants who could not understand the language of the statement experienced the short lag (the *décalage*) between the speaker's embodied words live and the interpreted speech in a disembodied voice through headphones. It is possible for the listener to concentrate only on the voice in the headphones for long stretches—it is much less effort—but outbursts, gestures, or other kinds of action that break the standard frame of courtroom discourse can draw the listener back in suddenly. The listener becomes aware of the experiencing, feeling, suffering body that speaks; the voices are reembodied in a moment of shock, though their words may not be understood. The procedures of simultaneous interpreting, supported by electronic and mechanical devices, structure the experience of testimony in this specific way.

The Frankfurt court did not employ the technological solutions used for the international tribunals, instead organizing the proceedings as a "normal" trial, with the interpreter sitting at a table with the witness, interpreting consecutively rather than simultaneously, so that their voices are heard together, and a relationship develops between them. It is a relationship of intimacy and tension, collaboration and conflict, within a structure of power that makes ethical demands of the interpreters: they are responsible for ensuring that a survivor of genocidal violence can speak, while also upholding the rhythms and hierarchies of the courtroom exchanges and protecting their own professional reputation.

The German-Polish-Russian interpreter Wera Kapkajew, who we will regularly encounter in this study, wrote in 1966, after the trial was over: "I believe that there has scarcely ever been a trial where such demands have been made of an interpreter" ("Kostenband für Frau Kapkajew," 1964–7, 37638/210, p. 41). Kapkajew was the only one of the translators and interpreters who left any public commentary about her experiences, but we do have some remarkable statements from her that give us an idea of the pressures that the interpreters came under during very long testimonies dealing with unimaginable horrors. As the interpreter who worked in open court with all but two of the eighty-odd Polish-speaking witnesses, and all the five Russian-speaking ones, she became well known, taking on a form of celebrity among journalists, as well as leaving clear memories with some of the witnesses. There are a couple of statements that she made toward the end of the trial, in summer 1965, that introduce many of the themes of this study and show how an interpreter can reflect on the questions raised by Franz Schuh's struggles to deal with George Preston's testimony.

In an interview with Uwe-Jens Petersen for the *Frankfurter Rundschau* newspaper, which had been closely following the trial, Kapkajew, whom Petersen refers to as Germany's most famous interpreter, is asked whether her work simply becomes routine. No, she replies, "I worry with every new witness about whether I catch the tone of his voice properly" (Petersen 1965: 265). Successful interpreting, in this view, is about understanding the voice of the witness and performing it in such a way that the listeners experience it directly; or perhaps more precisely, that they experience the interpreter's understanding of the voice.

In an interview with a Dutch television news program on August 19, 1965, released to coincide with the reading of the final verdict, Kapkajew goes further. When asked whether she identifies with the victims, she produces this complex answer:

> With the witnesses, one had to, not to identify with them, that is probably going too far, but to slip into the skin of the witness, and to completely become the witness as much as possible, to convey everything with his words, exactly as he does, choosing particular expressions exactly as he does, with derision in the voice or disapproval in the voice, with passion or the opposite, with a very great distance. (Wage 1965)

She is careful to avoid the idea of "identifying with the witnesses," an understandable caution when thinking about people whose experiences we cannot really share. Her answers show that she has ethical doubts about the temptation to claim the position of the victim. Nevertheless, her words show a tension between this ethical uncertainty and a view of professional practice that goes beyond simply imitating the manner of the witness.

She also talks about the need for the interpreter herself to preserve a professional distance while working and the resulting psychological and physical exhaustion:

> In the evening, when you come home, when you are interpreting for eight hours, when you experience a particular person's fate with them, and convey it, at that moment you feel nothing. You are the person who is doing that, so you experience it and convey it. And then one comes home and switches off, and then one feels like a squeezed lemon, there is no other way of saying it.

Aside from the physical exhaustion of eight-hour shifts, her choice of words to describe the psychological effects of interpreting is telling: the repetition of "erleben" (experience) shows an understanding of her work as sharing an experience with the witness. There is also a telling switch between "Sie" (you) and "man" (one) in her story, suggesting complex processes of distancing and self-observation.

She then tells an extraordinary story about developing sympathetic symptoms, which may give us an idea of the psychological pressure of the work or how she interpreted symptoms of stress or sickness. When the interviewer asks her whether the stress of work led to her becoming ill, she replies:

> Yes, and that was a remarkable story, that I—have to, I have to connect it in some way with the trial, because while I was working I developed a phlegmon—a

> condition that is typical for life in the concentration camps. All the witnesses reported, some more and some less, about cases of phlegmon, that they were sick, or that someone else died of it. In some way there was always talk of phlegmon, and in 1964, without having been through a concentration camp or being in a camp, I suddenly developed a 42-degree fever, blood poisoning in my arm, and was in hospital for 4 weeks.

Responding to this story, the interviewer presses her on the question of identification: "And in this way you identified with them, is that right?" Again avoiding the word "identify," her reply is fascinating: "That was how I experienced and lived through the trial with the witnesses" (So habe ich den Prozess mit den Zeugen miterlebt und durchlebt). The interviewer is clearly working toward a desire for identification with the witnesses, but Kapkajew carefully evades the question. Her insistence on words in the field "erleben/miterleben/durchleben" (experience/share an experience/live through) is striking: the interpreter vicariously experiences and lives through the trial with and for the witnesses.

Perhaps this is the ethical core: it is not a question of claiming an illegitimate position as victim or being able to identify with the experience of Auschwitz but instead sharing the experience of giving testimony as a form of solidarity. Avoiding the term "identification" used by the interviewer also shows a sensitivity to potential accusations of bias. In discussing her practice, she does not talk about her professional responsibility to the court but instead positions herself within a broader social discourse about authenticity and the voice of the witness, with an accompanying sense of how problematic this is.

The crisis of communication in the testimony of George Preston and the comments made by Kapkajew about her practice give us insight into what was at stake in the courtroom for interpreters and thus for the Holocaust survivors who had arrived in Frankfurt to give testimony. German courts did not require this kind of imitative performance from interpreters, so there is clearly more happening here than simple adherence to professional standards: beyond the questions of justice and evidence, the courtroom is the scene for a dramatic negotiation about the quality and value of the voices of survivor-witnesses and how they are heard. Many questions arise here. Under what conditions can a witness speak, and how exactly are they heard? How much influence and agency do they have in telling their stories when working with an interpreter within the unequal power structures of a courtroom? Why would a survivor trust an interpreter with this responsibility? How does a court ensure that it can trust the work of an interpreter? What is the contribution of translators and interpreters to the process of giving testimony in this context, and how do they make ethical decisions between the conflicting professional demands of the witnesses, the court, and the listening public? Finally, does the actual practice of an interpreter like Kapkajew conform to the way she describes it here?

Frankfurt Trial Witnesses Speak about Interpreting

Few of the witnesses spoke about the experience of having their words translated and their testimonies coordinated by interpreters. I will reflect on the words of four witnesses who did discuss the work of the interpreters, considering how they integrate thinking about interpreting into their account of giving testimony and how we might use their reflections to explore questions of trust and agency in witnesses' experience of interpreter-mediated testimony.

A radically negative view is given by Adrienne Krausz in 1996 in an interview for the USC Shoah Foundation (Krausz 1996). Here, Krausz discusses briefly in English her experience of giving testimony in Frankfurt, framing the experience in terms of betrayal, distortion, and anxiety about Holocaust denial. She states that she requested a Hungarian-German interpreter as her English was not good enough to testify at the time; this reveals a hierarchy of language preference, implying that she would have preferred to testify in English if possible. She goes on to make a series of highly critical observations:

> I realized that after about two sentences this guy was switching everything around that I was saying, in a malignant way you know, in a way like you would say today like the Holocaust did not exist, it was just a fiction of the Jewish mind you know. And I realized after about 2 sentences, I turned to the judge and said I would like to let the translator go, the Dolmetscher go, I want to depose in, I want to testify in German. The judge said to me but you said that you don't know how to speak German, and I say no Your Honour, I didn't say that I don't know, I said that I didn't wish to speak German. It so happens that I know very well German and I want to testify in German.

Asked by the interviewer how it felt, she says: "Terrible. I didn't want to go back but I wanted so much to testify against Capesius that I got over it." She concludes by saying that she traveled to Paris after three days as she didn't want to fly Lufthansa or have anything to do with Germany again.

Krausz here describes an extreme lack of trust in the integrity of an interpreter whose performance allies him with the perpetrators of genocide. The recording of Krausz's court testimony on October 29, 1964, shows no evidence of conflict with the interpreter Rolf Dienesch, though the recording is only switched on one or two minutes after the testimony starts: all that we miss are the judge's standard questions on the witness's identity. During her testimony, Krausz speaks excellent German with occasional support from the interpreter when she cannot find the correct expression. The relationship between them appears to be productive, but formal.

It is therefore not possible to establish whether the testimony proceeded exactly as Krausz describes thirty years later. There is certainly no evidence of conflict in the recording that we have, but it may have happened at the very beginning and been resolved by the time the tape begins. The key, however, is Krausz's framing of the encounter retrospectively in terms of trust and how the interpreting is associated with the worst possible breach of trust: radical denial of the truth-speaking of the genocide survivor.

Two of the witnesses participated in German-language oral history interviews with the historian Dagi Knellesen in 2005 as part of a project interviewing surviving participants in the trial forty years after the event. Ignacy Golik, a Polish former political prisoner who had worked as a Kapo (see Stengel 2022: 198–9), tells a story in German of being surprised by his own agency. He had always assumed he was speaking Polish during his testimony, but when he finally heard the recording of the testimony, he was surprised to discover that he had spoken German most of the time:

> Good heavens, Golik told this whole story to the court in German. Well, I forgot about that! I thought, that was back then, next to me the whole time was the, the lady, Wera Kapkajew, and I thought that she had translated it. And now I see that I, almost three quarters of it was me speaking German. (Golik 2005)

The Polish former political prisoner Anna Palarczyk has a different memory of the same interpreter: she provides an opportunity for exercising agency through a small act of deception at the micro level of interaction. The interpreter is described as tidying up the testimony of the witnesses. This is not a question of distortion, in Palarczyk's view, but of supportive behavior, allowing the witness to be heard in the best possible way:

> And at the table sat a wonderful interpreter, Wera Kapkajewa [*sic*], a woman who I will never forget. She translated better, better than it had been spoken. Although it was all true. All of it was true.
>
> All was correct. She didn't, just, one, one was, I became, and other witnesses, we were nervous, we, we did ... What we said was, well, not good! And she quickly, very quickly put it all in order and well.

> And it sounded much, much better than how the author had said it. (Palarczyk 2005)[1]

Palarczyk also describes how she used the presence of the interpreter as a way of taking control of the situation and giving herself time to gather her thoughts:

> Firstly, the judge asked me if I want to say it in German or Polish. I thought: First he will ask the question in German, I'll understand it.
>
> But the interpreter will have to translate it, then I have time to, to think, to think about what I should answer. And that was a good method. I made some time. Well, that was very, very good, that was, that wasn't so bad, not so bad.

Finally, Andrei Pogozhev, a Ukrainian former Red Army soldier, frames his Russian memoir around the experience of giving testimony in Frankfurt and the question of "good" and "bad" translators. Pogozhev, born in 1912 in Donetsk, fought in the Red Army after the German invasion of the Soviet Union but was taken prisoner soon after and transported to Auschwitz, where he experienced the murder and mistreatment of the Soviet POWs. He took part in a mass escape on November 6, 1942. After the war Pogozhev fell foul of the Stalinist suspicion of those who had been taken prisoner and experienced persecution along with his family as a "traitor." After Stalin's death, the former POWs were slowly rehabilitated, and Pogozhev published a memoir that acknowledged his experience while also attempting to write it into the Soviet narrative of wartime heroism (Pogozhev and Stenkin 2005; Pogozhev 2007).

Unusually, his memoir is framed by the experience of giving testimony in Frankfurt, supported by an interpreter called Vera, a Russian living in Germany who is keen to hear about the progress being made in her homeland. Vera is clearly modeled on Wera Kapkajew, who interpreted for Pogozhev, but she is described as nervous and emotionally overwhelmed by the situation, while Pogozhev portrays his testimony as a triumphant turning point of the trial.

Interpreters also play a significant role in Pogozhev's narrative of his time in Auschwitz: the POWs are accompanied by interpreters who work for the SS and who are all White Russian traitors employed by the SS to torment the prisoners. The text thus denies that there is a neutral position for interpreters to take up: they are part of a power structure and have to choose sides in the struggle. The figure of Vera allows him to perform his own rehabilitation and redemption as a former "traitor" without having to speak about the experience directly.

These four accounts deal with questions of interpreting and the person of the interpreter retrospectively; they tell us more about the context of the telling and the feelings connected with giving testimony than about the concrete situation in Frankfurt. In this sense, they are very revealing: talking about translation always entails talking about other things, and there can be no "pure" or value-free talk about translation. All of them make judgments about "good" and "bad" translations that are based on ethical, rather than purely linguistic, criteria: they use a narrative about interpreting in order to talk about agency, truth, honesty, the meaning of testimony, and above all trust.

Where Golik is surprised by the reminder of his own agency and achievement in speaking German during the testimony, Krausz describes being forced to speak a language that she knew well but had rejected: both of these stories are about control and the ability to shape the testimony situation, but they work with fundamentally different views of language and the role of the interpreter. For Krausz, the interpreter becomes a focus for anxiety about loss of control and not being believed, whereas in Golik's memory, the interpreter has taken on a supportive role, enabling him to speak in a difficult situation. Pogozhev has externalized the issue of trust and betrayal that he had to neutralize in order to perform his rehabilitation into Soviet society; as mediators between cultures, interpreters are seen to be fundamentally suspect in a context in which absolute loyalty must be demonstrated at all times. Pogozhev performs his own redemption by redeeming a translator-figure in his text: if she can be trusted then so can he. Palarczyk tells a story about her own ability to affect the testimony situation: the interpreter is a figure who "improves" the words of the witness, but the witness does not accept a passive role in the communicative exchange. Instead, she exploits the structure of an interpreter-mediated exchange to achieve her communicative aims and to be heard properly.

These retrospective reflections raise the question of whether Jewish and non-Jewish witnesses experienced the courtroom situation differently or came to different conclusions about the meaningfulness of the trial and the point of undergoing the stress of testifying. There is insufficient space here to discuss this issue in full, but Katharina Stengel's extensive study of the trial witnesses has shown that it is wise to avoid generalizations: a survivor's specific experiences in the camp system affected how the court responded to their testimony, and the witness's recollection and assessment of the trial was affected by their political stances and the memory communities they were active in (Stengel 2022: 516). We can certainly say that Holocaust denial is a more significant concern for the Jewish survivor Krausz in the 1990s than for the other survivors mentioned here, and her account of her trial testimony is overlaid with anxiety about trust, antisemitism, and the purpose of testifying.

For all these witnesses, the question of trust is fundamental, and the interpreter is not a neutral party. The interpreter is intimately involved in the survivor's performance of the role of witness or, at least, in how that role is understood and narrated in retrospect: questions of trust are inseparable here from urgent questions of truth and memory and the survivor's sense of the meaning and risks of testifying. Why would a witness trust an interpreter in this situation? What structures need to be in place to enforce compliance with the institutional setup preferred by the court? What other forms of trust may develop during an interpreter-mediated exchange that may encourage a witness to seek to achieve their own aims for their testimony, even in this complex, emotionally charged, and perhaps unfamiliar situation? Can a witness exploit the situation to establish trust in their testimony, where the institutional procedures of the court, with its insistent rituals of questioning, tend to suggest mistrust?

This book addresses the questions raised in this chapter by exploring in detail the work of interpreters and their interactions with survivor-witnesses at a single, high-profile, and historically significant trial: a multilingual communicative context of unequal power relations. It aims to show how a focus on interpreting can contribute to a broader understanding of the specific contexts in which survivors have given testimony and can help us to make visible the ethical and emotional challenges faced by testimony-givers and those on whom they rely to make their testimony possible.

The trial itself plays a central role in several different histories of the postwar Federal Republic: the history of the German justice system and its attempts to grapple with the legacy of the Holocaust (and by extension, post-Holocaust and other post-genocide trials more generally); the history of public memory of the Holocaust in Germany and other countries, especially Poland; the history of survivors' involvement in attempts to bring Nazi perpetrators to justice and the development of the public role of survivor-witness; the history of the Federal Republic's developing relationships in the Cold War context with Israel, East Germany, Poland, and other Eastern Bloc countries, as well as with international organizations representing survivors, in particular the International Auschwitz Committee (IAC) and the World Jewish Congress (WJC); the history of translation and interpreting as a profession; and the history of West Germany as a country of regular inward migration and multilingualism.

A translation-centered approach to the trial can give us significant insights into all these histories: the history of translation and interpreting cannot be written outside these specific contexts, and paying attention to the role of translation sheds light on issues that are otherwise not often foregrounded in historical writing. Listening carefully to the interactions between witnesses and interpreters helps us not only to understand the international scale and multilingualism of the victims and perpetrators of the Holocaust but also draws attention to urgent and challenging issues of language, communication, migration, and translation. My study is indebted to excellent recent scholarship on these questions (Degen 2008; Głowacka 2012; Hammel 2004; Insana 2009; Pollin-Galay 2018; Wolf 2016) and is intended as a contribution to this research on the effects of context—linguistic, communicative, cultural, discursive—on the act of testifying.

The highly visible work of sixteen interpreters in the public phase of the trial from December 1963 to August 1965 translating between German and eleven other languages (Czech, Dutch, English, French, Hungarian, Polish, Romanian, Russian, Slovak, Ukrainian, and Yiddish, with Polish by far the largest contingent) means that this trial has a place in the history of interpreting at post-genocide trials that has yet to be fully acknowledged. Beyond this, an uncountable number of translators and interpreters, some with formal training and institutional status but many without, contributed to the pretrial investigation and the international communication that made the trial possible at all. By reading the archive material for what it reveals about processes of translation and listening closely to the audio recordings of the interactions in court, this book shows how witness testimony is enabled and affected by the work of interpreters: it is a case study illustrating the vital contribution of translators and interpreters to creating, preserving, and disseminating knowledge about the Holocaust.

In the following chapters, I set out the scholarship on witnesses and interpreters that has been indispensable for formulating my own approach before moving on to detailed analyses of the exchanges in court. The rest of this chapter will provide some background on the trial and its significance.

The Trial: Background and Significance

On August 20, 1965, at the end of his reading of the verdict against twenty former Auschwitz personnel (nineteen SS and one prisoner functionary), Presiding Judge Hans Hofmeyer spoke the following words:

> In the twenty months of this trial, the court was required to experience mentally all the suffering and torment endured by the people in the camp, and which will forever be inseparable from the name Auschwitz. Many among us may for a long time not be able to look into the happy, trusting eyes of a child without

> seeing beyond, in our mind's eye, the hollow, questioning, uncomprehending, fearful eyes of the children who went on their final journey in Auschwitz. (20.8.1965, 88')

After a trial lasting a year and a half, following several years of investigations, the verdicts spoken by Judge Hofmeyer were seven life sentences for murder on multiple occasions, ten convictions for accessory to murder (one of whom, Dr. Franz Lucas, was acquitted after appeal), and three acquittals for lack of evidence.

Thus ended the most extensive criminal trial in the history of the Federal Republic, which lasted 183 days and in the course of which over 200 Auschwitz survivors had come to Frankfurt from nineteen countries to give testimony under the eyes of their former tormentors.

The prehistory of the Frankfurt trial is complex and dramatic and has been retold in detail in the works I refer to in this section (most recently Buck 2024: 153–72): there is no space here for more than a brief summary. The most remarkable, defining feature as far as this study is concerned is the international scope of the trial, the tension between the requirements of a West German trial, and the variety of voices, experiences, languages, and forms of expression brought to Frankfurt by witnesses from across the world.

The investigation actually originated in Stuttgart, in 1958, when the former camp Gestapo torturer Wilhelm Boger was identified. The judicial authorities there showed no great enthusiasm for the prosecution, and so the chief prosecutor of the state of Hessen, Fritz Bauer, took the opportunity presented by a cache of material handed to him by a journalist, that documented summary executions in Auschwitz, to have the investigation transferred to Frankfurt, where the investigation began in April 1959. The year 1958 represents something of a turning point in West German attempts to bring Nazi perpetrators to trial, with intense public interest in the trial of former SS Einsatzgruppe members in Ulm. A conference of West German federal justice ministers in October registered the urgency of prosecuting Nazi crimes and underscored the need for political backing for state prosecutors. The year also saw the creation of the Zentrale Stelle der Landesjustizverwaltungen zur Aufklärung nationalsozialistischer Verbrechen (Central Office of the State Justice Administrations for the Investigation of Nazi Crimes); based in Ludwigsburg, the Central Office was responsible for preparing and coordinating prosecutions of Nazi crimes committed outside the borders of the present Federal Republic (Weinke 2008; Hofmann 2018).

Fritz Bauer does not feature further in this study, as he did not lead the investigation and was not active in the courtroom, but it is worth acknowledging here his defining influence in instigating the investigation, gaining political support, creating the legal context, and structuring the trial for maximum public impact and educational value (Wojak 2001; Steinke 2013). The voices we hear on the recordings belong to the team of committed prosecutors that Bauer assembled in Frankfurt, who worked for several years with limited funding against institutional stonewalling and hostility. Bauer and his colleagues intended to construct a large-scale trial that they hoped would produce a moment of public introspection, education, and enlightenment. Bauer wrote and spoke extensively on the trial, appearing in public discussions and on television, valuing especially the opportunity to speak to young people who he hoped would work for social change and reflecting on whether the prosecutions and the extensive public discussion had produced the political, psychological, and spiritual transformation that he had hoped for (Renz 2015b).

International organizations representing victims and their interests were involved from the start. The judge Heinz Düx, who led the initial investigation, reminds us that the international attention and pressure operated as a corrective to the tendency of the justice system to delay and obfuscate (Düx 2013: 482). The trial archive contains extensive correspondence with the International Auschwitz Committee, the World Jewish Congress in New York, the Yad Vashem Museum, the Wiener Library in London, West German consulates in countries where survivors lived, police and judicial authorities in many countries, especially Poland, Czechoslovakia and Israel, and a deepening collaboration with the State Museum Auschwitz-Birkenau in Poland. Such organizations were essential in locating survivors and mediating between them and the court, building trust, and distributing the questionnaire that the Frankfurt prosecutors sent to prospective witnesses. The court's visit to Auschwitz in December 1964, in order to test the veracity of witnesses' statements about what could be seen and heard from specific points, was a key moment in the trial, and also a high point in the press coverage, with at least 200 international journalists accompanying the court (Steinbacher 2001).

The former general secretary of the International Auschwitz Committee, the Austrian former political prisoner Hermann Langbein, was instrumental in locating many of the trial witnesses in Poland and other Eastern Bloc countries at a time when the FRG had no official diplomatic relations with Poland or other communist countries (Stengel 2012). During the pretrial investigation, there were tensions between the prosecutors and Langbein, who went public with his allegations that the investigators were dragging their feet.

Judge Hans Hofmeyer opened the public proceedings on December 20, 1964, but the scale of the trial and the public interest meant that it had to move to larger premises in Frankfurt, the Haus Gallus. As many as 20,000 people attended the trial during its twenty months, including school parties (Steinbacher 2005: 146). On the recordings one hears moments when Judge Hofmeyer tells the audience to keep quiet, to stop eating or slouching or doing their hair; he also deals summarily with laughter or protests against the excuses made by the accused or the tactics of the defense. The intense interest of the audience in the courtroom is always audible.

The accused were certainly convicted, but features of the West German justice system produced verdicts that seem inadequate but were not out of line with other trials at the time. Murder verdicts were handed down for the low-level torturers and sadists, who had killed with their own hands, but they received shorter sentences than the maximum possible; those who worked at a higher level in the camp apparatus could not be shown to have directly committed murder in the way the crime was defined under the criminal law of the time. Only those who could be proved to have killed on the basis of certain subjective motivations—bloodlust, greed, sadism, ideological commitment—and on their own initiative could be convicted of murder. Others were convicted as "accessories" (*Gehilfen*), which carried a lighter sentence. The court was concerned that introducing what were considered legal innovations retrospectively might lead to constitutional challenges.

The key issue was that simply playing a role in the extermination machinery and knowing that actions would lead to death were not enough to secure a murder conviction: the court rejected Bauer's attempt to have the whole Auschwitz complex designated a single crime scene, meaning that each individual action had to be analyzed in painstaking detail. This procedural issue is the reason for the length and repetitive detail of the witness testimonies and is why the work of the interpreters was so important, intense, and exhausting.

There is a large and growing research literature on this single trial, much of which has been curated by the Fritz Bauer Institute in Frankfurt, which also runs a program of research and public education events. A number of scholars have discussed the legal background of the trial and have reconstructed the political and institutional difficulties encountered by the prosecution team (Wojak 2001; Bruder 2003; Steinbacher 2005, 2020; Wittmann 2005; Pendas 2006, 2013; Gross et al. 2013; Renz 2015a). There have been studies of the legal and historiographical questions (von Miquel 2001; Pendas 2009; Wagner 2010; Jasch and Kaiser 2017; Jasch 2021) and of the value of the documentation and testimony as historical sources (Renz 2009; Schlie et al. 2017). Alongside the trial archive, there were standalone publications of the extensive trial judgment and the history of the Auschwitz complex compiled for the court by the historians of the Institut für Zeitgeschichte (Buchheim et al. 1965). The key role played by historical expert witnesses in preparing the indictment was a defining feature of the trial (Wojak 1999; Turner 2018); their publications were also designed to reach a broad public.

Unless a member of the public had been able to attend the trial in person, there was no possibility to encounter immediately the voices of the witnesses, since recordings were made for the use of the court only, and no verbatim transcript was kept (on the survival and restoration of the recordings, see Beermann-Schön 2020). There was, however, excellent, committed reporting, which quoted directly the voices of both victims and perpetrators. In particular, the published collections of reporting by Bernd Naumann, Inge Deutschkron, or Rudolf Hirsch still give a powerful impression of the development of the proceedings, the voices and personalities of witnesses and perpetrators, and immediate public reactions, filtered through tough, questioning journalistic sensibilities fully engaged in the conflicts of the era (Hirsch 2001; Naumann 2013; Deutschkron 2018).

Historians have debated the resonance of the trial and its influence on public understanding of the Holocaust (Steinbacher 2005: 150–1; Steinbach 2015; Frei 1997; Benz 2004), and there has been important work in media history, asking specific questions about how the trial contributed to shifting public representation and discussion of Nazi crimes (Wilke et al. 1995; Arendes 2009; Horn 2009a, 2009b; Weinke 2009). Looking beyond the West German context, the trial was an event with international significance for the victims and their political organizations. The active interest of survivor organizations across the world indicates that the trial needs to be denationalized and placed in the context of international developments and debates about Holocaust memory, justice, and reparations. The voices of the victims remind us of the international, multilingual, and multicultural nature of the Holocaust. They remind us of German histories of migration and colonization in the East, the multilingualism of the communities that the Nazis destroyed or profoundly altered, the experiences of those who escaped the Third Reich, and postwar displaced persons, refugees, and expellees. There were also bilingual German postwar expellees among the court officials, interpreters, and defendants.

Katharina Stengel has analyzed in detail not only the vital role played by survivors in securing convictions but also the often painful challenges to their testimony in court due to their supposed lack of objectivity or inability to recall detail. In a challenge to a philosophical tradition of thinking about witnessing, Stengel suggests that it was the aggressive skepticism of lawyers that threatened to turn the Holocaust into an "event without witnesses." But looking beyond the courtroom, as Stengel makes clear, the public profile gained by survivors and the power of their first-person accounts had a profound effect on the developing public role of the victim-witness in the 1960s (Stengel 2022: 12).

Recognizing that the value of this testimony went far beyond simply establishing factual evidence about guilt or innocence, Hermann Langbein and a number of collaborators attended every session taking verbatim notes, which were then published in a two-volume collection with commentary (Langbein 1995). These versions of the oral testimony are indispensable as a literary-political intervention in the struggle for memory in the 1960s and are a testament to the committed antifascism of those who saw the preservation of the victim's voices as the key to historical understanding and social change. Nevertheless, they are multiply mediated, as are the written witness statements in the archive, and are transcribed in standard German, eliding the individuality of the voices, not to mention the fact that the German often originates from interpreters rather than the witnesses themselves.

There has been valuable research on the biographies of the witnesses themselves, with oral history interviews by Dagi Knellesen (Knellesen 2007) and Alice von Plato (von Plato 2001), and an extensive study by Katharina Stengel (Stengel 2022). This reflects a shift in the historiography away from a focus on the legal context, the crimes of the perpetrators, and questions of German memory culture toward a more individualized approach to the testimonies of the survivor-witnesses and an appreciation of the extraordinary richness of this material. This shift places the trial in a useful comparative context with developments in scholarship of restorative justice more broadly (see Thorne 2021) and permits us to ask very specific questions about the witnesses: Did they just want to have their day in court to tell their story? Did they have specific prosecutions in mind? Did they have political ambitions with their testimony? Did they find themselves frustrated with the way the questioning limited their options, or were they able to speak as they wanted? Stengel (2022: 414–40) gives the most detailed discussion of former witnesses' reactions to the experience of giving testimony. The recorded testimonies allow us to address these issues from linguistic and sociological perspectives and to think about translation, authenticity, memory, voice, and communication. This study continues this line of questioning: I focus on the survivor-witnesses and their voices.

Beyond the need to convict the accused, the prosecution set itself the task of building up a concrete picture of the Auschwitz complex as a concrete, living, and dynamically developing location within a much broader context of Nazi policy, secured with documentation and eyewitness testimony. The knowledge generated by the trial made Auschwitz relevant in a new way for anyone who wanted to engage with it: showing the contribution of translators and interpreters to this knowledge about Auschwitz is a key aim of this study.

Part I

People and Languages

1

The Witnesses and Their Language(s)

Who were the witnesses, and what did they bring to the trial? More recent research on the trial has shifted attention from the legal and historiographical issues connected with the prosecution of Nazi crimes toward the survivors themselves and their engagement with the trial both within and beyond the courtroom. There has been a welcome focus on the survivor-witnesses as active, and often critical, participants and observers, whose testimony in court or in pretrial questioning, correspondence, and commentaries make up vital sources for understanding their Holocaust experiences and postwar lives, and the possibilities of giving testimony under specific public conditions and pressures. For many survivors, this may have been the only time that they spoke in public about their experiences, so these documents are especially valuable. For others, giving evidence in court was part of their political self-understanding as a survivor; in particular the many witnesses who came to Frankfurt from Poland and Czechoslovakia, and the far smaller number of Soviet witnesses, had given courtroom testimony on several occasions already, and knew what it entailed.

During the public phase of the trial, with which this study is principally concerned, the witnesses who worked with an interpreter spoke ten different languages, with a rich variety of dialects and hybrid forms. The numbers do not reflect a representative sample of victim experiences as we might understand that today, with our greater insight into the history of the camp; instead, they reflect the priorities of the prosecution, the difficulty of contacting certain groups of witnesses, and the perceived usefulness of certain kinds of testimony.

Although this study focuses on the work of translators and interpreters in Frankfurt, the witnesses and their experiences of producing testimonies in collaboration with an interpreter must also be a central concern. I will avoid the tendency to describe certain witnesses as "difficult" or "problematic," as this reproduces the perspective of the court. I am also only going to discuss things that are relevant to the issue of interpreting, so a substantial proportion of the witnesses will not be mentioned here. This means that this study is not representative in terms of specific witness groups and their experiences. The large number of German-speaking witnesses are not discussed here: there is no space for the significant testimonies of German-speaking Jews and political prisoners, other former SS men, the wives of accused men who were called to testify, or the handful of German Sinti witnesses who testified to the mass murders in the "Gipsy Camp." This last group is an especially unfortunate omission, as their testimonies are striking and profoundly moving, and they were able to have their status as victims of Nazi racism acknowledged in public.

This study is not representative in another way, too: two-thirds of the witnesses who spoke with an interpreter were Polish speakers, representing both the importance of the evidence of Polish political prisoners in building the case and the extent and depth of the collaboration of the court with the Polish authorities. Each of them had an individual approach to giving testimony, and the relationship with the interpreter Wera Kapkajew developed in different ways: I have made a selection on the basis of illustrating different aspects of the interpreter's task and her response to them. The second largest group (fourteen) were Czech and Slovak speakers from Czechoslovakia: the court experienced some initial confusion about the difference between Czech and Slovak and eventually had to find a Slovak-speaking interpreter.

I have also given space to as many different languages as possible and thus to the work of the different interpreters, even where there is only a small number of witnesses. There are eight English-speaking witnesses, all but two of whom are Jewish survivors who had immigrated to the United States and now preferred to testify in English: the others are a former British POW, Charles Coward, and an American judge, Michael Musmanno, who briefly appears to give evidence about the Nuremberg trial. There are five former Soviet POWs, who all speak Russian, five French speakers, three each for Hungarian, Romanian, and Yiddish, and two Dutch speakers. It is notable that no witnesses testified in Hebrew: the small number who came from Israel either spoke German (Yehuda Bacon and Raya Kagan) or a mixture of German and Yiddish (Dov Paisikovic). Only two witnesses (Milton Buki and Dov Paisikovic) requested a Yiddish interpreter, but their testimonies as former members of the Birkenau *Sonderkommando* are so significant, and the work of their interpreter Moritz Grünblatt illustrates such significant issues to do with the interpreter's ethical choices that they deserve closer attention. Other witnesses, such as the *Sonderkommando* survivor Simon Gotland, employ Yiddish as part of their hybrid linguistic performance.

A distinction that is highly relevant for the trial but less so for the interpreting is that between witnesses called by the state and those who have brought a civil claim alongside the state (*Nebenkläger* or civil litigants). The *Sonderkommando* survivors whom I have just mentioned are part of this group, represented by the lawyers Henry Ormond and Christian Raabe, as are a group of witnesses from East Germany, represented by the East German prosecutor Friedrich Karl Kaul. They are questioned in the same way as other witnesses, but their representatives tend to encourage them to speak more generally and emotionally about the aftereffects of their experiences, and Kaul uses the opportunity to present the orthodox communist interpretation of Auschwitz as a product of capitalism.

Language choice is a significant issue for many of these witnesses: there is barely a single one who cannot speak or understand any German, and many witnesses try to address the court in German as a way of having their voices heard directly. Even those who do not will often insert German words or phrases when they wish to say something important, quote something said by an SS man, or demonstrate their understanding of camp language. This leads to varying degrees of hybridity in the witnesses' speech, often made more complex by specific forms of multilingualism that reflect the witnesses' origins and biographies. So, for example, there are witnesses whose origins lie in the multilingual region of Transylvania and who are called to give evidence against the defendant Victor Capesius, whom many had known before the war: their evidence can be given in Romanian, Hungarian, or German, or in the language of their new country of residence. These testimonies remind us of the multilingual nature of this region, of earlier histories of migration, language contact, and hybridization, as well as the tensions caused by nationalist movements in the prewar period: there is a subtext in some of these testimonies that tells us a lot about language politics and shifting identities. The court is a space in which Jewish survivors from Transylvania testify against Victor Capesius, with their words translated by interpreters who are former German expellees from the same region.

There are similar constellations with the Czechoslovak witnesses: former political prisoners and Jewish survivors testify with the support of interpreters who may be German expellees and in at least one case (Otto Stegmann) had been a Sudeten German nationalist activist in the 1920s and 1930s. A number of the defense councils were of a similar background and could follow what was said in Czech or Polish. The Soviet and Polish survivors speak with the support of an interpreter (Wera Kapkajew) whose family had been anti-Bolshevik exiles and whose husband had fought with a Russian SS unit.

The language choices made by Jewish survivors who had not returned to their country of origin are always significant and can lead to moments of telling linguistic hybridity, which interpreters must deal with: this is particularly the case with the French and English-speaking witnesses. If one thinks about the relationships in the courtroom in terms of these language constellations, then we can get a clearer understanding of what is being negotiated by witnesses and interpreters. Interpreting is never simply a question of translating, of course; instead, it is in this case about negotiating a potentially highly charged linguistic situation in which the interpreter is not a neutral party.

This chapter is concerned with the witnesses and their ways of speaking. What language(s) they speak and why is vital, but it is not the only issue. How do their experiences and the situation they find themselves in affect the way they try to manage the communication in court? What knowledge are they trying to impart, and how successfully can they do this? To what extent are their intentions and ways of expressing themselves compatible with the court's assumptions, procedures, and discursive practices?

In the first part, I explore current research on the Frankfurt witnesses and post-Holocaust courtroom testimony more generally. The next section characterizes some of the different groups of witnesses who spoke in court with an interpreter and considers how their experiences may have affected the way they gave testimony. In this chapter, I only refer to witnesses who spoke in the public phase of the trial and whose voices we thus hear on the recordings; there is only space to consider a fraction of these in any detail. The many survivors who overcame their misgivings to give evidence in the pretrial investigation, but whose testimony was in the end not required, are unfortunately absent here. Readers are referred to the extensive study by Katharina Stengel on the survivor-witnesses and to the oral history interviews by Dagi Knellesen and Alice von Plato, all of which I have drawn on in this chapter (Stengel 2022; Knellesen 2007; von Plato 2001).

One can only admire and pay tribute to the courage and commitment of the hundreds of survivors who contributed to the trial in ways ranging from filling out a simple questionnaire with details that they would prefer to forget to making the journey to Frankfurt to speak for several hours in open court.

Research on Trial Witnesses

In this section, I set out some recent research on the trial witnesses and their speeches. I am interested here in the discursive situation in which they formulate their testimony and in how scholarship on post-Holocaust trials has found ways of understanding this complex situation beyond questions of the evidentiary or historiographical value of their statements. How are we to understand these testimonies as communicative events unfolding through time and being created in the interaction of the parties?

As Katharina Stengel has said, trials were one of the few spaces in this period where survivors could be heard across the boundary between their solidarity groups and a broader public. This boundary-crossing is one of the defining features of the public role of survivor-witness, as it was developing in the 1960s, and despite the stress, power imbalances, and often hostility of the legal setting, many survivors felt that they had a responsibility to support the interests of justice (Stengel 2022: 84). The close connection with public testifying and trials is vital, since testifying in court aims at establishing factual, agreed, and confirmed truth about events rather than the more subjective features that have more recently come to the fore in thinking about testimony: biographical truth, trauma, the search for and questioning of meaning, and many other things. This is not to say that witnesses did not speak—or try to speak—about other issues that were important to them, but the courtroom was a compelling public stage for truth-telling.

The Eichmann trial had done more than any other to shape the image of the survivor-witness as a public figure on an international stage, and the prosecution in Frankfurt was well aware of the power of authentic speech by survivors giving testimony in a judicial forum. Post-Holocaust trials in Eastern Bloc countries had also drawn on the power of survivor voices for their public impact (Hájková 2020). Given the generally negative view of eyewitness testimony among specialist historians at the time, trials were often the only space beyond survivor organizations and communities that these witnesses could find an audience for their testimony: giving testimony thus took on an existential significance well beyond the concrete question of convicting individual perpetrators.

Stengel has suggested that the Frankfurt trial marks a moment in which survivors adopted the public role of survivor-witness in West Germany. Previously, survivors' public impact came through organizations and solidarity groups making political demands (including demands for justice) and often caught up in the conflicts and tensions of the Cold War. In the wake of the Eichmann trial, the Frankfurt witnesses began now to be perceived as individual survivors, as carriers or embodiments of memory, with authoritative, authentic voices speaking of ethical universals rather than making specific political challenges: "From now on, the former prisoners entered public consciousness with their memories, rather than with demands and campaigning" (Stengel 2012: 552).

The legal system gained almost all its knowledge about Nazi crimes from the narratives of survivor-witnesses. It is hard to overstate the significance of the language developed in the courtroom for public understanding of the Holocaust in this period: "The investigations and judicial proceedings were among the very few places where Nazi crimes were spoken about in concrete terms, so the question of *how* they were spoken about there also had a significance that extended far beyond the criminal proceedings" (Stengel 2022: 32). Thomas Henne has questioned approaches that discuss witness testimony purely with a focus on the reliability or otherwise of evidence. Employing a critical discourse analysis method, Henne shows how witnesses play an active role within a situation that is not structured according to their specific needs: they often "want to make their suffering the main subject of the trial," but the procedures of justice focus on the accused and the crime under consideration (Henne 2007: 81).

A witness is obliged to speak and act within a system that is geared toward the accused, both in terms of establishing his or her guilt or innocence and, in a liberal justice system, protecting the accused's rights. The witness must stand before the accused as an individual: they cannot speak as a group, and so collective solidarity dissolves into individual responsibility. Witnesses are required to report facts, and their own intentions and interpretations of these facts are irrelevant: the court interprets the facts at its disposal according to its rules of evidence. Nevertheless, it will become clear that the witnesses are very often speaking for others, on behalf of others, or to others: their knowledge about the camp has been gathered collectively, and different forms of solidarity have been vital for survival. Interpreters sometimes have to negotiate the issue of what a witness means when they say "I saw" or "I know."

The personal truth of the witness, whether this is an expression of purely individual experiences or of collective understandings or identities, is not the same as the truth criteria that the court works with, though it would be an exaggeration to say that they are diametrically opposed or entirely incompatible. Pendas puts it like this: "There was a clear contrast between the experiential truth of Auschwitz as a site of pain and loss and the legal truth of Auschwitz as site of minutely specifiable criminal acts" (Pendas 2006: 142). Pendas's view is significant, as it takes the witnesses and their experiences as the starting point for thinking rather than as a side issue in discussion of the legal problems. Employing an analysis of strategy and tactics drawn from de Certeau, Pendas goes on to suggest that witnesses may be able to exercise agency on a tactical level, that is at the level of individual interactions, while being unable to affect the overall structures and discursive authority of the court (Pendas 2006: 80).

Pendas does not extend this analysis, but other scholars have shown how survivor-witnesses at post-genocide trials are able to pursue their own aims and to be heard in ways that exceed what the court requires. For example, Stengel shows in detail how witnesses took the opportunity offered by their testimony for public self-justification, political and personal declarations, negotiation of individual and group identities, and many other things, in other words, "for the discussion of issues that were only tangentially relevant for the case itself" (Stengel 2022: 320).

Anna Hájková shows how historical studies of witness testimony can benefit from more informed attention to the narrative features of testimony as a genre. Tracing the testimonies of survivors of the Theresienstadt ghetto in postwar trials, she observes that witness testimonies are shaped to fit the context of the interaction, with the content remaining remarkably stable through time despite the shifting framing. Depending on their "experience and social capital," witnesses can influence the shaping of their statements (Hájková 2020: 82).

Hájková also draws our attention to the gendered assumptions behind the language of "hard facts" in testimony: male witnesses are more likely to be relied on for the "factual" accounts that structure a prosecution, whereas female witnesses' testimony may be either valued or discredited on the basis of its supposedly more emotional nature (Hájková 2020: 88). Certainly, the prosecution relied on a large number of testimonies by majority male German, Austrian, Polish, and Czechoslovak political prisoners in order to establish the factual basis of the prosecution: female political survivors such as the Austrian Ella Lingens or the Pole Anna Palarczyk gave key testimonies in this context but were in a minority.

The testimonies given later in the proceedings by survivors of the mass transports of Jews from across Europe, and in particular the Hungarian transports of spring 1944, were very different: there were proportionally more women in this group, and their testimonies tended to be considered more problematic, as they found it harder to provide a coherent account of their experiences in the terms required by the court. However, where the court needed to rely on women's testimony for an indictment—as in the case of the group of female camp interpreters who worked for the Political Department and testified against the torturer Wilhelm Boger—it did so.

An issue where gendered expectations become clearer is in attitudes toward the interpreters and the relationships that they develop with witnesses. In my discussion of the work of the interpreter Wera Kapkajew, I show how gendered views of the interpreters structure public commentary on her work. Since she interpreted for almost all the male Polish survivors and all the male Soviet survivors, listeners were hearing these male voices interpreted by a woman. Views of her skill as an interpreter were conditioned by gendered understandings of women's empathy and ability to submerge their personality to others': that this has little to do with her actual professional practice will become clear in my discussion of her work.

Research concentrating on the witnesses at the Frankfurt trial only began to emerge some thirty years after the trial ended, but there is now a rich literature of historical and oral history work documenting the biographies and experiences of many of those who spoke: Alice von Plato, Julia Wagner, Dagi Knellesen, Rebecca Wittmann, Devin Pendas, and Katharina Stengel have all made significant contributions to a historiography of witnessing at the trial. Wagner has explored how the speech of the witnesses was affected by the attitudes and behavior of the questioners in court, reminding us that testimony is a memory recreated in a specific situation and in dialogue with others: "Their choice of questions therefore determined which memories were of interest; their attitudes and behavior towards the witnesses made an impact on the situation of the interview and influenced how the narratives of the witnesses were shaped" (Wagner 2010: 344).

Wagner explores examples—such as the testimony of Josef Glück, whose priority was to tell the story of the separation from his wife on the ramp at Birkenau—where problems of communication arose, and the witness struggled with the requirements of the court. Her summary of the difficulties facing witnesses, and which shaped the way they spoke, is very useful:

> The circumstances in which the witnesses testified in court shaped the content and the form of their testimony significantly. The witness statements were not open narratives but were given in response to specific questions posed by the investigators, and later during the hearing also by the judges, the joint plaintiffs, the defense counsels and sometimes by the defendants. This means that themes and structure were to a large extent not determined by the witnesses themselves. The questions were geared towards their usability in legal argumentation and therefore extremely selective. While the court generally allowed the witnesses to take their time and to tell their story to a large extent in their own way, a concession which was met with criticism by some defense counsels, some witnesses were interrupted or guided towards the points which were of particular significance for the court .... The reasons for this procedure were not

> transparent to the witnesses. Yet, despite the regimentation of their narratives, the witnesses' narratives often eluded the needs of the court. (Wagner 2010: 354)

Wagner concentrates, for understandable reasons, on the moments of difficulty, where the needs of the witness were incompatible with the needs of the court. It is, however, worth recalling that many witnesses gave clear, skillful, committed, and dignified testimony, with an understanding of what was required of them. Wagner does not mention interpreters specifically in her useful analysis, but it is important to remember that interpreters participate actively in shaping the testimony situation, both in terms of supporting the witness in being heard the way they wish to be and in ensuring the witness adheres to the required discipline imposed by the questioning.

Knellesen uses oral history interviews with surviving witnesses to explore their memories of the experience of giving testimony; she offers an account in which witnesses reflect at a retrospective distance on their own agency and the gap between their understanding and the court's. In this view, the survivor-witness had been able to bring their individual stories of persecution to the court and have them discussed in public: "The strictly formal setting of the trial, which stood for the authority of truth, provided a forum for the survivors and their personal stories of persecution, which dominated the headlines over the next few months" (Knellesen 2007: 129).

So the context of communication makes the testimony possible and establishes a shape, but the judicial emphasis on establishing truth and factual evidence gives the stories legitimacy and ensures that they are seen as more than simply subjective memories. Although fewer than half of the survivor-witnesses were referred to in the final verdict since they did not pass the strict rules of evidence that the court imposed on itself, the other testimonies could still be associated with the legal truth claim when they were heard by observers (Wagner 2010: 355).

Knellesen's interviewees talk about being asked questions that have no relevance to their experience of the camp. Paul Schaffer puts his finger on the issue:

> The only thing that astonished me was one question from the judge, that I can't forget even today: "Did you see this violinist being killed?" as if back then we had had any desire or notion to take a look whether someone was dead or not. Really, that is the kind of question asked by a man who hasn't experienced it, who can't imagine that all I wanted was to hide so that no one would see me. And that obviously astonished me a bit, as it was a question from an inexperienced man, at least in this area. (Knellesen 2007: 131)

We see here an important clash between different modes of understanding and ways of creating knowledge out of experience: it is obvious to Schaffer how the other prisoner was killed, but there were things he could not bear to watch directly. For the court, this raises questions about the value of knowledge that is not directly based on eyewitness testimony, while for Schaffer it shows that the court has little understanding of the situation that the prisoners found themselves in. One of the key tasks for the interpreters is to mediate between these different ways of knowing, to organize the discourse of witnesses in such a way that it registers as valid testimony in court.

Other witnesses show that they were able to manipulate the situation in order to pursue their own aims. Here, Imre Gönczi tells a story about how he was able to educate the judge by going off on a tangent once he has given direct evidence against one of the accused:

> And I was supposed to give evidence against this Klehr. And during my testimony I organized things so I could speak about everything. Not just about the question of Klehr. I talked about Klehr quickly, and then I got started: Hygiene Institute, human flesh and all the rest, and that brought everything to life, because the judge didn't know anything about the things I was talking about. I was very nervous, but I prepared myself mentally. (Knellesen 2007: 131)

In these interviews, the witnesses stress their own agency and strategic ability to make the trial about more than just the narrow question of legal guilt: the courtroom is a space in which views of the trial and what knowledge is to be conveyed clash and are negotiated. Despite the retrospective nature of the interviews, with a corresponding tendency to construct a narration stressing their role as agents of their own fate, they are helpful for structuring our own view of the recorded testimonies, ensuring that we see the witnesses as active participants in the communication.

Knellesen questions the assumption that witnesses' speech should be seen as a product of trauma. The possibility of speaking about the experience has less to do with the return of repressed trauma than with the social framework in which speech is possible, the interactions with other participants, and the structure of reactions to it (Knellesen 2007: 135). Naturally, many witnesses' speech is at times highly emotional, and there are moments of inarticulacy and outbursts of anger, and it is tempting to focus on these heartbreaking moments at the expense of understanding the whole communication and the intentions of the witness in the round. These oral history interviews remind us that we should at all costs avoid thinking of the witnesses as passive or helpless: they are subject to a system of institutional and discursive power but are still able to find ways of being heard.

The most significant account of the witnesses at the trial is the recent study by Katharina Stengel, which goes into far more extensive detail than I am able to here. Considering a number of trials up to the last of the Frankfurt trials in the 1970s, Stengel traces the involvement of survivor organizations in the planning and investigation of post-Holocaust trials, as well as the debates among German lawyers concerning the value of eyewitness testimony. She provides extensive biographical material and discusses methodological approaches to witness testimony, which I have drawn on here.

A significant feature of Stengel's study is its clear view of the individuality of the witnesses and their ways of speaking about their experiences: the rejection of reductive views of courtroom testimony is an important advance that opens up possibilities for doing justice to the detail of interactions between individuals in the courtroom (Stengel 2022: 19). There is a rich research literature on post-Nazi trials, but until relatively recently it has concentrated on the legal history perspective (e.g., Weinke 2002; von Miquel 2001; Freudiger 2002). Witnesses and their experiences played a limited role in this literature, often only as a source of problems for the investigators. This is of a piece with a tendency in earlier Holocaust historiography to downplay the value of survivor testimony as evidence. It was left to survivors and their representatives to produce a victim-focused counter-historiography that wrote history using the memories and voices of those who had suffered the most. A key actor in the German-language context was Hermann Langbein, who, along with fellow survivor-scholars and campaigners such as H. G. Adler, produced accounts of Auschwitz structured around witness testimony, most importantly the collective volume *Menschen in Auschwitz* (*People in Auschwitz*) and a substantial radio feature (Langbein 1972; Langbein 2004; Adler and Langbein 1961).

The important works on the trial by Devin Pendas and Rebecca Wittmann, which are another key source for this study, shifted the perspective toward the witnesses and took a more critical view of the operation of the justice system. Taking a critical legal studies approach, Gerd Wamhof has explored how judicial reality is created performatively through narrative in the courtroom, which is a location in which knowledge is created and negotiated (Wamhof 2009). This is a vital step forward in that it allows us to see interpreters not simply as translating language but also as participating in interactions through which specific types of knowledge are formulated: knowledge about Auschwitz, the perpetrators, and the victims, certainly, and knowledge about survivors as witnesses and the nature of testimony.

Who Were the Witnesses?

One of the remarkable features of the new wave of West German trials of Nazi perpetrators that began in the late 1950s was the internationalization of the investigations: survivors of the genocide were scattered throughout the world, and it was no longer sufficient to get evidence from people who happened to have stayed in Germany after the war. Extraordinary efforts were made to locate witnesses with the vital help of organizations that represented survivors, in particular the International Auschwitz Committee (IAC) and the World Jewish Congress (WJC): this is a long, complex, and fascinating history that Stengel has traced in detail (Stengel 2022: 129–85).

Far from being silent, unwilling, or unable to share their traumatic experiences, survivors, as Stengel shows, were in the 1950s and early 1960s often more than willing to engage with the German justice system and contribute to the prosecution of perpetrators (Stengel 2022: 63). The Eichmann trial had given an international profile to survivor-witnesses and had centered their testimonies dramatically: the First Frankfurt trial benefited from the willingness of hundreds of survivors to be interviewed either in Germany or abroad and come to Frankfurt to speak in public. This willingness began to evaporate in the 1970s for several reasons: disillusion and cynicism at the inadequacy of the sentences for mass murderers, exasperation at the treatment meted out to survivors in court, in particular the hostility of certain defense councils, and changing priorities in the perceived meaning of giving testimony, shifting from attaining justice to preserving memory (Stengel 2022: 62).

The willingness of witnesses to participate was severely tested from the start, however. The Frankfurt prosecutors prepared a questionnaire to be sent out to prospective witnesses around the world—though principally the United States—asking for details about the length of time spent at Auschwitz, whether they could identify any SS guards, and whether they had witnessed specific criminal acts. The WJC provided translations of the German into English and Yiddish and helped to locate potential Jewish witnesses. The responses to this entirely inappropriate way of gathering evidence from survivors range from denial of knowledge, accounts of extreme suffering and loss without naming perpetrators, or angry denunciations to fuller accounts with information that was more useful for the prosecution.

The forms are a fascinating source in their own right, demonstrating different survivor responses to a catastrophic failure of communication and understanding: Stengel discusses them in some detail. For the purposes of this study, the most relevant issue is the way that the witnesses' knowledge is formulated and how it contrasts with the court's knowledge practices. Stengel's key insight here is that survivors were not simply helplessly expressing suffering but anticipated an understanding of the violence of the Holocaust that the justice system would only adopt later, namely that being present at and contributing to the operation of an extermination camp was sufficient evidence of participating in the crime, and there should be no need to provide detailed eyewitness evidence for every small action as part of this process (Stengel 2022: 217). It is vital to keep this perspective in mind, as it reminds us that survivors have a clear understanding of the issues and an active, political interest in the context and significance of their testimony: they are not passive or helpless, simply wanting to give expression to suffering, but their testimony has a purpose in the context of its articulation. There were some kinds of testimony that the court's practices were better able to deal with than others.

Initially, no support was provided for witnesses arriving in Frankfurt to give testimony: expenses were paid and hotels booked, but there was nobody to meet or guide them until voluntary organizations stepped up to play that role. Also, it was not until the 1970s that jurists began to see survivors as individuals who—whatever the quality of their evidence—may find the process of testifying in itself traumatic and who therefore may require targeted support (Stengel 2022: 101).

The evidentiary bar for witness testimony was also set very high: convictions in post-Holocaust trials were not made on the basis of a single witness testimony, even though this standard was not set in law (Stengel 2022: 60). The practical consequences of this were that survivors who had come to Frankfurt to give evidence found that their individual voice was not sufficient to convict any of the perpetrators: this must have come as a shock to people who had little experience of the legal system and had come to expect their testimony to be valued. The question of trust here is key: survivors who provided testimony for collective publications, such as those put out by Langbein, were used to having their words treated as truth. The IAC, whose representatives understood the legal requirements well, did spend time assessing the testimonies that they received, but their standards were far less narrow than those employed by the courts themselves.

The case against the accused relied to a significant extent on eyewitness testimony, given the lack of documentary evidence for the crimes that were being prosecuted: this put at times intolerable pressure on the witnesses and led to lines of questioning and challenges that they were not prepared for. Individual crimes had to be described in minute detail and corroborated by other evidence, and witnesses were challenged constantly on lines of sight, precise dates, exact identification of perpetrators, and secure sources of knowledge. The questioning of witnesses could thus proceed for several hours, especially if they were working with an interpreter, and could feature moments of conflict and long, difficult negotiation over detail and precision, all of which the interpreters had to deal with. Many German jurists, especially those prosecutors who spent time with survivors in the course of their investigations, had an understanding of the problems that the witnesses faced, but this did not lead to changes in legal practice until much later (Stengel 2022: 55).

My study is concerned with the witnesses who worked with an interpreter, but a brief account of the different witness groups may give useful context. Stengel makes the important point that the court worked with categories of witness that were essentially drawn from Nazi systems of classification: political prisoners divided into national groups, Jewish prisoners defined as such through Nazi racial categories and the consequent experiences of deportation and violence, "Zigeuner," "antisocials," criminals (2022: 42). The experiences of these different groups were vital in order to build up a picture of the camp, but it meant that the survivors had no opportunity to define themselves in their own way.

The legacy of these Nazi categories in postwar West Germany meant that those that had been assigned the labels antisocial and criminal as grounds for imprisonment were not invited to testify in open court, as their testimony could be challenged on the basis of "character." Further, the evidence of more "privileged" prisoners, who had been able to observe and gather information, tended to be trusted more than that of other victims (Stengel 2022: 27).

The majority of the witnesses who took the stand were German speakers, either Germans or people whose German was good enough to dispense with an interpreter. There were a significant number of German and Austrian political prisoners and Jews whose testimony set the tone at the beginning. There are extraordinary German-language testimonies from a group of German Sinti survivors, as well as a group of multilingual Jewish women who had worked as interpreters in the Auschwitz "Political Department," witnessing the torture and murder carried out by Wilhelm Boger. Stengel (306–45, 394) has written about these witnesses in detail. The other large group of German-speaking witnesses comprises former SS men and camp personnel, who were called to give evidence: many of them had already been either tried and amnestied or "denazified," and so they had little to fear from the trial, as long as they did not incriminate themselves further. Some defendants' wives were also called, as was the widow of the former commandant Rudolf Höß. I am not concerned with these figures, though they would make an interesting study in linguistic strategies of blockading, evasion, and denial.

Given the point-blank refusal of most former SS personnel to provide any useful information, the court relied on survivor-witnesses to build up a picture of the topography, history, and daily activity of the camp: this was a vital element of the prosecution strategy, as Auschwitz needed to be presented as a concrete crime scene understood in terms of structures, relationships, and interactions between people, lines of sight, sources of knowledge, behavior that was considered "normal" and "abnormal." This was also a key element of the educational aim of the prosecution, which was so important to Fritz Bauer's intentions.

Of the non-German survivor-witnesses, the Polish political prisoners make up by far the largest group: the first witnesses were interviewed in October 1959, and their testimony was vital right from the beginning of the investigation. Their range of experiences, the length of time that they stayed in the camp, their strategy of observation and information gathering as forms of resistance, their willingness to work positively with the court to gain prosecutions, and the support of the IAC and the Auschwitz Museum were indispensable. It is this group that provided the prosecution with its initial basis of knowledge about Auschwitz, its history, and operation (Stengel 2022: 190). The kinds of knowledge these prisoners brought with them affected the court's ultimate understanding of the camp and thus the formulation of the indictment and the patterns of questioning in the trial's open phase (Stengel 2022: 207).

All of them had different perspectives and personalities, different levels of German and ways of expressing themselves, leading to different kinds of interactions with the interpreter: Wera Kapkajew worked with all but two of them. The overwhelming majority were male, which creates an interesting dynamic in their relationship with the female interpreter. I am only going to be able to discuss a small fragment of this fascinating group, whose testimony did more than most to make the prosecutions possible: I will also concentrate on issues that affect their language use and which are relevant to the work of the interpreters.

Citizens of a communist country with which the Federal Republic did not have official diplomatic relations being questioned in evidence was controversial at the time and went against the official political line of the Federal Justice Ministry: the state of Hessen went its own way here, with an awareness that the success of the prosecution depended on the evidence they could bring with them. They tended to be young at the time of their arrest for resistance activities, with a level of education that made them useful as scribes or medical orderlies in the Auschwitz Main Camp. These positions enabled them to collaborate in gathering knowledge, archiving it, and smuggling it out. This clandestine work had formed the basis of the collections of the Auschwitz Museum and explains not only its richness but also its biases and blind spots. The director of the museum Kazimierz Smoleń, who had developed a close working relationship with the Frankfurt prosecutors during the pretrial investigation, gave evidence in open court on May 25 and 29, 1964 and April 22, 1965.

Their testimonies are very varied, but most of them share an understanding of how the evidence needed to be presented in court, speaking for the most part clearly and directly and with a focus on reconstructing processes and structures as well as individual experiences: as resisters, they tended to see themselves as part of a collective rather than as isolated victims. They differ in how they express emotion, in their confidence in presenting evidence, and, significantly, in how they define their relationship with the other participants: some are collaborative and flexible, others more aggressive and mistrustful, which leads to complex interactions with the interpreter, who has to manage the situation.

They were also aware that the kinds of declarative rhetoric common among communist survivors were unlikely to produce results in Frankfurt: Stengel presumes that Langbein had a hand in briefing them about appropriate language use at an early stage in the investigation and rewriting some of the initial depositions they passed through the IAC (Stengel 2022: 188). Their status as resisters, with a place within the political memory landscape of the postwar Polish state, meant that many of them had never stopped talking about, thinking about, and researching Auschwitz, placing it securely in the context of the German occupation of Poland, and commemorating the dead. They had also often spoken at the postwar trials in Poland and had an understanding of the political significance of the proceedings.

Despite this, one of the particular challenges faced by the political prisoners when giving testimony arose from the conception of knowledge that they operated with, which clashed with the court's requirement for individual eyewitness testimony. For the politicals, knowledge in itself was not neutral but already a form of resistance: gathering accurate information, sharing and assessing it against other evidence, collating it, and passing it on were forms of resistance in their own right, necessary but extraordinarily risky. The knowledge the prisoners present in court is thus collective rather than individual: fellow prisoners' words are trusted as much as the evidence of one's own eyes. The court, however, could not accept evidence on the basis of collective understanding

("Everybody knew this") but demanded direct, individual eyewitness testimony for every criminal action.

This can lead to uncomfortable moments of absurdity, as when witnesses are questioned about the mass killing of prisoners by Josef Klehr using phenol injections: for the witnesses it is obvious through long observation who wielded the syringe, even if they were not able to see every detail of the action. Many of these political survivors were experienced witnesses who knew what kind of evidence the court required, but there are occasions when interpreters need to manage a communication that threatens to break down or become a conflict, for example, when witnesses are persistently questioned on where they were standing in relation to a closed door or drawn curtain.

The reasons for the quality of their evidence could also form the basis of challenges by the defense: their group solidarity and knowledge gained through subsequent reading and exchanges with other survivors was attacked as evidence of bias and collusion, leading to some dramatic scenes. There were also attempts to play up national conflicts between the different groups of political prisoners, who were always careful to stress the internationalist nature of the camp resistance movement: the defense called surviving witnesses from the Organization of Ukrainian Nationalists in an unsuccessful bid to discredit the powerful testimony of Józef Kral, a key witness for the prosecution. Franziska Bruder has written about this feature of the trial in more detail (Bruder 2003; see also Stengel 2022: 265–7).

By the time the court had heard dozens of testimonies by former political prisoners, it had built up a picture of how the camp operated that it could use to corroborate, back up, question, and interpret the testimonies of witnesses who came afterward. A compelling aspect of the trial is listening to how the court learns and creates its own knowledge as it goes along, building on the work of the historians who had contributed to the indictment and filling the outline in with detail drawn from the human experiences narrated in court.

As Stengel indicates, the problem here was that the survivors of the mass transports of Jews from across Europe to Birkenau, who gave testimony later in the proceedings, were speaking in a situation in which an understanding of the camp—how the command structure worked, what was important, and how the behavior of the SS could be interpreted according to the court's legal categories—had already been established (Stengel 2022: 60). Considerable attention is paid to the process of "selection" on the ramp at Birkenau but, extraordinarily from a contemporary perspective, the "industrial" mass killing in gas chambers receives less attention than individual acts of sadism. The court seems helpless in the face of what we now consider the defining feature of the Holocaust, as it cannot be reduced to a single action carried out by one identifiable individual driven by motivations captured in the legal definition of murder and willing the action himself in full awareness of the consequences.

Also, much of the evidence by political prisoners was concerned with studying and understanding the behavior of the SS guards and kapos: this was vital for survival and could then be used in court to identify and describe their actions in terms relevant to securing convictions. But it also meant making distinctions between forms of behavior that were irrelevant for the operation of the gas chambers: the question of whether a particular individual was sadistic or lenient, or what his motivation might have been, was inadequate for understanding the reality of the process of murder.

So, in a very different way to the political prisoners, many of the Jewish witnesses found themselves answering questions that they either could not answer or seemed irrelevant, confusing, or offensive. For example, when trying to describe the agonizing moment of separation from family members on arrival, witnesses could be asked instead to describe exactly who was standing where, who made what gesture, who appeared to be giving orders, who was wearing what uniform, and so on. These are moments of intense negotiation, collaboration, or conflict between the participants in which the interpreters play a defining role in organizing the interactions.

This conflict of perspectives had been an issue since the 1950s. Jewish survivors were often not able to provide the kind of evidence that the courts required: they had little overarching understanding of how the camp system had functioned, and their testimonies were often characterized by gaps and uncertainties, which, as Stengel points out, was more representative of the camp experience than the evidence presented by the politicals: "The 'ordinary' Auschwitz prisoners, who were not active in survivor organizations, had often not yet found a narrative for their stories; their personal experiences were not embedded in a larger story, and they had no explanation or interpretation of what had happened to them" (Stengel 2022: 93).

For the Frankfurt trial, the detailed preparation of the indictment was intended to bridge this gap between these "different worlds" of experience, but the problem remained, and witnesses often found the lines of questioning—even from the prosecution, with whom they shared the intention to convict the accused—difficult to understand. The interpreters play a key role here in trying to negotiate these issues, often reorganizing the statements of the witnesses into a form that is useable by the court: they at times seem to be mediating between different worlds.

A small group of witnesses provided what may be the most extreme challenge for the court and for the interpreters, namely the survivors of the Birkenau *Sonderkommando*. This was the first time that the work of the Jewish *Sonderkommandos* had been described at a trial. The prosecution counsel Henry Ormond, who represented the civil litigants (*Nebenkläger*) in the trial, had ensured that these witnesses were called to speak: the state prosecutors had evidently decided not to use their evidence, perhaps because the operation of the gas chambers themselves was so hard to analyze using the standard criteria for a murder conviction, but Ormond clearly intended to ensure that these voices were heard. As Stengel has shown, Ormond's questioning often allowed witnesses to give a more general overview of violence in the camp and to talk about the legacy of their experiences in their later lives: something that the prosecution did not for the most part consider relevant (Stengel 2022: 183).

The witnesses Filip Müller, Dov Paisikovic, and Milton Buki belong to this group, while others, like Simon Gotland, are also able to speak about *Sonderkommando* experiences. They all, in different ways, present complex linguistic issues for the court and the interpreters. The extremity of the experiences they describe is beyond the capacity of the court's linguistic practices to deal with: a trial relies on a shared understanding of the rules and of what knowledge is under negotiation. But if witnesses are describing a world that the court's language cannot grasp, then the negotiation on the basis of shared assumptions becomes impossible, and the knowledge gained becomes "precarious" (Stengel 2022: 286). Interpreters find themselves in a position in which they are trying to make these experiences available for understanding and judgment by the court: there is no neutral position to take up here, and their ethical choices are complex.

Conclusion

It is clear by now that it is not possible to reduce the survivor-witnesses' ways of speaking in court to a single common denominator. Different groups of witnesses, with different collective or individual identities and with different experiences to draw on—before, during, and after their time in Auschwitz—frame their testimony in different ways and find it more or less easy to operate within the court's discursive framework.

Even within a testimony, the witness will vary their speech, shifting their attitude toward the situation and the experiences they are describing as the communication and the relationships between the participants develop. There are times when Devin Pendas's account of witnesses' helplessness in the face of hostile questioning does seem to describe what we are hearing, but for the most part—even in the most emotionally harrowing moments—the witnesses are actively pursuing their own aims and seeking to be heard in ways that they can control. They share the aim of achieving prosecutions but may not share the court's understanding of the camp or view of knowledge and may have other aims: they may want to name and pay tribute to the dead, make political statements, educate, accuse, or speak to audiences beyond the court. Their strategies vary from moment to moment and are at times successful ans at others, catastrophically unsuccessful.

The court possesses the institutional power to set the terms of the exchange and the genre of talk and to assert its discursive authority when it deems it necessary: it determines what testimony means in this context, but its understanding of what testimony might mean for survivors is flawed. Witnesses have to work within this structure or make the risky strategic choice to push against it; conflicts arise when intentions are thwarted, witnesses' understandings of testimony clash too clearly with those of the court, and where relationships break down. These overarching power imbalances should always be borne in mind when listening to and analyzing the intricate detail of the interactions in court: the witnesses' language use is a product of many factors interacting in this specific context. Ultimately, it is my choice to pay attention to their individuality, agency, and active role within the communicative relationships in this unequal context. This, in turn, allows us to bring out the complexity of their interactions with the interpreters and understand the ethical dilemmas they faced.

In the next two chapters, I turn to the interpreters, their biographies, and the context in which they worked.

2

Interpreting in Context

Writing the history of translating and interpreting always entails drawing on, reinterpreting, expanding, or challenging other histories. The purpose of this study is not simply to locate the Frankfurt trial within translation history and give it its appropriate status and visibility there but to ask how an approach that makes visible the issues of language, communication, and power, with which translation history is concerned, can contribute to an understanding of witness testimony and the conditions under which survivors are able to speak.

In order to understand the situation in which the translators and interpreters found themselves working at this significant historical moment, it will be useful to put their work in the context of training and employment in the postwar, post-Nuremberg Federal Republic. Research in interpreting at post-genocide trials has mostly focused on the high-profile tribunals set up in the wake of genocidal events: there has been important research on the Nuremberg Tribunals (Gaiba 1998; Skinner and Carson 1990; Behr and Corpataux 2006; Rumprecht 2014), the Tokyo tribunal (Takeda 2010), and the United Nations tribunals following the genocides in former Yugoslavia and Sierra Leone (Elias-Bursać 2015, 2019; Kelsall 2009). In all these cases, the tribunals employed simultaneous interpreting, which had been made possible by technological innovations; the scholarship has reflected this, discussing questions of accuracy, bias, monitoring processes, and the effect of the experience of interpreting on the individuals who carried out the task.

By contrast with the international tribunals, German post-Holocaust trials have been structured as "normal" trials following the standards and procedures of the German penal code (*Strafprozessordnung*). The work of interpreters has therefore been governed by the same regulations, which require the interpreter to be present at both the nonpublic pretrial evidence-gathering phase and the public trial itself. Rather than speaking through a relay system from a different room, as for the Eichmann trial, or present in the courtroom but enclosed in a glass box, as at Nuremberg, the Frankfurt interpreters sat at the same table as the witness and spoke into the same microphone. Their physical proximity to the witness is a vital element in the dynamics of the relationship between the participants: the intimacy of their relationship in a stressful situation makes these testimonies endlessly fascinating. There was also no elaborate, bureaucratic process of monitoring, quality control, and post hoc correction of transcripts in the Frankfurt court, as there was at Nuremberg and in all the subsequent United Nations tribunals. Unless there was a direct challenge in the courtroom, the words that the interpreters spoke were the final word.

In the rest of this chapter, I will draw on existing research into the history of court interpreting in the early Federal Republic, providing a different context for the interpreters' work: the trial contributed to a watershed moment in the history of translating and interpreting in Germany, as well as to the history of Holocaust memory. The 1960s saw debate about the professionalization of court interpreter training and about the role of interpreters in a society becoming rapidly transformed through mass labor migration. All this is happening while the interpreters are plying their trade in public in the Haus Gallus.

The history of interpreter training in Germany has been traced by scholars including Katrin Rumprecht, Wolfram Wilss, and Christiane Driesen (Wilss 1999; Driesen 2018; Rumprecht 2014). Although training courses for interpreters had existed in Germany since the 1930s, no specific training for court interpreting was offered until later in the century. A number of the Frankfurt interpreters—as far as I have been able to establish—had had legal training, which gave them an understanding of the task and the discourse, but whatever their background or qualifications in interpreting, none of them had had specific training in courtroom work.

The first school offering systematic interpreter training in Germany was established in Mannheim in 1929, merging with the University of Heidelberg in 1933. Nevertheless, it was not until the 1950s that training began to be offered alongside academic study: this coincided with discussion about the acceptability of non-German qualifications for work in the Federal Republic, an issue that had significant consequences in the context of the Frankfurt trial. New training schools—in Germersheim and Saarbrücken—were founded in the French occupation zone after 1945, followed by others, such as the Munich Sprach- und Dolmetscherinstitut in 1952; in East Germany, the Leipzig translation school founded by Otto Kade in 1950 provided professional training and academic study, largely in conference interpreting (Pöchhacker 2004: 131).

Training became increasingly formalized through the 1960s, with more institutes opening that began to offer specialized training in court interpreting: a school opened in Frankfurt while the trial was in progress. The introduction of more standardized examination regulations in the 1960s was part of a move toward clear, shared definitions of professional practice and obligations, and a national conference in 1970 dealt with fundamental questions of training: should training concentrate on language expertise or specialist subject knowledge (Wilss 1999: 159)? A feature of this process of "professionalization" is a political desire to employ "reliable" interpreters and exclude where possible the informal practices of language brokering and community linguistic support that migrant and minority communities depend on in their interactions with employers or bureaucracies. There is an unusually frank admission that interpreters cannot take up a neutral position in the record of a meeting in the Hessen Chamber of Industry and Commerce that took place on February 27, 1961. During a discussion of the issues raised by the employment of "foreign workers," one of the participants suggests that "German" interpreters will do a more reliable job than "foreign" ones:

> *German* interpreters are most suitable for ensuring successful linguistic communication between employer and the foreign employees. Employing a foreigner is not recommended, since the interpreter always has to carry water on both shoulders [i.e., balance responsibilities] and a German interpreter is better suited to representing the German interests towards the foreigners. ("Beschäftigung und Ausbildung ausländischer Arbeitskräfte," 27.2.1961, HHStAW 507, 7670b, 4)

"German" and "foreign" are not defined here, so it is hard to know whether the difference is one of citizenship, linguistic ability ("mother language"), professional vs nonprofessional, or some other nebulous distinction between individuals. The German idiom—carrying water on both shoulders—suggests an awareness of interpreting as a tricky balancing act, but the speaker also assumes that the interpreter must always represent one set of interests rather than mediating between them in a neutral way. It is clear here that representatives of powerful interests—the employers and their organizations—treat with suspicion interpreters who belong to the same community as the workers. It is a zero-sum game: being trusted by one side means being mistrusted by the other. Incidentally, there is no sense here that it might also be in the "German" interest for all workers to have their interests represented and needs met. Of course, this discussion is not about court interpreting, which has its own legal structure, which I discuss below, but it illustrates the context in which interpreting is being developed as a professional activity entailing specific forms of institutional trust that act as criteria for selection, inclusion, and exclusion: who is entitled to speak for whom?

Since the founding of the Bundesverband der Dolmetscher und Übersetzer (Federal Association of Interpreters and Translators, BDÜ) in 1955, translators and interpreters had developed a stronger sense of professional identity and solidarity, developing professional codes and campaigning for better pay and conditions; this was an international development, supported since 1953 by the International Association of Conference Interpreters. In Chapter 3, I discuss a case in which an interpreter makes reference to the standards proposed by the BDÜ in requesting (unsuccessfully) a pay rise.

The entrenching of systems of institutional trust through education and qualification requirements, bureaucratic regulation, and access to the benefits of professional status (however precarious these may be for translators and interpreters) has a direct effect on relationships between translators or interpreters, their employers, and the survivor-witnesses whose testimonies they translated. To put it bluntly, are the mechanisms by which an institution like a court ensures trust in translators and interpreters the same as the needs of survivors of genocidal violence for a relationship of trust with the person who speaks for them and performs their testimony in another language? This is one of the fundamental structuring questions of my study and is the ethical motivation for weaving together an account of the Frankfurt trial with the history of interpreting.

Thus, as well as a key moment in the history of post-Holocaust justice in Germany, the Frankfurt trial took place at a turning point in the development of interpreting as a profession. I would also argue that these developments cannot be separated from the history of West Germany as a country of significant migration, diversity, and multilingualism, with consequent challenges for language policy at moments when these issues are noticed and addressed by policymakers. The trial was impacted by the history of Germany as a country of continual movement of people across borders: the mass deportations of victims of the Holocaust and the dispersal of many survivors throughout the world; other Nazi policies of violent population transfer across occupied Europe during the war; the mass movements of Displaced Persons and German expellees and migrants from the East, their transit through or settlement in West Germany; refugees from Eastern Bloc countries once the postwar borders had hardened; and the postwar reemergence of mass labor migration into West Germany.

The question of who is entitled to translate and how trust is created and maintained is vital here. The processes of professionalization described by Wilss mean that there is no opportunity for witnesses to select who will interpret for them on the basis of more personal forms of trust (e.g., the interpreter belonging to the same victim community or being chosen on the basis of personal acquaintance). When given the choice during pretrial statements outside Germany, we find evidence of witnesses bringing friends or family members to act as trusted language brokers, and witnesses sometimes complained that their words were misrepresented by court-supplied interpreters during the pretrial investigation (I discuss some examples in Chapter 6). The archive materials do not allow us to assess the truth of these allegations, so we should note instead how witnesses may project anxieties about being misunderstood or anger or dismay at having their evidence challenged onto a figure they identify with the court: the interpreter's subordinate position within the court hierarchy and the intimacy of the relationship with the witness means that challenging them is a less risky, face-threatening action than directly challenging the judges, prosecutors, or defense councils.

In October 1965, the Hessen Justice Minister issued a decree stating that translators and interpreters can only be sworn (*vereidigt*) for legal work if they have passed a qualifying state interpreter examination in Germany (see *Justizministerialblatt Hessen* 1965: 459). An interpreter must also be twenty-one years old, resident in Hessen, and possess the "required personal reliability." The educational infrastructure was now well enough developed for the state to redefine its access criteria to the profession: in the context of the difficulties encountered by the Frankfurt court in finding interpreters with appropriate expertise for some languages, the new criteria explicitly exclude the many bilingual or multilingual refugees, migrants, and expellees from Central and Eastern Europe who had been applying for work as interpreters on the basis of language competence. For example, the application in April 1967 of a Czech speaker for work on the grounds of his linguistic ability was turned down with reference to the decree (Letter of April 14, 1967, "Dolmetscher und Sachverständige, Landgericht Limburg/Lahn," HHStAW 462, 1387, o. Bl.). More seriously, it would also exclude from post-Holocaust trials many fellow survivors whom the witnesses might be more likely to trust and feel comfortable with on the basis of shared experiences.

In terms of the institutions of a liberal justice system, these developments are legitimate, as they help to support the constitutional guarantee of equal access to justice and the right of the accused to a fair trial. But they also demonstrate some of the issues that arise when a regular court comes to consider genocide or other forms of mass violence: it is not a forum in which the needs of survivors for an opportunity to testify to their experiences can be met in full, even though this was part of the intention of the prosecution and is what many of the survivor-witnesses anticipated. Furthermore, none of the Frankfurt interpreters were trained court interpreters, and none had a specific understanding, informed by research, of the issues presented by interpreting for genocide survivors. Even those who had training in interpreting and a legal background—by no means all of them—were still trying to understand the task as they went along.

We have no evidence for whether any of the Frankfurt interpreters engaged with the history of the Nuremberg tribunals or exchanged experiences with the other interpreters. Perhaps the nature of the Frankfurt trial as a "normal" court meant that the Nuremberg, Tokyo, and Eichmann trials were considered to be of a different order, and the interpreters and their employer did not consider their relevance. We know that the interpreters had to study the historical materials produced by the prosecution and familiarize themselves with the specialist language of the camp, but there is no open reflection on the history of interpreting or consideration of the especially distressing nature of the material or of the ethical issues raised by working with survivor-witnesses: that the interpreters thought hard about these issues is, however, clear from their behavior in court, as I show in the second half of this study.

Historians of interpreting in Germany have discussed the ambiguous employment status of court interpreters. Interpreting had been common in German-speaking courts since the late eighteenth century, and a law requiring an interpreter to be present in cases where a defendant could not understand the proceedings was introduced in Prussia in 1822. The multilingual and multicultural Austrian Empire had already introduced a similar law in 1803. The requirement for court interpreting was codified in 1879, after German unification (Balaei 2004: 30).

These developing features of liberal legal systems in the nineteenth century focused on the right of defendants to understand the case being made against them and were anchored in law and practice. After the Second World War, the Basic Law (*Grundgesetz*) of the Federal Republic affirmed the right to equal access to the law; access to court interpreting was guaranteed on this basis and later through the European Human Rights Convention.

None of these conventions, which focus on the right of the accused, include the right of the witness to understand everything beyond the questions that they answer; they are expected to deliver their testimony and depart. But at a post-genocide trial, survivors may want to recount their experiences and pay tribute to those who have died and may feel excluded or hurt when they are not able to follow the rest of the proceedings. This can have an effect on how they act in court, presenting the interpreter with a set of ethical choices that may go beyond the institutional expectations placed on them.

Despite the importance of interpreters' work in securing the constitutional right to a fair trial, their employment conditions and the status of their work have often been unclear. In the period in question in this study, the work of court translators and interpreters was covered by the law on expert witnesses or *Sachverständige* (Gesetz über die Entschädigung von Zeugen und Sachverständigen, 1957: from here on referred to by its official abbreviation *ZuSEG*). Despite this, translation and interpreting work was not considered equivalent to the testimony of an expert witness. Both expert witnesses and interpreters are considered to bring expertise to the court to assist it in forming a verdict, but the ambiguity arises from the fact that the work of *Sachverständige* constitutes evidence, but that of interpreters does not. So the work of the historians who provided such vital research for the Frankfurt indictment is considered a contribution based on the experts' own knowledge, whereas the interpreters' contribution is to mediate evidence provided by others.

Interpreters, in this view, do not create or supply knowledge. They require some legal expertise in order to do their job but cannot employ this expertise in order to comment on legal issues or advise witnesses. The boundary between clarifying through helpful translation and commenting or advising is hard to draw, and there are times when interpreters operate informally as expert witnesses during a testimony. Interpreters were also unable to argue that they brought expertise to court beyond a very narrow definition of translation as creating linguistic equivalence, which affected their ability to argue for appropriate levels of pay. As I will argue, interpreters do, in fact, collaborate in creating knowledge about witnesses, witnessing, and the language that can be used to talk about the Holocaust: there are, after all, other kinds of knowledge. This role of the interpreters, which is a key element of this study, is performed within and sometimes against the institutional discourse of the court.

In practice, of course, they coordinate the communication, advise on linguistic and cultural issues, negotiate and clarify meaning, filter for relevance, solve problems, and make ethical choices moment by moment; they also had to conduct research into relevant aspects of language use by the camp administration and the prisoners, as well as the language used by historians to describe the spaces and operation of the camp. Some interpreters also offered the witnesses assistance with aspects of bureaucracy, for example, filling in expenses claims.

The court tolerated, and often acknowledged, this supportive behavior informally on the part of interpreters who had developed institutional trust: some were able to "get away" with more than others. Nevertheless, it always exceeds the structuring fiction of court interpreting—that the interpreter is simply transmitting meaning "word for word" from one participant to another—and the Presiding Judge Hans Hofmeyer retained the power to discipline interpreters who exceeded the expectations of the role in specific ways, for example, acting in ways that undermined the discursive authority of the court by appearing to act on behalf of the witness. Small moments like this display and reinforce the limits the court places on the agency of witnesses.

Effectively, the role of both translators and interpreters at the trial is to ensure that translation disappears as an issue and is invisible rather than transparent. Their job is to produce written or spoken text that can act unproblematically as evidence in the ways defined by the legal system. They guarantee the truthfulness of the reproduction of the original with their names, ensuring that any problems that arise are seen as their responsibility rather than arising from the court's own linguistic practices or its attitude toward the speech of witnesses.

At the time of the Frankfurt trial, there was no provision in the German code for criminal proceedings for a verbatim transcript to be taken down by court officials; instead, a summary was made, marking important moments in the testimony, key events, and denials or affirmations on the part of the accused. The law was only changed in 1965, just as the Frankfurt trial was reaching its end, requiring a summary record of the content of witnesses' statements, though still no verbatim transcript. This means that judgment could only be made on the basis of what was spoken in court and the judges' assessment of the evidence. The interpreters' words become the text from which the judgment is written, and the institutional requirement for interpreters, as well as translators, was to produce original texts that superseded the texts that preceded them.

There is a telling change in the examination regulations for translators and interpreters applying for sworn status in Hessen that came into force in 1966. The previous regulations, issued by the Hessen Culture ministry in 1955 ("Erlass vom 1.6.1955," *Amtsblatt des hessischen Kultusministeriums* 1955: 166), had slightly different requirements for translators and interpreters. For translators, the summary of quality criteria reads:

> The applicant must demonstrate:
>
> Secure command of German and the foreign language and knowledge of the relevant linguistic and specialist reference works;
>
> Fluency in written expression in German and the foreign language, secure grasp of grammar and idiom, and faultless style;
>
> Ability to adapt to the demands of the text in question and its linguistic character [Sprachform], and the ability to anticipate potential misunderstandings and misinterpretations and to eliminate [ausschalten] them with appropriate translation choices.

For interpreters,

> The applicant must demonstrate:
>
> Secure command of German and the foreign language and knowledge of the relevant linguistic and specialist reference works;
>
> Fluency in spoken expression in German and the foreign language, secure grasp of grammar and idiom, and the ability to anticipate potential misunderstandings and misinterpretations and to point them out while translating;
>
> Correct pronunciation and intonation, good memory and concentration, quick understanding, empathy, confident performance.

Alongside generic differences we find one very interesting contrast: translators are expected to anticipate issues and deal with them in a way that ensures that problems of understanding do not arise, whereas interpreters are expected to draw attention to potential problems as they work. In other words, they are expected to employ their expertise to assess and describe problems and make explicit to the other participants their understanding of them.

In the new regulations ("Regelung von Gebührensätzen und Vorbereitung von Prüfungsordnungen aufgrund des Gesetzes zur Ordnung des Handwerks," 1966, HHStAW 507, 10842, 12), which update some of the requirements, this particular discrepancy has disappeared, and interpreters are expected to show

> Secure command of German and the foreign language in pronunciation and intonation, orthography, grammar, vocabulary, and style;
>
> Particular fluency in spoken expression;
>
> Concentration and empathy, allowing him to anticipate potential misunderstandings and misinterpretations in translation and to eliminate [ausschalten] them in translation;
>
> Flexible and confident performance;
>
> Familiarity with the practical requirements of interpreting.

Interpreters are no longer expected to draw attention to problems but to anticipate them and ensure that misunderstandings do not arise. This small change makes a large difference: where the earlier examination assumed that understanding was to an extent a responsibility shared among all participants in the communication, the new criteria place sole responsibility onto the interpreter. One small window that allows communication and understanding to be negotiated visibly under the guidance of the interpreter has been closed: becoming a sworn interpreter means learning to take sole responsibility and not trouble the client with issues of communication and understanding.

A further issue to note here is that translators and interpreters are understood to be mediating between different "peoples" and "national" cultures. The examination regulations require "sufficient familiarity with the state institutions and the political, economic, geographical and cultural conditions of the people [Volk] in whose language the test is being taken" (5). This understanding of translation and interpreting is driven by the economic needs of the nation-state, for instance, in communication with foreign business and political representatives. In correspondence from 1961 to 1962 concerning the founding of an institute for translator training in Frankfurt, the Hessen Ministry of Education stresses the needs of international companies, political relationships, and the developing role of the Federal Republic in foreign development and aid ("Einrichtung von Instituten zur Förderung der Entwicklungshilfe, insbesondere in Hessen," 1961–2, HHStAW 507, 10548).

Understanding translators and interpreters as mediators between static and separate national linguistic cultures clearly has little relevance for work—such as court interpreting—that often takes place in communication situations characterized by multilingual speakers and linguistic hybridity. Interpreters often find themselves in a position where they are obliged to pin a witness, who is communicating in hybrid form, to a single language to be able to translate properly. This has the effect of constructing the witness as the problem—a person with deficient language skills—rather than understanding that their way of speaking may be meaningful in this context. At a later date, interpreters' expertise would be acknowledged through the introduction of the term *Sprachsachverständige* (linguistic expert witness), though as Wilss acknowledges this did not clear up the problem, as it limits the defined expertise to "linguistic" issues, without a clear definition of what this means (Wilss 1999: 14).

To sum up, the interpreters at the trial were working within a professional situation that was developing dynamically and which put them in a complex institutional position of essentially unresolvable tensions. Adding to this the extra layers of complexity, emotional intensity, and public interest of this extraordinary trial, then it is clear that the conditions under which they worked made extreme demands and required flexibility, stamina, specialist knowledge, fleet-footedness, ethical sensitivity, an ability and willingness to reflect on their practice, and clarity of purpose. Few of these qualities were explicitly acknowledged in the statutes that governed pay and conditions for translators and interpreters: the ZuSEG law mentions specialist knowledge, the "difficulty" of the specific language, and potential loss of other earnings.

We should therefore always keep in mind that they are working in a situation in which the complexity of the task and the skills required were not recognized formally in any of the relevant institutions but were taken for granted in practice on the quiet, as the trial would be impossible without them. In cases of difficulty, the court could fall back on an ideology of interpreting as simply transmitting statements word for word from one language to another: when something goes wrong, the responsibility lies with the interpreter who has sworn an oath on the basis of this ideology or with a witness who cannot speak appropriately.

The extraordinary variety of the multilingual communication that made the trial possible gives us—and must have given the participants at the time—a clear impression of the international scale of the genocide and the multitude of ways of speaking about it. In order for the legal system to perform its task of formulating judgments, this material must be transformed into a set of documents in a specific form of Standard German. The potential unruliness of multilingual, often hybrid, survivor voices must be shaped and ordered—perhaps tamed—to operate as a German concern: the professional context of the translators' and interpreters' work is designed to ensure that this happens smoothly, or at least appears to happen smoothly, leaving no traces of uncertainty on the surface of the text. An elaborate system of professional trust operates in favor of the institution and its needs: what this means for the work of the interpreters and the needs of the witnesses is the subject of the rest of this study.

3

Who Were the Interpreters? Biographies, Pay, and Conditions

This chapter is perhaps the hardest to write, as biographical information on the vast majority of people who translated and interpreted at the trial is sparse or impossible to come by. With one exception, Wera Kapkajew, those who translated and interpreted did not speak in public about their work and left little trace in the archive beyond information on rates of pay: a vital source, which I discuss in the second half of this chapter but not enough to be able to make judgments about their work on the basis of biography. This is in stark contrast with the first Nuremberg Trial, whose interpreters have left behind a rich literature of autobiography and professional commentary, in awareness of the historic nature of the occasion as well as the fascination with the new technology being employed.

The Frankfurt translators and interpreters may have had many reasons for not speaking in public despite the fact that the historic nature of the trial was clear to everyone. There was no new technology to discuss and so no broader interest in interpreting in its own right: it was intended to be a normal trial with normal (consecutive) interpreting procedures. The interpreters were sworn to the court and may well have felt bound by codes of confidentiality and the need not to take risks that might endanger their employment. Most of the interpreters may simply have gone back to their usual routine after working for the court. We have no record of any informal interaction, reflection, or discussion between them, apart from some important statements by Kapkajew, which I discuss at the end, and a few traces in the archive, which tend to concern employment conditions.

This means that we are left with reflections on interpreting that occur live during the interpreted testimonies themselves and which tell us something about their understanding of the task and how it is negotiated during the proceedings. In this section, however, I will set out what biographical information we do have in order to give some background to the voices that we hear on the tapes. The number of individual translators and interpreters who contributed to the trial from initial investigation to final verdict is literally uncountable. Many are anonymous, working within organizations or in informal support of survivors who are providing information; prospective witnesses themselves translate back and forth between languages and discourses, trying to formulate their experiences in ways that the court can work with; translation and interpreting processes are present below the surface of many texts and statements, without being immediately detectable. We need to bear this in mind when thinking about the few identifiable individuals who are discussed in this book: the vast majority of translation activity is anonymous, spontaneous, evanescent, and swiftly absorbed within the larger processes of an institution or hidden within a document. But it is this work that makes the Holocaust visible and graspable at all.

The individuals discussed here represent no more than the tip of the iceberg, and the named visibility of their activity means that they are not representative of the whole. Nevertheless, this visibility is what allows us to investigate their working conditions, their agency, and the ethical choices that they make. I will devote most of this chapter to the sixteen interpreters whose voices we hear, but there are other individuals whose translation activity made a significant contribution and whose achievement it is worth acknowledging. Beyond the Frankfurt legal authorities, there are several centers of translation activity, for example, the WJC, the IAC, and the Israeli police. In Frankfurt, there are a number of individuals whose names occur regularly in the archive, working quickly to make documents and depositions available and—where they have sworn status—to confirm with a stamp the accuracy of received translations.

The name that occurs the most is Elisabeth Grimmeisen, who had been working as a clerk of the Frankfurt court (*Justizangestellte*) since at least 1954. As an employee already responsible for a range of administrative duties requiring legal knowledge without formal qualification as a lawyer, she also takes on extensive translation work, for the most part from Polish and occasionally correspondence in English. She also stamps and authenticates translations. It is not clear what formal qualification in translation or other experience she had. The most likely explanation is that she was a bilingual German speaker from the eastern territories who fled to the Frankfurt area at the end of the war: this remains speculative, however.

Whatever her qualifications, she has clearly accumulated enough institutional trust to be commissioned to translate witness testimony, which she does quickly and effectively. There is also a record of her acting as an interpreter during the pretrial investigation: she interprets during the questioning of the Polish witness Jan Sikorski on May 16, 1960, although Sikorski claims at the end that he has been able to follow the questioning and that Grimmeisen has only had to translate in a few cases (37638/33, 5537–43). From the beginning of the investigation, she translates substantial documents, for the most part witness statements sent by the Polish authorities or the IAC, and authenticates translated texts. It is not clear how this translation work is reconciled with her other duties, but she clearly plays a vital role in enabling the investigation to get off the ground, contributing to the smooth running of the proceedings and official communications, and doubtless also working in multiple informal ways to maintain her position and status: not untypical for female employees in this kind of institution. I comment on her rates of pay for translation in the next chapter.

The sheer amount of Polish-German translations produced by the investigation means that we have a number of names of translators who contributed significantly to the court's work. Wera Kapkajew does a large amount of translation work alongside her interpreting, as does Arno Fuhrmann, who does not take interpreting work. Fuhrmann is a qualified engineer who is accredited with the court in Frankfurt as a translator (his stamp gives his name and title as Ing. A. Fuhrmann). There is no other information on his background and qualifications in the archive, but it is a reasonable assumption that he was another refugee from the East who had found a niche in the Federal Republic using his language skills.

A number of other translators also seem to be refugees from the East: as in the case of Heinz Otto Beer, who translated from Hungarian, or Otto Stegmann, who translated and interpreted from Czech. Their qualifications tended to be legal rather than in translation: we have more biographical information for Stegmann, which I discuss later in the section on the interpreters. Their language skills were extremely useful in this period of mass movement from East to West and restitution claims for lost property: it may well be that this work sometimes provided a useful backup for individuals who had not been able to find a secure footing in the legal profession in West Germany.

The archive does not usually contain the letters of application written by prospective translators and interpreters, but one letter from Kurt Schneider, who took one commission in 1960 from the Prosecutors Office for checking and confirming Hungarian translations or potentially retranslating them (37638/40, 6711), gives us an insight into the way these refugees integrated themselves into the system. On February 5, 1950, he wrote to a court in Hanau, Hessen, applying to be accepted into the list of accredited interpreters in Italian, Hungarian, and Romanian. He lists his experience as working for the courts in Frankfurt, teaching at the Berlitz School, and working as a freelance translator: this is how he pays for his studies at Frankfurt University. He ends the letter with the statement, "I am a German (*volksdeutscher*) refugee from the South East." In an added remark he says that he realizes that he should include his denazification certificate (*Spruchkammerbescheid*), but he has not, as he hopes that his employment at the court in Frankfurt will be sufficient: in other words, he suggests he would not have been employed there if there had been an issue with his denazification ("Angelegenheiten der Sachverständigen für das Landgericht," 1936–53, HHStAW 470/124, 220).

Dora Frank also belongs to this interesting group of German-Romanian-Hungarian translators, presumably all originally from the same region: she is employed to deal with the complex correspondence concerning a group of witnesses from Romania, who had been difficult to locate and were not initially permitted to leave the country (e.g., letter from Heinz Düx to Magda Szabó, 17.8.1962, 37638/72, 13263). In the register of translators and interpreters for the court in the neighboring town of Hanau, Frank is recorded as a sworn translator since February 1952, giving her profession as "housewife": this suggests that translating was considered merely to be a supplement to her main domestic duties ("Verzeichnis der Dolmetscher und Übersetzer beim Landgericht Hanau, 1951–59," HHStAW 470/125, o. Bl.). It is not clear when she was accredited to work for the court in Frankfurt. It is not always clear what qualifications they have, but people in the position of these refugees are the ones potentially affected by the Hessen Justice Ministry decree of 1965, limiting employment as accredited translators to those with German qualifications.

There is a similar group of translators who work with Czech and Slovak, and who in at least one case (Otto Stegmann) we can identify securely as of Sudeten German origin (see his versions of statements by Margita Schwalbová and Erich Kulka in December 1961, 37638/60, 10935–40). I discuss Stegmann in further detail later in this chapter, as he acts as an interpreter during the public phase of the trial, and we have more detailed biographical information for him. Stegmann is employed for most of the Czech-German translation work, with Johann Kresse taking on some of the work. I discuss Kresse's attempted negotiation over pay rates in the next section.

There is a very small amount of translation from Hebrew, which is perhaps surprising giving the extent of the collaboration with the Israeli police. For the most part, translations were where necessary made before sending the material to Germany. So Hebrew translation commissioned by the court is limited to translated extracts from published texts by survivors: for example, a certain Dr. Lichtigfeld is commissioned to translate extracts from a book by Israel Gutman (letter from Düx, 28.3.1962, 37638/65, 11997).

Western European languages are a minority concern with this trial. There is little translation from English, despite the international scope of the investigation: most of the correspondence with international organizations representing survivors is conducted in German, and witnesses living in English-speaking countries often provide testimony in other languages. When they are interviewed in English in West German consulates in the United States, Canada, or Australia, their statements tend to be translated on the spot before sending to Frankfurt. Familiar bureaucratic procedures produce enough trust in these versions that the court will accept them. In Frankfurt, English translation is taken on by a number of different people, including Elisabeth Grimmeisen, Julius Steuer, and Wilhelm Schneider-Ludorff, who also works as an interpreter.

Translations from French, Dutch, and Norwegian reflect the court's need to build a picture of the mass deportations from Western Europe: names that appear with some frequency are Erik Ziese (Norwegian), Siegrid Weiberg (Dutch), Erika Diedrich (Dutch), Albert Herrmann (French), and Erwin Stroetzel (French). Diedrich also acts as interpreter, as does Stroetzel: he is present for one of the most dramatic incidents in the pretrial investigation, which has consequences for the interpreter Schneider-Ludorff in the main trial. During the questioning of the French survivor Charles Corrin in Frankfurt in April 1962, Corrin claims he saw the defendant Stefan Baretzki on the "Ramp" at Birkenau during the "selection" of prisoners. Confronted with this evidence, Baretzki calls Corrin a "vulgar liar," for which he is fined 300 DM ("Ordnungsstrafbeschluss," 16.4.1962, 37638/72, 13342). Corrin is an interesting witness who has clearly had a difficult experience with testifying at the trial: the conflicts continue during his testimony in open court on July 27, 1964, where he carefully monitors and criticizes the interpreter Schneider-Ludorff. I discuss this event in Chapter 9.

A small, but consequential role is played by the Ukrainian scholar Dr. Olexa Horbatsch, who gained a Chair in Slavonic Studies in Frankfurt in 1965. For the court, he translated an article by the Ukrainian nationalist exile Borys Witoschynski concerning conflicts between Polish and Ukrainian prisoners in Auschwitz and read it into the record in open court on July 3, 1964 (37638/113, 466).

What I have set out here is really just the tip of the iceberg, but I hope to have given an impression of the intensive translation activity and the scores of translators involved, working under very different conditions and in many different countries. Certain groups and patterns do emerge, however: for example, the many former refugees and expellees from German-speaking Central and Eastern Europe who earned a living with translation. We also find evidence of the willingness of foreign judicial authorities and the political representatives of survivors to translate witness statements and correspondence into German before sending them to the court: translation here becomes a contribution to attaining justice. The court needs their work in order to build up a picture of the international scale of the prisoner population at Auschwitz, ensuring that the trial can go ahead at all means relying on specific forms of institutional trust that translation can be taken for granted.

The Interpreters in the Open Court Phase of the Trial

This section will set out what biographical information is available for the individuals who are the main focus of this study: the sixteen interpreters whose voices we hear on the recordings of the trial. It will also summarize the extent of their work and introduce some of the issues that I will be discussing in the analytical chapters. The uneven availability of information means that some individuals will have no more than a couple of lines, while others can be written about in more detail. For this reason, I will not be able to draw any secure conclusions about interpreters' practice based on biographical data. I should also stress that the availability or otherwise of biographical information will have no effect on how much space I devote to a specific individual's work in court. This section is designed to provide some background information and a brief portrait.

Michael Benesch interpreted from Czech and Slovak. He was brought in to replace the interpreter Ottmar Schamschulla on November 6, 1964, after the latter's work had come in for harsh criticism in the court. Benesch had already had to step in for Schamschulla after it became clear that Ján Weis, a witness from Bratislava, was speaking Slovak: the court appears not to have considered the issue of Slovak-speaking witnesses before this point. Benesch establishes himself as the court's preferred interpreter: he goes on to interpret for eleven Czech and Slovak-speaking witnesses. For the most part, they report on the transports from Theresienstadt and the so-called Theresienstadt Family Camp in Birkenau.

Benesch was clearly not a sworn court interpreter in Frankfurt, as he has to be formally sworn in in court. From this we learn that he was thirty-three in 1964 and employed as a research assistant at the College of Education in Frankfurt: so he is a researcher in pedagogy and presumably also a teacher trainer. His qualifications are unknown, but there is a record of a Michael Benesch gaining his teaching degree in Frankfurt in 1954, with the subjects History and Catholic Religion, and a dissertation entitled "The Endangerment of Young People under Communism" ("Lehramt an Realschulen [Mittelschulen]: Bahl – Buß [Benesch, Michael]," 1954, HHStAW 801, 22). This may not be him, but the age profile is correct. Benesch may well be either an expellee from Czechoslovakia or someone who left the country for West Germany when still very young.

Rolf Dienesch interpreted from Hungarian and Romanian. We first hear of him in the archive in a note to the pretrial statement of the Hungarian Jewish survivor Alfred Ehrenfeld, who had come from Sweden to testify on July 2, 1962. The original interpreter, Dr. Heinz-Otto Beer, a lawyer, was unable to appear and so recommended his cousin Rolf Dienesch, who was sworn in, giving his age as thirty-four (37638/70, 12892). Beer and Dienesch were presumably both of Transylvanian German background: Dienesch's work interpreting from both Romanian and Hungarian suggests this. Dienesch continues to take on translation and interpreting work after this, interpreting for the four witnesses who request a Hungarian translator (Adrienne Krausz, Paul Pajor, Albert Ehrenfeld, and Lajos Schlinger) and the one (Magda Szabó) who speaks Romanian. Dienesch is singled out for harsh public criticism in the much later video testimony by Adrienne Krausz, which I discussed in the introduction.

Erika Diedrich interpreted for three Dutch-speaking witnesses in open court, in March and April 1965, in the final weeks of the proceedings. One of these testimonies (Celine van der Hoek, April 12, 1965) is extremely brief, but the other two (Abraham de la Penha, March 26, 1965, and Rosje Corper-Blik, April 12, 1965) are useful examples of how an interpreter needs to deal with problems created by witnesses who try to bypass her and speak directly to the court. Diedrich was sworn in as interpreter for the Frankfurt court on October 9, 1964, in the middle of the trial, having previously worked for the court in Hanau. Clearly there is a perceived necessity for a Dutch interpreter at this moment, as these witnesses can talk about transports to Auschwitz from Western Europe, though the archive contains no detail of her employment beyond this.

Hilde Firtel (whose name we sometimes find in the archive as Fietel or Fiertel) did a small amount of interpreting between French and German: for Dounia Wasserstrom, April 24, 1964, Louise le Porz, November 27, 1964, and Paul Schaffer, January 11, 1965. It is not clear from the archive how she came to be working for the court, as she had no formal interpreting or legal training and was not a sworn interpreter at the time: she has to be sworn in formally at the beginning of Wasserstrom's testimony. She had gained experience interpreting for the Allied authorities after 1945 and in the 1960s was making a living as a writer and translator (she gave her profession as *Schriftstellerin* (writer) when she was sworn in). Her previous life had been dramatic, however. Born in Vienna in 1910 to a wealthy Jewish family, Firtel studied composition and conducting, eventually choosing to become an orchestral conductor, with some success in the early 1930s. The family's economic difficulties led her to turn to playing piano in variety theatres, which offered a steadier income.

In 1937, she moved to Milan, working as a German and French teacher and secretary and converting to Catholicism. After being denounced as a communist agent, she left Fascist Italy for Manchester, where she continued to work as a teacher, translator, and journalist. Here, she encountered the Catholic lay apostolic organization Legio Mariae, to which she devoted the rest of her life. She joined the US Army as interpreter, returning to Germany in 1944, where she built up the German branch of the Legion, persuading the German bishops to support this lay organization that had been regarded with suspicion in the pre-Second Vatican Council hierarchy. By the time she interpreted for the Frankfurt court, she had given up her role in the Legion and was producing translations, autobiographical works, and biographies of Catholic figures. She died in Frankfurt in 1991 (see Korotin 2016).

Moritz Grünblatt interpreted for the two witnesses who requested a Yiddish interpreter in the public phase: Dov Paisikovic, October 8, 1964, and Milton Buki, January 14, 1965. Grünblatt had been located through the Frankfurt Jewish community (see Stengel 2022: 401). It has not been possible to establish more information about him.

Erwin Jarolim interpreted for a small number of Czech-speaking witnesses: we have recordings of him working with Rudolf Rybka, October 19, 1964, Artur Radvanský, October 9, 1964, Max Kasner, October 15, 1964, and for the second day of the testimony of Filip Müller, October 8, 1964. He appears only to have worked for the court in October 1964. Biographical information is sparse, but his profession is given as *Bank-Oberinspektor*: he is not a professional interpreter, but perhaps one of the group of German refugees who supplemented their income with translation work. His work comes under challenge in court, and he eventually has to be replaced: I discuss these challenges further in Chapter 9, as they give us useful information about the court's quality criteria and the tensions between witness, interpreter, and court.

Wera Kapkajew is mentioned frequently in this study: I cited witnesses' reactions to her work in the introduction and will discuss the press interest in her work and person in Chapter 7. The next section of this chapter sets out her reaction to challenges to her hourly pay as interpreter, which was well in excess of the others named here. This information is pulled together in another publication, where I explore her work and the way she was able to fulfill and manipulate role expectations in order to build a career (Davies 2022).[1] In this section, I set out what is known about her biography for easier comparison with the other interpreters.

Born Wera Mirman in Poland on November 22, 1918 to a family of Russian émigrés, she had studied Law in Vilnius (since 1922 part of Poland) before the German invasion; after 1945, she ended up in Frankfurt, becoming a sworn translator and interpreter for the state of Hessen. There are significant gaps in what we know of her biography, which has been pieced together from obituaries published on her death in July 1984 (Kamiński, 1984; Kapkajew, 1984). In particular, details of how and when she arrived in Germany are vague: her anti-Soviet background makes it likely that she fled before the advancing Red Army. Initially, she taught Russian and trained as an interpreter, being sworn in as a court interpreter in Frankfurt from November 1958 ("Verzeichnis der Dolmetscher und Übersetzer beim Landgericht Hanau, 1951–1959," HHStAW 470, 125).

Oleg Beyda and Igor Petrov have established that she was connected through her husband with Russian collaborators who fought alongside the Wehrmacht: after the war, she married a man who had fought with a notorious unit of Russian Nazi collaborators, the Kaminski Brigade, which was eventually absorbed into the Waffen-SS, taking part in the suppression of the Warsaw Uprising. They settled in Frankfurt, where Wera worked as translator and interpreter (Beyda and Petrov 2017). It is clear why this connection would have been obfuscated after 1945, and it is unlikely that the Polish survivors for whom she interpreted would have known, though one can imagine their reaction. It is tempting to speculate on her inner conflicts when interpreting, but we have nothing to go on beyond the statements she made to journalists, which naturally avoid this aspect of her biography. Of all the interpreters at the trial, she is most skilled in establishing and maintaining trust and positioning herself in relation to the different, and often conflicting, expectations from different sides (institution, witnesses, press) of the role of interpreter.

Kapkajew continued to translate and interpret for the Frankfurt court, working for the subsequent Auschwitz trials and being recommended in 1965 for the Central Office of the Land Judicial Authorities for the Investigation of National Socialist Crimes, indicating that she had built a career and reputation around this kind of work ("Ahndung Nationalsozialistischer Straftaten," Band 21, 1965, HHStAW 505, 2616, 111). Her most significant translation project in the field of Holocaust testimony was Wiesław Kielar's important Polish text *Anus Mundi*, which she translated into German in 1979. Kielar had given testimony at the Third Frankfurt Trial in 1968, so Kapkajew may have met him in this context.

Kapkajew's unusual pay and status at the trial meant that she left a substantial trace in the archive, with the record of a conflict over her pay and expenses giving us fascinating insights into how interpreters' work was assessed in relation to the voices of the witnesses in the trial and what difficulties were seen to be associated with conveying these individuals' experiences: I discuss this issue in the next section. The earliest audio recording of her work is the recording of the testimony of Tadeusz Paczuła, on April 30, 1964. After this she appears regularly in support of testimonies by Polish- and Russian-speaking witnesses. The last Polish witness whose testimony she interpreted was Edward Burakowski, on April 26, 1965; the last Soviet witness, for whom we have evidence of her work, was Pawel Stjenkin,[2] on November 2, 1964, though she may also have interpreted for the final Soviet witness, Nikolaj Alexejew, three days later.

There are useful sources for her work accompanying the court's trip to Auschwitz in December 1964. The trip is well documented in the archive (HHStAW 461, 37638/93), and important historical research on the court's visit gives us a fuller picture (Pendas 2006: 178–82; Steinbacher 2001). Since most of the Polish participants could speak German, she may have played only a supporting role in most cases. There is also evidence that she worked with the group of volunteers led by Emmi Bonhoeffer, who supported non-German witnesses during their time in Frankfurt.

Janusz Kluźniak interprets for Polish-speaking witnesses when Wera Kapkajew is unavailable. We have recordings of his work with Władysław Gwoździk, July 17, 1964, Paweł Danel, April 22, 1965, and the director of the State Museum Auschwitz-Birkenau Kazimierz Smoleń, April 22, 1965. He had already interpreted for the court during the pretrial investigation, in the questioning of Tadeusz Szewczyk (16.5.1960, 37638/33, 5587). He was thirty-eight at the time of the public trial. On February 14, 1964, he had written to Hofmeyer applying for work with the court: "During a conversation with the Polish journalist from Bonn, Mr. Podkowiński, I was informed that you require a Polish interpreter for the Auschwitz trial" (37638/92, 17835). The journalist mentioned here may well be Marian Podkowiński, at the time the correspondent in West Germany for *Trybuna Ludu*, the newspaper of the Polish United Workers' Party. This gives us an impression of the kinds of informal networks that interpreters drew on in order to establish contacts and further their careers, stepping from outsider to insider status: it may also, more speculatively, give us an insight into Kluźniak's political connections or sympathies. I discuss Kluźniak further in the second part of this chapter on pay and conditions, as he challenged his hourly rate.

Johann Kresse had been a sworn interpreter in Frankfurt since August 1962: he gives his "Muttersprache" as German and is registered as offering interpreting in Czech, Hungarian, and Slovak ("Verzeichnis der Dolmetscher und Übersetzer beim Landgericht Hanau, 1951–1959," HHStAW 470, 125). Thus, it is likely that he was another postwar expellee from Czechoslovakia. I discuss Kresse's work in more detail in the second half of this chapter, as he challenged his rate of pay.

Ottmar Schamschulla (also Othmar Schamschula) interpreted for a number of Czech-speaking witnesses: we have recordings of his work with Alfred Wetzler, November 5, 1964, Viktor Lederer, November 5, 1964, Alois Vašut, November 5, 1964, Ján Weis, November 6, 1964, Ota Fabian, November 6, 1964. He was likely the father of Dr. Walter Schamschulla, a scholar of Czech and other Slavic literature at Frankfurt University (later at Berkeley), who also worked for the court: they were German postwar expellees from Czechoslovakia. Schamschulla's work is discussed further in Chapter 9.

We have one recording of the English-German interpreter *Regina Schmidt-Ott* (Helen Goldmann, September 3, 1964). She gives her profession as *Hausfrau* (37638/208, p. 78).

Wilhelm Schneider-Ludorff interpreted for a small number of French-speaking witnesses, though he also translated documents from English for the court. We have recordings of the testimony of Charles Corrin and Simon Gotland, both on July 27, 1964; in the case of Gotland, he had to be replaced by Wera Kapkajew, as the communication began to break down (see Chapter 12). We have a certain amount of biographical evidence in the archive due to documentation gathered for a disciplinary hearing in 1960, the details of which need not concern us here. We should be aware that these biographical details are taken from his own postwar account, so they should be treated with all due caution.

In many ways, Schneider-Ludorff was the typical legal insider, able to bridge the transition from the Third Reich to the Federal Republic with little difficulty. Born in 1911 in Offenbach am Main, and thus—unlike the majority of the interpreters—a local born and bred, he studied law in Frankfurt and Berlin from 1934 to 1938, moving on to work for the Reichskommissariat für die Preisbildung in Berlin, a department of Goering's Four-Year Plan ministry responsible for maintaining price controls. After the invasion of France, he took up a post in the occupation authority in St Germain, before fighting in North Africa from 1942, until he was taken prisoner in Tunisia. He was a POW until 1946, returning to Germany to work for the United States occupation authorities and train and qualify as an interpreter (he leaves no record of where he trained). He is recorded as admitted for courtroom interpreting in Frankfurt from 1948 and was licensed to practice as a lawyer again in 1949. In the CV supplied with the documentation, he claims to have been included in the Christmas Amnesty of 1948, thus requiring no denazification documents to allow him to take up his work again. The slight professional hiccup of disciplinary proceedings against him seems not to have jeopardized his further career ("Personalakte Schneider-Ludorff, Wilhelm Christian Friedrich," HHStAW 505, 5287).

Franz Schuh did English-German interpreting for a number of witnesses: we have recordings of his work with Lili Zelmanovic, December 3, 1964, Charles Coward, February 19, 1965, George Preston, March 4, 1965, Arthur Woloski, March 4, 1965, Boris Piękny, April 22, 1965, and the American judge Michael Musmanno, March 29, 1965. As with the other English and French interpreters, he may have gained experience working with the Allied authorities, but there is no further biographical evidence in the archive.

There is more evidence available for the career of *Otto Stegmann*, who interpreted between Czech and German: like the other Czech interpreters, he was a German expellee from Czechoslovakia, but in this case we have more evidence of his prewar activities. Stegmann had done a large amount of written translation work for the court, translating correspondence and authenticating translations of Czech-language witness statements. His contribution to the public phase of the trial is minimal, but fascinating: he is present for the testimony of Imrich Gönczi on June 8, 1964, but beyond providing his personal details at the beginning, he is not required, as the questioning is conducted entirely in German. More strikingly, he also works on the first day (October 5, 1964) of the testimony of the Slovak *Sonderkommando* survivor, Filip Müller, who went on to write a significant testimony and to contribute to Claude Lanzmann's *Shoah*. He supports Müller in speaking German, and the interaction between them develops in a fascinating way (see Davies 2021).

It is worth looking at the evidence for Stegmann's biography, despite his minimal contribution to the public trial, as it gives us insight into the careers of translators and interpreters from German-speaking Central and Eastern Europe who made their home in West Germany. Born in 1899 in Budweis/České Budějovice,

Stegmann studied law at the German University in Prague between 1918 and 1923, gaining his doctorate.[3] He went on to practice law in his home town, while becoming active in the nationalist political-cultural organizations dedicated to "protecting" the culture of the German minority in Czechoslovakia: he seems to have had a high office in the Deutscher Böhmerwaldbund in the early thirties. He continued to work as notary and lawyer during the war and was also a sworn interpreter, though there is no evidence of formal qualifications. After the war, he worked as an interpreter until his expulsion in 1947, when he moved to Frankfurt and began to practice again. His daughter, Erika Stegmannová-Klöss, wrote an autobiographical account with memories of her father's life (Wagnerová 1993: 64–72).[4]

His biography—sparse as it is and with many gaps—helps us to understand some of what was at stake in the Frankfurt courtroom: the legacy of prewar nationalisms and multilingualisms was being negotiated, with Holocaust survivors encountering people with a (partially) shared cultural background but who may have played some part in preparing the ground for the destruction of their communities. The courtroom is steeped in political, cultural, and linguistic histories beyond the immediate context of Auschwitz.

The interpreters' varied backgrounds tell us much about the way formal and informal networks operated and how individuals were able to build careers in the early years of the Federal Republic, characterized as they were by mass migrations and multilingualism. It is striking how Germans originating from Eastern Europe were able to find work, but there is only one Jewish survivor represented here, Moritz Grünblatt; though we should also not forget that the Catholic convert Hilde Firtel only escaped the Holocaust through good fortune and that we do not have secure biographical information for all the interpreters. It seems likely, though, that apart from two Yiddish speakers, none of the Jewish survivors who spoke in open court had their words interpreted by a fellow survivor.

I conclude this chapter with a look at the interpreters' pay and conditions, considering what this says about how interpreting is valued and understood within the institution and about the interpreters' ability to intervene on their own behalf.

Pay and Conditions

The pay and institutional status of court translators and interpreters were regulated by the law governing the employment of *Sachverständige* (expert witnesses), the Gesetz über die Entschädigung von Zeugen und Sachverständigen (ZuSEG 1957). The Frankfurt trial made extensive use of the testimony of historians as expert witnesses, in particular in drawing up the indictment: since this material, representing alongside the extensive judgments a thorough account of the history and functioning of the Auschwitz complex, was to be published, the prosecution hoped that it would serve as a source of public education beyond its purely judicial function (see "Schwurgerichtsanklage" and "Urteil" in Gross et al. 2013: 105–583; 575–1236; also Wojak 1999).

The work of expert witnesses can, in certain defined contexts, be counted as evidence at trial. The ambiguous status of translators and interpreters within this system arose from the fact that their work does not count as evidence, even though their employment was governed by the same law. This situation was reformed in 2004, though issues remained (see Balaei 2004). However, the concrete actions of interpreters and the uses to which their expertise is put in court demonstrate the falseness of any distinction between translators or interpreters and other expert witnesses. For example, the first time that Wera Kapkajew's name is mentioned during the court proceedings comes in a discussion drawing on her linguistic and legal expertise in translating and, significantly, correctly understanding the previous verdict of a Soviet military tribunal ("Verlesung des Urteils zu Oswald Kaduk," 13.3.1964).

The ZuSEG (§16 (3)) set rates for written translation per line, with a base rate of DM 0.30, rising to up to DM 1 per line for specialist technical or medical texts or "other especially difficult translations." It determined the hourly rate for interpreters in line with the rate for expert witnesses. The hourly rate was set between DM 7.50 and DM 15 per hour, depending on the necessary specialist knowledge or difficulty of the task (§3 (2)). The precise rate of pay is set by the court (in effect, the presiding judge), but the expert witness and the state have a right to appeal (§16).

The only circumstances in which these rates can be exceeded is when it can be shown that the individual has suffered an unreasonable loss of earnings due to the duration of the work or has had to spend a significant amount of time engaging with scientific or scholarly material (§3 (3)). Qualifications or experience do not play a role in determining the rate of pay, and emotional stress or other potential psychological effects are not mentioned explicitly.

The power of the presiding judge to set pay rates, within the limits set by the law, means that the archive contains some useful information about how translating and interpreting were evaluated by the court. Our archival sources for institutional attitudes are sparse, though, and so it is impossible to build up a complete picture; the most significant discussions of translation, such as assessments of individuals' work, will have taken place informally and have left no archive trace. Our best source for understanding how institutional actors viewed translation and interpreting in practice is through an analysis of the live courtroom interactions, where they are confronted with situations that challenge established procedures and require intervention. Nevertheless, it is possible, using the available archive sources, to go some way toward establishing the ideologies of translation that circulate within the institution and that affect how translators' and interpreters' work is evaluated. Anthony Pym's question—what happens when translation and interpreting become visible as contested objects of knowledge?—is a useful way to structure this investigation (Pym 1999).

The archive provides us with details about the pay rates for individual translators and interpreters without, in most cases, any evidence for the reasoning behind differential rates. We can extrapolate from the criteria set out in the ZuSEG to draw some cautious conclusions about what kinds of work the court defined as "more difficult" or as requiring "specialist knowledge"; caution is required here, though, as it is impossible to establish to what extent the loss of other earnings played a role in setting rates of pay.

As so often with this trial, we find the standard procedures being tested by the extraordinary scale of the proceedings, the nature of the crimes and experiences under investigation, and the linguistic problems presented by the testimonies. The ZuSEG contains no criteria for emotional strain or for linguistic issues beyond the perceived difficulty of the language involved and the need to study specialist vocabulary; however, the phrase "difficulty of the task" (Schwierigkeit der Leistung) contains potential ambiguity that can be exploited. There are also no official criteria covering the quality of an individual's work, as opposed to the challenges of the material, but considerations of quality must have played a role in the selection of individuals for specific tasks and clearly also in setting pay rates.

Some interpreters also contributed to the smooth functioning of the trial in more informal ways, in particular working with the witness support groups and providing advice for witnesses in form-filling. This kind of activity was vital, but it could be perceived as compromising the interpreter's neutrality. It is therefore perhaps surprising that no objections were made to informal contacts between interpreters and witnesses, not even on the part of the defense team, who otherwise took every opportunity to allege collusion between witnesses.

As I will show at the end of this section, most of these issues—including the activities that are not included in the ZuSEG criteria—could be used to set pay rates for interpreters, indicating a degree of flexibility and awareness of the extraordinary nature of the work involved but setting a complex set of hurdles that interpreters had to take before attaining the required levels of trust. The sources we have to draw on, for the most part, document the agreed rate per line for translating or per hour for interpreting: if there was any formal or informal negotiation over these rates, there is no trace left in the archive. As Heike Demme clarifies, the invoice submitted is actually a *Kostenfestsetzungsantrag* (application to fix costs), implying that negotiation takes place and the institution is able to set the final amount according to its own assessment (Demme 2017: 24). So we are left drawing inferences about how specific kinds of work were valued by the court. In the following, I will give an overview of what seems to have been the norm for the trial and then concentrate on a small number of cases where negotiations or appeals become visible, allowing us to draw more concrete conclusions.

A trial archive is not structured around making translation visible: translation is a means to the end of documenting the process of evidence-finding and judgment. Translation is therefore not exactly invisible but visible to the extent that its visibility contributes to demonstrating the legitimacy of the proceedings. Pay rates for the sworn translators are documented carefully in the trial *Kostenbände* (volumes 190–211 of the trial archive) and occasionally in other correspondence; since these costs are subject to audit and appeal (one of the legitimizing practices of the justice system), they must be accessible and extractable from the archive.

Witnesses and their representatives were not always aware that the court could meet translation and interpreting costs, so we also find correspondence elsewhere. For example, Simon Gotland wrote to the court from Paris offering his testimony in what would become the Third Frankfurt Trial (1967–8), which ended with convictions for two German prisoner functionaries, Bernhard Bonitz and Josef Windeck. Gotland offers to find other witnesses but asks for financial support for translating their letters into German, as the witnesses he knows are laborers who cannot afford the fees themselves (Letter 22.2.1963, HHStAW 461, 37656/02, 15). Gotland's letter exposes some of the extra obstacles placed in the way of many working class and poor survivors: the court will make its own translations of letters, but the witnesses need to know this and feel empowered to ask.

The *Kostenbände* show significant variations in the pay rates for sworn translators and interpreters, and it is not always easy to establish clear reasons for the differences.[5] Negotiations may well have happened informally before invoices were submitted, but the court seems to have accepted wide variations. For translations of witness statements and other documents, the court paid between DM 0.45 and the exceptionally high rate of DM 1.50 per line. So, for example, Franz Schuh received DM 0.60 per line for English-German translation (e.g., DM 0.60 for translating legal documents into English, 37638/208, p. 113) while Johann Kresse received DM 0.80 for Czech-German (37638/208, p. 71), as did Otto Stegmann (37638/208, p. 7), and Elisabeth Grimmeisen received DM 0.45 for Polish-German (37638/208, p. 37). It is not always clear what specific commission these rates refer to, so we are not able to judge the technical complexity of the work. However, the court did consider the languages of Eastern Europe to be "more difficult" than those of the West, so this may explain why Schuh's work was paid less than Kresse's, for example. As I show in the second half of this section, Kresse was an individual who was prepared to object, hustle, and negotiate over his pay with reference to the rates recommended by professional organizations. This may explain why his per-line rate for an "Eastern" language is higher than that of Grimmeisen, who was an employee of the justice ministry and thus perhaps not in a position to negotiate.

The highest rates were claimed by Wilhelm Schneider-Ludorff, who translated from French and English for DM 1.50 (37638/211, p. 90). There is nothing to suggest why he should earn a rate three times that of Grimmeisen for translating from Polish. He also earned the highest hourly rate that the law allowed for interpreting (DM 15 per hour for the testimonies of Charles Corrin and Simon Gotland on July 27, 1964: 37638/208, p. 39). Speculatively, one could say that as a lawyer who had practiced during the Third Reich and was a local rather than a refugee from the East, he was an insider, even though he had been disciplined for professional misconduct, and seems to have negotiated for himself a better rate.

Negotiation over rates was possible. The Hungarian-German translator Heinz Otto Beer submitted an invoice for translating Hungarian witness statements, in which he proposed a higher rate: "Since the texts are in places hard to understand—the witnesses do not write their native language well—I have taken the liberty of invoicing for a rate of DM 0.50 per line." (December 5, 1960, 37638/42, 7244). The rate that Beer asks for here is still comparatively low, however: an indication that the freelancers who worked for the court were not comparing notes and working together for fair payment. Apart from Schneider-Ludorff, none of the translators receive the amount recommended by the BDÜ at this time (DM 1 per line) as appropriate for this work, but there are occasions when translators use reference to their professional body to seek more appropriate recompense.

The Czech-German translator Johann Kresse refers to the BDÜ rate in an attempt to challenge his pay for translating survivor testimonies: this occurs during the preliminary investigation for the third trial, led by Heinz Düx, but it demonstrates something about the contrasting attitudes toward translation within the judicial system. In a letter to Düx in January 1964, Kresse refers to the standard rate set by the BDÜ and complains that he is not receiving this:

> The last time I submitted a translation of transcripts from Czech your colleague only approved a charge of DM 0.80 per line. This was the fee I was paid. Since the tariff rate is DM 1 per line and I am obliged by my association (BDÜ) to adhere to this tariff, I reserved the right at the time to approach you for payment of the difference of DM 0.20 per line.

The reply—drafted in a handwritten note on January 13, 1964—is extraordinary:

> According to §19 of the Act on the Compensation of Witnesses and Experts, the rate for a line with an average of 15 syllables is DM 0.45. Only in the case of specialized texts, technical or medical expert opinions, and particularly difficult translations can the rate be increased. DM 1.00 per line was justified because most witnesses describe their experiences in Auschwitz using special camp terms, requiring the reader to possess knowledge of conditions in the camp. This initially creates difficulties for the interpreter. Through your translation work you should now be familiar with these conditions, so that in the event of any further translations of statements about the Auschwitz concentration camp a rate of DM 1.00 per line can no longer be offered. (37656/19, 18150)

Effectively, this means that the more expertise a translator gathers, the less they can be paid: translators are not paid on the basis of experience or quality of work but purely on the basis of the specific qualities of the text, as assessed by the court. We begin here to see conflicts arising from the collective organization of translators and interpreters, asserting a professional identity beyond an individual relationship with the employer.

The hourly rates for interpreting tended to cluster around the higher end of what was permitted by law: for the most part, interpreters earned DM 12 or DM 15 per hour for the main trial, though rates were much lower for work during the pretrial investigation, normally set at DM 7.50. Evidence is lacking to draw clear conclusions about the reasons for discrepancies. The specific language seems to have made little difference, and rates varied as much between interpreters in one language as between different languages. During the main trial, Hilde Firtel earned DM 15 for French (37638/211, p. 33; her name is misspelled Viertel here). Otto Stegmann received DM 15 per hour for Czech (37638/208, p. 117), but

Ottmar Schamschulla received DM 10 (37638/208, p. 128). For English, Regina Schmidt-Ott received DM 10 (37638/208, p. 78), while Franz Schuh received 15 (e.g., 37638/209, p. 3); for Dutch, Erika Diederich received DM 10 or DM 12 (37638/209, p. 45, p. 49), and Moritz Grünblatt DM 15 for Yiddish (37638/211, p. 73). Some received varying rates: for example, Rolf Dienesch received DM 12 for Romanian (e.g., for the testimony of Magda Szabó on August 24, 1964, 37638/208, p. 65) and DM 15 for Hungarian (e.g., for the testimony of Albert Ehrenfeld on August 17, 1964, 37638/208, p. 54). For Polish, Janusz Kluźniak received DM 15 (37638/209, p. 61) when he stood in for Kapkajew, contrasting with her hourly rate, that was set at the very high DM 20 per hour.

The supposed "difficulty" of the language pair seems therefore to have played no role in the decisions. With the exception of Wera Kapkajew, female interpreters seem to have been less likely to earn the highest rate than male ones, which may be down to the law's reference to loss of other potential earnings: so Regina Schmidt-Ott, who gave her profession as "housewife," earned less for English than Franz Schuh, and those interpreters who were qualified lawyers tended to earn a higher hourly rate. The numbers are too small here to draw any firm conclusions, though, without further concrete evidence.

The archive contains little direct comment on interpreters' work, but there are a small number of cases that give us an insight into how they were seen within the system. Johann Kresse also raises a complaint about his rates for interpreting, and the internal correspondence that arises from this gives us an insight into the institutional views of the task of the interpreter. After a session interpreting in court for the witness Erich Kulka, on April 17, 1964, Kresse approaches Hofmeyer to complain about his hourly rate, referring to the much higher rate he received when working during the pretrial investigation. Hofmeyer makes a handwritten note of this meeting, for the attention of the prosecutor's office:

> The interpreter Johann Kresse has presented himself … and declares: I interpreted in Czech on April 16 and 17, 1964. I was paid an hourly rate of DM 7.50 for this work. I do not agree with this hourly rate. The translation in this trial is very difficult, as it has to be very accurate and is also done in front of the general public. I therefore request an hourly rate of DM 15. I have already translated for the public prosecutor's office in these proceedings and have always received this amount. My application is based on §§ 3 and 15 ZuSEG. In my own experience, the interpreters of the eastern states always receive the maximum rates if the subject matter of the translation justifies it. The interp. has declared that he will never work for the court again if he only receives the minimum rate.

> The interpreter Frau Kapkajew has already made a similar request. Herr Kresse would be grateful for an early decision. (37638/92, 17906)

Kresse addresses here some of the difficulties of the trial situation—the need for absolute precision in translating evidence and the high public profile and consequent pressure—but he has formulated it in a way that downplays the exceptional situation. Hofmeyer's own view is that this objection is justified, though he takes a different angle: "Eastern" languages are considered to be more difficult, bringing higher rates. We also have a hint here that Wera Kapkajew had made a similar complaint about her pay: I discuss her exceptional institutional position below.

Kresse's strategy of brinkmanship—threatening to quit—does not seem to impress the Prosecutor's Office. Staatsanwalt Vogel replies on April 27, 1964, with a certain dismissiveness:

> I do not consider it necessary to increase the hourly rate for the interpreter Kresse. The reason given that the translation work was particularly difficult because the translation "has to be very accurate and is also done in front of the general public" is not sufficient reason for an increase in the hourly rate, since this fact should be self-evident in the case of translation during an ongoing trial. Furthermore, I am of the opinion that the work of Herr Kresse as an interpreter for the Czech language can by no means be compared with the work of Frau Kapkajew as interpreter for the Polish language. (37638/92, 17908)

The sarcastic tone in which Kresse's appeal is dismissed indicates that he has not managed to formulate his reasons adequately, that is, in a way that refers to the concrete provisions of the law governing interpreters' pay. In Vogel's comments about Kapkajew we also gain an insight into the internal discussion about interpreting: Kapkajew is considered to be the better interpreter, justifying her higher pay. The ZuSEG does not allow for pay differentials in terms of the quality of individuals' work, so this shows that institutions were willing to employ informal quality criteria when they felt it necessary; this is not, however, made public in correspondence with Kresse.

The negotiation continues in a reply from the trial judges (Hofmeyer, Hotz, and Perseke) to Vogel on May 8:

> This reason alone does not justify an increase in the average maximum rate of DM 7.50 pursuant to §§ 17.3 (2) of the ZuSEG; in particular, it must be taken for granted that the translation from a foreign language is correct.
>
> However, it should be recognized that the subject matter of the proceedings and the degree of difficulty of the Czech language made demands on the interpreter's

> specialist knowledge that exceeded the normal case, so that an hourly rate of DM 10 seems appropriate.
>
> An increase to DM 15 is not justified. Such an hourly rate must be reserved for special services, e.g. for the translation of the testimony of an expert witness, for which special technical knowledge is required. (37638/92, 17910)

The trial judges thus appear more sympathetic to the achievements of the interpreters than the prosecutors, having a clear view of the importance of their work.

In the case of Janusz Kluźniak, the Prosecutor's Office supports him in an appeal against a manifestly unfair rate for the pretrial investigation. From May 16 to 18, 1960, he interpreted for the questioning of Tadeusz Szewczyk. He appears to have worked for the three days, but a note at the end suggests that Kapkajew was brought in to translate the whole transcript verbally back into Polish for the witness so that he could confirm it (37638/33, 5587–600). His submitted invoice for DM 8 per hour was reduced to 5, as the material was not seen as requiring technical terms or specialist knowledge (Letter from the judicial officer at the court [*Rechtspfleger*], 9.6.1960, 37638/192, p. 70). His appeal based on the technical difficulty of the material—medical language and the description of technical processes—was successful, and his rate was raised to DM 7: the court accepted that the work required "above average ability and specialist understanding" from the interpreter (handwritten note, 17.8.1960, 37638/192, p. 75).

Kapkajew herself was also interpreting on these same dates for Leon Czekalski, explaining why Kluźniak was brought in for Szewczyk. An invoice for this work shows her asking for a higher rate of DM 8 per hour because, as she puts it, "technical, difficult processes needed to be translated" (37638/192, p. 23). Czekalski's testimony (461, 37638/33, 5568–85) describes his observations of the operation of gas chambers and the sadism of individual defendants: in order to justify the higher rate, Kapkajew needs to use language reflecting the formulations in the ZuSEG law, which talk about "technical," rather than emotional, difficulty.

This testimony is, however, no more difficult than Szewczyk's in a "technical" sense. So we find that both interpreters asked for a higher rate of DM 8 per hour, but one had his rate reduced, while the other's was raised. The fact that Kapkajew is brought in at the end of Szewczyk's testimony may give us a clue that the court valued her work more highly. She may also be able to gain the court's trust through what we might call strategic honesty: her invoice for work done in June 1960 actually asks for the hourly rate to be reduced to DM 6 since, as she says, the witness was able to make parts of his statement in German (37638/192, p. 12; this refers to the questioning of Władysław Fejkiel, 7.–9.8.1960: 37638/35, 5790–807).

In all of these cases, pay rates are discussed in terms of the technical difficulty of the material and the use of specialist lexis, though Kresse is given credit for the "difficulty" of Czech as an "Eastern" language. Other grounds—for example, the stress of a high-profile public trial or the emotional extremity of the material—are not valid, which tells us something important about the way the court understood the work. The final example will show how Kapkajew begins to push against this restrictive interpretation of the law in supporting her claim to higher pay.

Her work for the main trial in April and May 1964 began at the highest rate of DM 15 per hour (plus standard sums for travel and other expenses), but from June she was paid DM 20 per hour, a sum that was not allowed for in the law and that exceeded what the other interpreters received. There is unfortunately no documentation of the thinking behind the court's decision to raise the hourly rate to DM 20: it was clearly taken very quickly, once Kapkajew's expertise and value to the court became clear. However, once the trial was over, the *Bezirksrevisor* (district auditor) wrote to the court on September 29, 1966 with an objection to the unusual hourly rate. This correspondence is very revealing for what it says about specific language ideologies and views of the professional status of interpreters and what their work actually involved. The auditor writes that the highest rate of DM 15 is allowable because of the difficulty and rarity of Polish, as well as the specialist knowledge required for the work, but that the law does not allow a higher rate ("Kostenband für Frau Kapkajew," 37638/210, p. 36).

In his handwritten draft reply of November 15, Judge Hofmeyer gives a detailed and sympathetic account of the professional difficulty of the work and the extent of Kapkajew's contribution to the trial and shows an awareness of the linguistic complexity of many of the witness statements. Hofmeyer begins by noting that Kapkajew's work for the court meant that she had been unable to pursue her usual employment for many months. He continues,

> Beyond this, the quality of the interp.'s work far exceeded the normal extent. She had to convey the true sense of statements that were often in dialect or given by people who were barely able to speak Polish (Yiddish). Because of her previous legal training, the interp. not only understood the meaning and intention of the questions, but was also able to explain them to the person being questioned, in so doing providing an invaluable service to the court. The quality and value of her work for the court thus fall under the provisions of § 3 Abs. III Ziff. a ZuSEG, as without her ~~activity~~ [crossed out in original] participation the work of the

> trial would have been in doubt, as was shown by experiences with other interps. ("Kostenband für Frau Kapkajew," 37638/210, pp. 37–8)

Hofmeyer draws attention to the linguistic difficulty of the work, with the interpreter having to deal with witnesses who could or would not express themselves in a particular language or in standard linguistic variants. This statement simplifies the complex situation in which the witnesses found themselves: the way they speak is seen as a sign of linguistic deficit for which the interpreter must compensate. In particular, the dismissive view of Yiddish as a sign of linguistic confusion or deficit tells us a lot about the language ideologies that characterized the court's work.

Hofmeyer also draws attention to Kapkajew's legal training. Qualifications and training are not mentioned in the regulations as grounds for elevated rates of pay, but Hofmeyer's letter contains an implicit critique of this absence: only her legal training enabled her to perform as required in the role. Hofmeyer's letter demonstrates a genuine appreciation of the skill of a good interpreter, though it is notable that the responsibility of unsuccessful interpreting lies clearly with the interpreter: the court requires smoothly operating communication of a particular kind and is not prepared to consider that its own communication practices, and in particular its attitudes toward witnesses who are victims of genocide, may be part of the problem. The interpreter's job is to deal with the linguistic deficit of the witness and to convey "the true sense of statements" ("den wahren Inhalt von Aussagen"). This statement makes clear that the court placed no value on the tone of voice or manner of speech of the witness and on the interpreter's skill in conveying this. The potential emotional load on the interpreter is also not mentioned here, as "the difficulty of the task" (ZuSEG §3 (2)) seems to refer only to technical, rather than emotional, difficulty.

Since the district auditor does not seem to have accepted the court's arguments, Kapkajew herself was required to write in support of her case. Here, she shows herself able to negotiate the internal, administrative discourses of the legal system as well as public interest in the witnesses. Her letter on December 12, 1966, is a masterpiece of rhetoric and legal positioning and is also very revealing about her view of the value of the interpreter's work and how it should be formulated in this specific context. She sets out several reasons: loss of earnings owing to the unusual length of the trial; the psychological strain of the work; the linguistic and legal problems requiring a high degree of professional competence and specific expertise; and the need to satisfy the requirements of the court when dealing with unusually difficult material:

> My work as interpreter in the proceedings ... which lasted nearly two years, was understandably so demanding that I had to severely limit or give up completely my other work as translator and interpreter.
>
> Besides the especially difficult and psychologically demanding material that I was translating continually, I had to master many Polish dialects, feel my way into what was said and convey it in German. I believe that there has never been another trial where such demands have been made of an interpreter. On some days, I had to convey the words of three or four witnesses of different levels of education, speaking different dialects and with different personalities, in such a nuanced and accurate way that none of the closely observing court officials had any grounds to object. Quite apart from the fact that an interpreter at this trial was expected to know all the specific language of camp life and understand and convey them accurately in both Polish and Russian. ("Kostenband für Frau Kapkajew," 37638/210, p. 41)

Here, she does not argue that she had to imitate the witnesses, or empathize with them, but that she has to deal with specific linguistic problems, including dialects and nonstandard sociolects, and interpret them correctly, under constant observation. Thus, trust is created and defended through professional expertise and specialist historical and linguistic knowledge and by responding to instances of control and checking which potentially threaten her professional status. She does mention—but only in passing—the psychological strain of the work, but this cannot be centered in this letter as it does not feature in the criteria justifying differential rates of pay. By contrast with the description of her work in the interview, Kapkajew's letter argues for trust on the basis of expertise rather than on ethical commitment: here, she presents herself as taking the side of the court rather than the witness.

The rate of DM 20 per hour is finally confirmed on January 9, 1967, in a document ("Kostenband für Frau Kapkajew," 37638/210, pp. 46–50) that takes up almost verbatim the arguments of Hofmeyer and Kapkajew. It makes no reference to the psychological strain of the work, which is not relevant to the regulations but confirms the other grounds: unusually high workload leading to loss of earnings, the difficulty of the linguistic problems, and her specialist legal expertise. It also adds new grounds, namely that she carried out tasks above and beyond her contracted hours, for example, helping the Polish, Czech, and Russian witnesses with their paperwork. We are given the impression of an indispensable and ever-present employee of the court whose energy and expertise are barely compensated even by the unusually high rate of hourly pay.

Conclusion

The assessments of the work of Kapkajew, Kresse, and Kluźniak give us an insight into the internal discussion of translation and interpreting that influenced the pay and conditions of the people who made this multilingual trial possible. We have the impression—as so often with this trial—of a real tension between an awareness of the exceptional nature of the work and an institutional need to maintain a sense of normality and legitimacy. An increasing awareness of the vital role of interpreters can be traced through some of the decisions on rates, and it becomes clear that there are informal internal evaluations of interpreter performance that do not map onto the provisions of the law but that affect pay. The official criteria for rewarding interpreter performance cannot acknowledge the key role that they play in enabling testimony nor the emotional burden of the work, so supporting interpreters' work means trying to find ways of making the provisions of the law work in their favor.

In order to gain the highest institutional acknowledgment of their work, interpreters have to work hard at accruing both "thick" and "thin" trust, that is, trust based on personal relationships versus trust based on institutional or bureaucratic procedures, for example, the approval of qualifications: they must fulfill professional obligations while also developing status and personal approval with significant individuals within the institution. If they are able to do this—as in the case of Kapkajew—they can then bring to the table arguments that are not specifically detailed in the legal criteria, mentioning for example the emotional strain of the work. In most cases, however, these extra criteria play no role, and the court has no mechanism at all for acknowledging the harrowing nature of the work or for understanding that "difficulty" may mean more than simply complex, specialist language.

Finally, we should note that the needs of witnesses, their understanding of the role of translator and interpreter, and their experiences with their work play no role in this process. This is an entirely internal, institutional discussion. An explicit ideology of correctness, accuracy, and objectivity, along with implicitly employed criteria of trust, ensures that interpreters and translators work according to institutional expectations. But the scale of the trial and the nature of the material push against expectations and ideologies of translating; we get a hint of this in the discussion of pay rates, but it becomes far clearer when we observe the interpreters working live.

Part II

Methods

4

Voices, Power, and Trust

Recent scholarship on interpreting has addressed issues of power, trust, and inequality in the courtroom. I intend to consider what aspects of this discussion allow us to analyze the courtroom interactions closely and understand what is at stake for survivors bearing witness to Holocaust experiences. The focus of my study will be on how the interpreters understand the ethical significance of their task and how this affects their interaction with the witnesses, and I will concentrate on aspects of their interaction that are relevant to this discussion. Naturally, in this specific institutional situation, any "challenges" to power occur at a level of detail that does not act as a threat to the institution: giving testimony at a trial is an act that reaffirms the institution and its discursive practices. The survivors become witnesses in a way that is available to them in the context of speaking. But witnesses, working with their interpreters, are sometimes able to make challenges either in the detail of the interaction or by projecting their voice beyond the confines of the court's practices to contribute to broader ethical and political imperatives. They may "be heard" in different ways.

In this section, I will set out how I read the interpreted testimonies, what questions I ask and what I am looking for in the exchanges. I read the recordings first and foremost as linguistic events unfolding in time in a specific present context rather than as representations of the past. In other words, I do not read the testimonies as a key to understanding Auschwitz as a historical location or the events that the witnesses lived through—though there are still untapped riches in this collection—but as a source that reveals something about the communicative, linguistic, and collaborative dimensions of testimony.

At the beginning of this discussion I want to make clear my own ethical position on the question of agency and intentions, which will have a direct effect on my analysis. Unless there are clear reasons not to, I assume that the witnesses are in control of their speech and are making active choices within the constraints of the communicative situation: this is how I read George Preston's outburst against Bednarek, which opened the introduction. This means not making assumptions about preexisting determining factors, intentions, or psychological states unless they are displayed in the interaction and the participants orientate themselves toward them. I do not exclude the possibility that witnesses' language use is determined by trauma, for example, but I find it ethically problematic to assume this on the basis of listening to an interaction. Assuming that the witnesses are making choices and exerting conscious agency gives them the dignity of political actors in a context of power, rather than being the passive objects of an analysis that assumes that I understand their motivations better than they do.

This means that I prefer to explore the testimonies as dynamic processes that emerge in interaction between participants rather than as reflections of cognitive processes or psychological states. I acknowledge the usefulness of cognitive linguistics approaches in interpreting studies, but my focus is on the details of relationships and interactions, so I do not employ them here. This will mean being explicit when faced with things that I can't know, and where there is doubt, coming down on the side of assuming that the witnesses know what they want and are pursuing conscious aims.

The work of Ellen Elias-Bursać on interpreting at war crimes tribunals has provided vital insights into the complexity of the interpreters' tasks. Interpreters are always in a situation of obligation toward multiple agents: employer, accused, witnesses, judges, and lawyers, with the added pressure of high public visibility in an emotionally fraught and politically contested trial (Elias-Bursać 2015: 3). They work between parties who compete over the sense of words, the interpretation of what is said, the reliability of memory, and the meaning of experiences of extreme violence (Elias-Bursać 2015: 143). What happens in court can have an effect on how witnesses are viewed, how testimony is formulated and heard, and how the crime is understood beyond the courtroom. Where issues of translation and interpreting become visible objects of contestation in the courtroom, they always stand as a proxy for other negotiations and conflicts to do with memory, guilt, experiences of pain, loss, and anger, and responsibility toward truth and the memory of the dead.

Elias-Bursać notes that translating and interpreting within an institution entail accepting and affirming the institutional system of values, its mission, and its linguistic practices, so the language professional must align their voice with that of the institution. Just as becoming a witness in court affirms and reproduces the court's practices and its construction of the "legal witness," acting as an interpreter affirms and reproduces the linguistic practices that support this construction. There are, however, always multiple competing discourses within and beyond an institutional context that not only complicate the task but also offer potential routes for challenge (Elias-Bursać 2015: 250). Interpreters can have significant power within the exchange itself as co-constructors of the interaction but within a broader institutional and discursive structure that they have little influence over. Resisting, challenging, or pushing back is difficult in terms of professional ethics, institutional practices, and expenditure of energy, potentially resulting in loss of face, damage to institutional status, and professional sanctions.

Professional codes and standards of behavior tend to reflect a view of the interpreter as transparent, invisible, passive, neutral, and detached: a language processor rather than an active participant. But they are figures who "fulfil a function in the institutional system of control," even though their position within that system may be precarious or ambiguous, depending on their employment conditions: they have power within the interaction rather than in the institution (Wadensjö 1998: 13). Importantly, the power is given by the institution but is not reducible to the needs of the institution:

> Interpreters can exercise this unique power by adopting certain verbal and non-verbal strategies to coordinate the communication … to negotiate, check, and rebalance the power relations, thus exerting a certain influence on the direction and outcome of the interaction. (Mason and Ren 2012: 238)

During a long testimony, the interpreter will establish a relationship with the witness that helps the communication to proceed smoothly but may transgress institutional expectations and potentially attract sanctions. The quality of the relationship as it develops tells us a lot about the interpreter's view of their task and who they may identify with: do they identify with the witness, the institution, their professional group, or with some more abstract set of ethical principles? And how do the witnesses and other participants respond? (Mason and Ren 2012: 240–1) The interpreter may act to empower the witness and to give them a voice, but that voice may be displayed or performed in such a way that it conforms to the court's preconceived ideas.

This ambivalent situation, enabling communication that could not otherwise happen, reproducing the effects of power while also being subject to them, and challenging power at the micro level while reinforcing it at the macro level, makes ethical decision-making indispensable but complex. Interpreters, who tend to have access to linguistic resources that those they interpret for may lack in their own language (an understanding of judicial procedure and language, for example), can act to empower them but may also represent them in a way that conforms to the court's terms of reference for a "good" or "bad" witness.

Rosemary Moeketsi's study of interpreters working in South African courts has shown that they often feel compelled to take action that would be considered unethical according to professional codes, for example clarifying aspects of a complex question, in order to rectify the imbalance (Moeketsi 1999: 91). This shows interpreters taking positive, and potentially risky, action to intervene on behalf of a speaker at the micro level of interaction in order to shift the balance momentarily: as I will show, the Frankfurt testimonies display many instances of this kind of intervention on behalf of the witnesses, with varying degrees of success. For the testimony of a Holocaust survivor, these issues can have a profound influence on the experience of testifying and on vital questions of trust and being heard.

The presence of the interpreter not only enables mediation but also creates an impression of irreducible difference that needs to be "overcome" in a specific way; the presence of an interpreter draws attention to difference and acts as a focus for communication problems. In effect, the ideologies of language and communication on which the work of the court is built define interlingual communication as a problem that can be fixed by an interpreter rather than as an issue of power. The speech of the survivor-witnesses tests these ideologies in a variety of ways, and the interpreter must expend considerable energy dealing with the consequent tension.

Moira Inghilleri suggests that professional codes provide reassurances that the role of the interpreter is clear: they encode ethical conduct as a matter of neutrality and faithful reproduction and disguise the political and social relationships in the dialogue situation (Inghilleri 2012: 33). There is a clear separation between the languages being spoken, and there is a defined semantic content that can be mediated and understood, with problems arising from the witness's expression or the interpreter's work rather than in the interaction itself. In Inghilleri's view, the role of professional codes is to disguise the power differentials in the situation (26).

Interpreters often find themselves in situations of ethical conflict: who are they obliged to? What does ethical behavior mean in this specific situation? Dean and Pollard have proposed understanding interpreters' work as a form of active ethical reasoning in practice rather than simply as a display of technical expertise. Dealing with the unpredictable nature of communicative encounters, interpreters engage in teleological reasoning—focusing on outcomes and the consequences of actions—rather than simply following a deontological ethical framework, that is, one drawn from externally imposed norms and rules (Dean and Pollard 2011: 157). They solve problems dynamically as the communication develops, considering the interests of the different parties, including their own, before acting (29). Because they must act publicly according to the codes they have signed up to, they often deal with issues that arise "under the radar" and are generally left alone to resolve clashes (32).

Professional codes and standards, as well as the forms of monitoring that accompany their work, lead interpreters to believe that they may only deviate from norms surreptitiously. Since they are nevertheless constantly evaluating the concrete situation in which they are operating in terms of its complex ethical dynamics and engaging in behavior that reflects this evaluation, they may find themselves in a position of ambiguity, tension, or conflict.

In a post-genocide trial, these ethical dilemmas are intensified as the stakes are much higher for all involved but especially for the witness, who is not simply providing evidence for a crime but also reporting on profound experiences of violence and loss. For this reason, my reading is fundamentally about relationships rather than questions of accuracy, how they develop over time within an exchange, and how the participants understand what they are doing and position themselves toward each other and the material they are dealing with.

Ian Mason reminds us that communication is a process of negotiating meaning rather than transmitting prepackaged messages. So an interpreted testimony situation does not consist of the preformulated memory being transmitted through an interpreter but is a process of negotiation over memory, language, and the meaning and nature of testimony in a specific context (Mason 2006: 2). It is less important to compare the propositional content of source utterance and translation than to describe the behavior of all parties and the attitudes and understandings that structure that behavior (Mason 2001: 54).

The role of "interpreter" is complex, having as much to do with organizing an interaction as with translation, working within a complex network of role expectations, opportunities, and constraints. Cecilia Wadensjö's discussion of this issue draws on Erving Goffman's participation framework to bring out the complexity of roles in an interpreted exchange: participants are engaged in constant evaluation of their own and others' performance of their roles, assessing the social identities that are on display and the qualities that are required to perform the role. In this view, "witness" and "interpreter" are roles that are constantly negotiated and challenged during an exchange (Wadensjö 1998: 86). "Interpreter" is the name of a professional status, of a specific function within an institution defined by bureaucratic structures of qualification and access, of an individual who carries the label "interpreter" in a specific interaction, and of a role carried out at a specific moment within an interaction. Any individual may carry out the role of interpreter in an interaction in court, but the "text" they produce will not "count" unless they are "sworn": are fellow survivors entitled to interpret, and who decides which form of trust is more important? What happens when different participants have conflicting perceptions of the role of the interpreter (advocate, adversary, member of the institutional establishment, etc.)? How is the perception of interpreters affected by other social factors: gender, membership of a survivor or perpetrator community, nationality, age, shared or conflicting background, or autobiographical experiences? Likewise, many people may lend a (helpful or unhelpful) hand at translating within an interaction, but only one will have the label "interpreter": what happens to a testimony when the supposedly clear channels of mediation are disrupted?

Questions of how an interpreter responds to a witness's statements may influence the impression that a speaker makes. Sandra Hale has put it this way: "Interpreters feel the pressure to improve on the style of the original, fearing that if they maintain the convoluted structure, hesitancy and incoherence, they will be judged as incompetent" (Hale 2007: 200). The interpreter's response to speech that he or she regards as incoherent—or could potentially be seen as incoherent in the court's terms—can have a profound effect on how the speaker is regarded as a witness. In a post-genocide trial, with its specific focus on the voice of the survivor-witness, this issue becomes especially fraught: the witness's speech may only appear incoherent to the court because its criteria for judging it are unable to grasp a different form of coherence or an emotional, embodied form of knowledge.

This presents the interpreter with an ethical choice between institutional expectations that require "word for word" interpreting of an incoherent statement and a face-saving behavior that clarifies and organizes what the witness says: the interpreter is regularly faced with these choices between different forms of ethical reasoning, and the interpreter's attempts to act in protection of the witness may also ensure that the witness's own way of speaking and knowing is lost.

Susan Berk-Seligson has shown how the interpreter exerts "a controlling force over the impression that the witness is making on the jurors" by altering the pragmatic intent of their speech (Berk-Seligson 2002: 145). The interpreter controls the flow of the testimony, determining rhythm, pace, speech, and silence and deciding what is heard and what isn't (Berk-Seligson 2002: 86). Even in a courtroom, with its strict rituals of communication, the interpreter may still be managing a situation with a lot of "side talk" and thus deciding what is heard, what is "on and off the record" (Wadensjö 1998: 191). They may process a fragmented account into a more fluent narrative, raise the register of witnesses' speech, "standardize" working-class speech or dialect, or disguise the hybridity of multilingual speakers' testimony. They often expand witnesses' shorter statements with particular linguistic strategies that alter their pragmatic force, for example, rephrasing statements, reorganizing longer passages, or inserting material that may only be implied in the original; softening criticism of the court or other individuals in order to preempt conflicts that the interpreter would have to resolve; inserting or deleting hedges and hesitations, politeness forms, modal particles (the latter are a characteristic and highly expressive feature of German speech, which cause problems in translation). They may also make interventions that weaken or intensify the presentation of individual agency in the situations described, foregrounding or backgrounding individuals within the event, shielding the speaker from exposure to criticism or shame (Berk-Seligson 2002: 99–100).

Mason and Stewart have shown how witnesses and interpreters engage in "facework" during interpreted exchanges. Giving testimony is a "highly face-threatening speech event," so a witness may use hedging, shifts in modality and register, off-record speech, and other behaviors in order to negotiate and protect face (Mason and Stewart 2001: 63). But the interpreter may also be engaged in complex face-saving behavior, either on behalf of the witness, trying to present them more favorably and give a good impression of their competence, or on behalf of themselves, trying to ensure that they are not held responsible for any perceived miscommunications, delays, or other problems. The interpreter may, for example, add or delete hedges in translation, affecting the perceived strength, confidence, or certainty of an utterance and changing its illocutionary force. These are factors that are vital for the perceived quality of eyewitness testimony in court, and shifts can have significant consequences, affecting the perception of the witness's coherence, confidence, and competence (Mason and Stewart 2001: 56).

Berk-Seligson suggests that such interventions, which happen for the most part "below the radar," may make the testimony sound more precise and coherent but at the expense of feeling weaker and less challenging, or more appealing, subservient, or obedient (2002: 131). Survivors' testimony often implicitly challenges the court's power and linguistic practices, and interpreters are left with a choice as to how to respond. An interpreter who is considered "professional" or trustworthy by the court may well be one who ensures witnesses' speech is presented in a form that presents no challenges, thus avoiding blame for problems. As Wadensjö has established, the more secure the accumulated institutional status and trust of the interpreter is, the more leeway they have to deal with problems and conflicts in ways that do not disrupt the work of the court (Wadensjö 1998: 133). They work within the court's power hierarchy to "counter anything identified as a threat to the shared interaction order" (Wadensjö 1998: 191), helping to determine how blame is attributed when problems arise: ultimately, though, such situations demonstrate how limited the interpreters' power actually is, as the power does not originate with them. They exercise power on behalf of the judge.

Anthony Pym shows that the interpreter is seeking coherence within each of the languages spoken in court, trying to ensure that what is said makes sense in terms of the progress of the interaction (Pym 1999: 274). This form of coherence-seeking behavior has consequences for how the witness is seen in court. The court regards communication through an interpreter as a clear, linear process of "bridging" between two separate worlds of expression, framing the witness as passive: the witness speaks, the words are transmitted through the interpreter and then received by the hearers, and vice versa. But communication in the Frankfurt court in particular is dynamic and often multilingual or hybrid, with witnesses and other speakers understanding aspects of what is said, communicating in different ways, bypassing the interpreter, and passing the role of "interpreter" between them. Aspects of meaning always bypass the person designated as interpreter—gesture, intonation, or fragments of language that other parties believe they understand—and the interpreter is faced with a choice as to how to deal with such events. Do they try to restore "order," intervene in different ways, or simply give up?

We should note here that such dynamic, hybrid activity is a normal feature of communication in groups; it only appears "chaotic" because the court's practices assume a simplified model of formal dialogue. So restoring "order" in this situation is an exercise of power on behalf of the court, and the interpreter has access to specific behaviors which allow him or her to intervene and take control: they can determine whose turn it is to speak, ignore one or more speakers, determine what order things are translated in, or, in a more drastic move, actively silence one of the speakers. Once order has been restored, the interpreter may return to things that were said during the conflict and translate them, ensuring that everything is heard, but the source of the conflict passed over (Wadensjö 1998: 193). I will pay attention to such situations in which communication is seen to "break down" in order to explore the interpreters' position within the power hierarchy.

I will also explore the moments when interpreting becomes "visible" in a way that is relevant to the court's discourse, where there is "talk about talk," in Wadensjö's words, the interpreter's role, behavior and skill become the center of attention and the interpreter's role may shift toward that of commentator or expert witness (Wadensjö 1998: 192). There is a tension between the constant visibility of interpreting, with the processes of consecutive interpreting drawing attention to the interaction of voices, and the court's insistence that only certain things may be "heard." When listening to these interactions as testimony, we can try to understand the quality of the interactions beyond the legal requirements for witness testimony, but moments when this structuring tension becomes visible are very telling, so they will be a focus of my discussion.

How are interpreters monitored, by whom and using what criteria, and under what circumstances are they challenged? Unlike in other post-genocide trials, there was remarkably little accusation of bias at Frankfurt (Ellen Elias-Bursać has described such an allegation at the UN Tribunal for the former Yugoslavia [2019: 341] but makes clear that genuine bias in interpreting is very rare). There are, however, multiple challenges to interpreters' competence, coming from prosecution, defense, and occasionally a witness: I will explore these moments in terms of institutional trust, considering how competence is assessed by the different participants and what they appear to want from an interpreter.

Trust

Giving testimony in court is an inherently risky activity; witnesses testify to experiences of genocidal violence in the country of the perpetrators, under the eyes of former SS men, and in a court whose procedures involve the insistent questioning of victim testimony according to criteria that seem to have no relevance to the survivor's experiences and knowledge. As Adrienne Krausz made clear, a lack of trust at an individual level can come to represent a sense of radical doubt in the very historical truth of the Holocaust. For a survivor giving testimony in an overarching context characterized by doubt, establishing a relationship of trust with at least one of the participants in the exchange is a potential means of mitigating risk and maintaining a sense of control at the micro level of interaction.

Much of the interpreting studies literature on trust has explored the perspective of interpreters and their professional need to establish trust with clients and employers. Interactions between participants in interpreter-mediated exchanges can be read as involving negotiations of trust at different levels. The court wants to perform its legitimacy through its regulations and rituals, the witness wants to not only show they are a good witness but also achieve their own goals in giving testimony, and the interpreter has a complex set of things to negotiate: professional standing (which requires attaining the trust of the institution) and also making ethical choices about their role and responsibilities vis à vis the persons they are translating for.

William Altano has described the relationship between the court interpreter and the witness in terms of trust and dependence: the interpreter is not just a translator but a "guide through the emotional labyrinth of the alien court system … one fixed point in the whirl of this hostile environment, seen by the witness as an ally, a mentor and, at times, a confident" (Altano 1990: 98). Giving testimony potentially involves a threat to well-being, honor, and sense of self, so the court interpreter is "perched precariously between professional impartiality and a complex link to the witness" (100). In an analysis of interpreter–client interactions, Julia Wagner has explored witnesses' potential reasons for suspicion: they perceive (often rightly) hostility behind questions that doubt aspects of their testimony and find it hard to understand why even "friendly" questioners are asking for precise clarification of details they may find irrelevant, such as technical details or dates, descriptions of surroundings or of the appearance of perpetrators. Their perception of the role of the interpreter within the courtroom constellation is vital (Wagner 2010: 352). Interpreters provide not only a link to the proceedings but also potentially a sense of discomfort at the public display of dependence or inability to understand. For this reason, the "behavioral aspect of the witness-interpreter relationship" is as important as the linguistic, and trust must be negotiated continually while the testimony proceeds (Altano 1990: 99).

Andrea Rizzi, Birgit Lang, and Anthony Pym propose that historians of translation pay attention to the ways in which "translators and interpreters exchange their trust" (Rizzi, Lang, and Pym 2019: 4). We should "pay attention to trust: to the emotions and logics by which people do, indeed, allow translators to speak on behalf of others" (8). Interpreters work within a field of tension between establishing and maintaining the trust of the institution that commissions their work (represented by individuals who perform roles within that institution) and performing their own role in such a way that the witness trusts them sufficiently that the exchange can take place as effectively as possible.

Lang, Rizzi, and Pym differentiate between "thin" trust, that is dependent on impersonal social relations (such as systems of training, accreditation, professional standards, employment conditions, and the oath sworn by the interpreter), and "thick" trust, that arises from interpersonal relationships and personal confidence. The interpreter relies on establishing "thin" trust and maintaining a reputation for trustworthiness within impersonal (and bureaucratic) systems: they enter the system through a qualification process and then perform their role under constant monitoring of expected standards of performance. As a way of reinforcing their status, they may also strategically develop "thicker" trust in personal relationships with important individuals within the system who are empowered to make judgments about trustworthiness. In this way, interpreters working within an institution are able to amass both thin and thick trust as a resource, becoming a worker acknowledged as reliable and willing to work as the institution requires: the "go-to" person for particular tasks. As I will show, this status allows an interpreter to act in different ways during a testimony, to "get away" with things that others cannot.

Within the power relations that characterize a courtroom, the witness's need to trust the interpreter is of a lower institutional priority than the court's insistence on what it defines as good professional practice. But for a witness who has come to court to give testimony on experiences of violence, loss, grief, or trauma, trust in the interpreter is the most important factor determining their feelings about the experience. So for the interpreter to present as a professional—establishing thin trust on the institution's terms—may not be sufficient or indeed may lead the witness to actively mistrust the interpreter for embodying or taking the side of a hostile institution. Andrei Pogozhev's testimony presents an extreme version of this problem: interpreters in the camp worked for a hostile institution (the SS), while "Vera" established a relationship of "thick" trust with the witness within another hostile institution (the court) through her emotional responses, personal interest in the survivors, and shared national identity.

Interpreters, then, need to signal trustworthiness to the witness as well as the institution, but they need to do it in different ways. Unless they are familiar on a professional level with the work of court interpreters, witnesses may well favor signals of thick trust that can be judged in terms of a more intimate relationship as the testimony develops over time. An interpreter in court is able to work within the regimes of institutional trust while making small decisions about the relationship with the witness. Such decisions can be based on many different factors, from institutionally focused ones (for example, a perceived need to bring the witness on board, or to exercise discipline, in order to ensure the smooth running of the interaction or to save face and signal their competence or control) to ethical decisions in support of the witness. Such decisions may be affected by any number of factors that the participants may deploy to define their relationship as intimate or distant, sympathetic, or antipathetic (shared cultural background or historical experience, gender, class, political sympathy or antipathy, and many others).

In the course of a long testimony exchange, trust is signaled and negotiated continually and in multiple ways. In her extensive and original study of the work of interpreters in postwar Polish trials, Małgorzata Tryuk (2015: 32) has set issues of trust in the context of conflicting expectations and understandings of the nature of the interpreter's work:

> Only an experienced interpreter realizes that a request by an official to "please just interpret" glosses over something much more complicated in situations when the participants to a communication have differing status, education, and life experience, and above all aim to accomplish different objectives.

Thinking about trust as a resource deployed by interpreters in their work, as Tryuk does, enables us to understand interpreters as active social agents both in the macro-context of relations between and within institutions and the micro-context of specific participants in a testimony situation interacting with each other. Interpreters' work in a courtroom reproduces existing social relationships and hierarchies, but they are also subjects who reflect on their understanding of the context and the expectations placed on their work and are making decisions based on a delicate and precarious balance: the more institutional trust they have gathered, the more flexibility they can allow themselves in their work, and the more trust they can develop in the—temporary and evanescent—relationship with the witness, the more comfortable the witness will feel. There are many variables that affect the negotiation of these forms of trust as a testimony proceeds, and when they clash with each other, as they frequently do, the interpreter has a choice to make where to situate themselves within a hierarchy of institutional power and norms of behavior: do they risk their professional standing in support of the witness, or do they act as an agent of power and reaffirm the hierarchy? Such decisions have to be made constantly and have significant effects on the ability of witnesses to be heard.

Tryuk makes the important point that interpreters are perceived to be powerful in a courtroom, meaning that their work must be carefully scrutinized and monitored by all sides (2015: 128). Cornelia Vismann puts it more strongly, claiming that interpreters are seen as powerfully able to affect the proceedings and therefore represent a threat to the court's discursive power; this means that various control mechanisms have to be imposed (2019: 239). The court has a spectrum of formal and informal control mechanisms at its disposal, ranging from the repetition of a question or a friendly reminder of the translator's task to the ultimate sanction of dismissal. By contrast, a witness's possibilities for intervening in cases of mistrust or doubt are far more limited: even a cautious challenge to a translation is a risky act.

Tryuk suggests that codes of conduct and professional conditions, such as the swearing of an oath, are on the surface founded on the concepts of faithfulness, neutrality, and confidentiality. This represents an "idealistic understanding of the multitude of activities involved in interpretation … The courtroom reality is marked by more complicated and ambiguous conditions. A courtroom is a place where a number of different persons wish to show they are in charge of various aspects of a complex situation" (Tryuk 2015: 99). Further, "the presence of the interpreter also partially disrupts the ritual governing the court's procedural agenda … increas[ing] the complexity of the proceedings and introduc[ing] an element of unforseeability" (Tryuk 2015: 103). So Tryuk proposes a more appropriate set of concepts to understand interpreters' actions in an institutional context: trust, power, and control. Trust in interpreters is always incomplete and contested and so has to be negotiated, controlled, and monitored.

Questions of control are vital for an interpreter performing several roles at once in a long testimony: they have to carry out a complex assessment of the situation while performing the role in a way that manages a successful interaction and also fulfills expectations of an interpreter's work. The witness may expect things from the interpreter that he or she is unable to provide, or only inconsistently; so the interpreter's active management of the communication may seem hostile or supportive at different times, whether or not it is intended that way.

Witnesses may focus their attention and desire to attain trust on the interpreter, rather than the court officials, as the interpreter is more "accessible," not only in terms of language use but also as a conduit for their own voice, words, intonation, even gesture: the witness sees him or herself reflected in or performed by the interpreter. This is a relationship that can oscillate rapidly between intimacy and distance, trust and distrust, and it can leave the witness feeling passive and victimized (Krausz) or provide opportunities for agency and creativity (Palarczyk).

In her study of interpreter-mediated interactions in public services, Cecilia Wadensjö has suggested that participants in exchanges—including the ritualized exchanges of the courtroom with its extreme power imbalance and limited possibilities for witnesses to affect the proceedings—are able to mobilize concrete resources in the interactions in order to achieve tactical aims. For example, a witness is able to draw on shared social identities with the interpreter in order to exercise agency in her testimony and, at times, to take up a critical stance toward the proceedings at the micro level of individual interactions (Wadensjö 1998: 191). Although it is rarely possible to challenge the management of the proceedings as a whole, a witness can take the opportunities available in the detail of the interaction with the interpreter in order to be heard as they want to be, even if they are not "heard" by the court (I discuss this distinction later).

Tryuk's argument that questions of trust, power, and control are more significant for understanding the relationships in the courtroom than questions of accuracy, faithfulness, and impartiality is key here (2015: 103). If we take this claim and use it to shift our focus to the perspective of the witness, we can ask vital questions about how witnesses are able to formulate testimony under these circumstances and how they experience the situation.

Consecutive Interpreting

Finally, I will comment briefly on the mode of interpreting that is employed in the trial, namely consecutive interpreting, in order to differentiate it clearly from the procedures of simultaneous interpreting, familiar from the Nuremberg, Tokyo, and Eichmann trials, as well as other post-Holocaust and genocide tribunals. Debra Russell and Kayoko Takeda have produced a useful initial definition of consecutive interpreting, which allows us to acknowledge the interpreter's role in managing the communication:

> Consecutive interpreting (CI) is defined as the process of interpreting after the speaker or signer has completed one or more ideas in the source language and then pauses while the interpreter transmits that information … "Long consec" is a phrase used to describe consecutively interpreting a lengthy passage (over several minutes) or possibly an entire speech at a time, usually with the aid of notes, while "short consec" refers to consecutively interpreting a short passage, possibly a word to a few sentences, with or without the aid of notes. (Russell and Takeda 2015: 96)

The duration of the initial statement usually falls between these two extremes: very long statements are more likely to be found in the setting of a conference or formal function than in a courtroom. But the timing can vary considerably, depending on factors like the point in the formal proceedings (for example, when the witness recounts in open court the testimony previously given to the investigating judge or the state prosecutors, as opposed to the phase of more insistent cross-questioning); the skill of the interpreter; the assertiveness or otherwise of the interpreter and the witness; the kind of experience that is being related (for example, detailed descriptions or highly emotional testimony); the nature of the interaction with other participants in the courtroom; and levels of trust that have developed during the testimony. During a session of consecutive interpreting dealing with experiences of violence, degradation, resistance, and loss, the duration of statements and the participants' turn-taking behavior can tell us a lot about their attitude toward the experiences being recounted.

The definition by Russell and Takeda should be taken as an ideal type: it is the expected norm for consecutive interpreting in court, and deviations from it tend to attract censure. The standard norm disguises a key factor that determines the distinction between interpreting and other kinds of translation: *interpreting involves translating language and managing an interaction while maintaining a fiction that it only involves translation*. The interpreter is at the center of these three activities—and takes responsibility for them—but all participants in the exchange are engaged in all three to a greater or lesser extent, so it is a joint activity (I prefer joint to collaborative, as the interaction is not always characterized by positive collaboration).

Thus, there is no "pure" consecutive interpreting: it is characterized by the overlapping of different modes of interpreting around a dominant normative model. Consecutive interpreting requires the participants to learn a certain discipline in their behavior and accept that the interpreter manages the rhythm and pacing of the exchange. But the rule that prohibits simultaneous speech is often transgressed: the tension between the norm, its transgression, and how this behavior is evaluated by the participants characterizes this form of interpreting.

Participants frequently deviate from the expected pattern of orderly turn-taking for reasons connected with what is occurring in the interaction and their relationships with each other: material may go untranslated, turns may be missed or interrupted, or other participants may believe that they have understood without needing translation. Other participants may take on the role of "interpreter" when they feel they have something to contribute, or there may be moments of metalinguistic discussion of translation (for example, challenges) that disrupt the pattern. Departures from the expected pattern tend to center issues of language and translation or the person of the interpreter, and it is often the interpreter who has to repair the interaction: how they do this tells us something about their ethical choices and their attitudes toward the witness and the institution. The interpreter is always visible and cannot be ignored in a courtroom, but perhaps we can say that there are times when their visibility becomes visible.

Whatever the expectations placed on interpreting in court, there is no lengthy exchange where consecutive interpreting as defined by Russell and Takeda is the only mode employed. Beyond the disruptions to the norm that I have just discussed, interpreters (and occasionally others who take on the "interpreter" role) may resort to summarizing statements where they feel it is appropriate, or when what is said exceeds their skill at that specific moment, or to whispered simultaneous interpreting (*chuchotage*) when they are trying to keep a witness informed about exchanges between other participants.

Chuchotage breaks the norm that only one voice should be heard in the courtroom at a time so that all participants hear everything equally. However, this norm tends to be upheld only for the panel of judges and lay magistrates, the defense and prosecution councils, and the accused (it is fundamental to the principle of a fair trial that the accused hears and understands everything). The witness is in fact the only exception to this: there is no obligation for the witness to understand all the discussion in court, as they are there only to provide testimony and be questioned on it. But for survivors, the feeling that things were happening beyond their control and understanding could be infuriating, as it made clear that their experiences were not the central concern. An interpreter who is sensitive to this and has made an ethical choice to exceed courtroom norms in support of the witness may then provide a whispered translation, summary, or commentary on what is happening. Whether the presiding judge permits the interpreter to speak "privately" to the witness like this depends on a range of factors, including the level of trust the interpreter has built up with the institution and which they can expend in order to "get away" with breaking a norm.

Some of the scholarship on consecutive interpreting has stressed its negative features. William Altano suggests that it presents a complex cognitive challenge for all participants that disrupts the naturalness of speech: thoughts are not permitted to develop fluently in speech, which in turn affects the thought processes themselves, and there is often a need to cycle through sequences several times in order to get things right. Longer narratives are broken up into manageable chunks, affecting how the story is told. This means that a witness or defendant whose words are being interpreted can appear incoherent if they find this complex cognitive challenge difficult or are not used to working with an interpreter (Altano 1990: 98).

These critical discussions of consecutive interpreting examine the problematic nature of certain kinds of interaction in court and are thus aimed at improving interpreter training, courts' understanding of the nature of interpreting, and the ability of accused persons to access justice and of witnesses to be heard adequately. By contrast, Katrin Rumprecht points out that, despite the extra time required for it, consecutive interpreting offers advantages, in that the interpreter does not have to be completely subordinate to the speech rhythms of the speaker: the interpreter can define their own tempo and rhythm and thus can choose how to represent these aspects of the speaker's speech in ways that may be more useful or appropriate (Rumprecht 2014: 160). Thus, consecutive interpreting allows the listener to hear the original speaker and then to hear an interpretation and representation of that speaker's speech.

Sandra Hale and Jemima Napier remind us not to neglect the physical and spatial aspects of the interactions and in particular the intimacy of the relationship between speaker and interpreter:

> The position of the interpreter in relation to the other participants may affect the dynamics of the interaction and the way the witness is perceived. Standing or sitting next to an alleged offender, whispering in his ear, as is the current practice with spoken language interpreting when interpreting simultaneously, may be perceived by the jury as confirmation of the defense case that this defendant is harmless, or it may suggest that interpreter and witness belong to the same "team," with the assumption that there is no impartiality on the interpreter's part. The positioning of the interpreter in court, therefore, may also affect the perception of his/her status as an independent and competent professional. (Hale and Napier 2016: 352)

Cornelia Vismann's account of court interpreting takes this further, allowing us to analyze the interpreted testimonies as processes of meaning-creation and witnessing. In her media historical study of German courts, Vismann makes an argument about the significance of consecutive interpreting, asking why the German court cannot use the technology for simultaneous interpreting that had characterized the Nuremberg and Eichmann tribunals. After all, this would save an immense amount of time in a very long trial. Several arguments present themselves immediately: the potential expense; the lack of interpreters with the appropriate training; the fact that it would mark this trial out as "special," putting it in line with the Nuremberg or Jerusalem trials, at a time when the West German authorities were keen to demonstrate the legitimacy, independence, and effectiveness of their own court system, avoiding the appearance of a "show trial" or special tribunal.

Instead, Vismann argues that consecutive interpreting in court draws attention to the quality and immediacy of the speaking voice, which is estranged (*verfremdet*) by the technology of simultaneous interpreting. Interpreting technology disrupts the processes of a "normal" court, requiring different rules and spatial practices; many participants in the proceedings, including those who will come to the verdict, do not directly experience the voices of all the speakers. For the reasons outlined above, a regular German court requires access to the voices of all the speakers, even where the language is not understood. German judges feel empowered to assess the authenticity of testimony on the basis of the witness's vocal performance; such a judgment must be made on the basis of a complex assessment of impressions made by the witness's voice and the interpreter's performance. There are examples of witnesses being asked to speak up or move closer to the microphone, even when speaking a language that others in the court cannot understand.

At this point, Vismann makes a move that turns the critical views of consecutive interpreting in court on their head and makes them productive for understanding issues of languages, communicative relationships, and witnessing in court. Consecutive interpreting "celebrates its translations on every level, making linguistic discontinuities [Sprachbrüche] visible and audible" (Vismann 2019: 230). Consecutive interpreting allows those listening to hear and compare the voice of the speaker and the interpreter's rendition, to come to conclusions about how the speaker's voice may reflect honesty, authenticity of memory, and inner emotional states, and to make judgments about the interpreter's performance on the basis of this.

There is a tension between the physical presence of the witness and the estrangement of the voice through interpreting that is played out in every testimony in different ways: how does the interpreter understand this issue, and what choices do they make in response? How does the witness respond to the use that is being made of their words, and do they intervene on their own behalf in order to take control of their voice? How does the court regulate the tension between the requirement for immediacy and the fact of highly visible interpreting?

Vismann's reflections provide a way of linking questions of voice and agency in Holocaust witnessing with the linguistic practices of the court and the activity of interpreters without narrowing our focus to technical questions of accuracy and equivalence: the court is a theatre of voices crossed by discursive practices of power that create a conflict between what is permitted and what is forbidden and between different conceptions of authentic and false speech, useful and unnecessary testimony. The presence of the interpreter makes these tensions visible and has a decisive influence on the proceedings.

The behaviors of all participants in an interpreter-mediated testimony are complex, dependent on how they understand and react to the situation as it unfolds: conflicts between different conceptions of testimony and conflicting role expectations for both witnesses and interpreters are common, and moments of communicative breakdown are telling, since they expose the different pressures on witnesses and interpreters in this stressful situation. I will also look at moments where communication appears to be functioning smoothly but where power is being exercised without attention being drawn to it: who benefits from a situation in which power operates smoothly?

Taking my lead from the scholarship discussed here, and extending it to encompass the particular stresses of post-Holocaust testimony, I explore how the role of "Holocaust witness" is negotiated between the participants: "witness" is an identity that is always in the process of becoming and is negotiated in the tension between judicial concepts of witnessing and a broader social identity constructed from notions of accuser, bearer of individual and collective memory, educator, representative, and spokesperson for a survivor community and for the dead.

5

Sources and Transcriptions

The most important sources for this study are the recordings of interpreted witness testimony, which have been digitized and transcribed in a collaboration between the Fritz Bauer Institute, the Hessen State Archive, and the Deutsches Rundfunkarchiv. The value of these recorded testimonies has been acknowledged by historians, but there is still work to do in evaluating them as sources in their own right. Although my approach does not work with the historian's source-critical methods, my study draws on invaluable recent work by historians such as Werner Renz, Katharina Stengel, and Rebecca Wittmann (Renz 2009; Stengel 2022; Wittmann 2005). As Renz has put it, the recordings are a source that "conveys the psychological situation of the survivor-witnesses giving testimony in a German court in personal confrontation with the perpetrators" (Renz 2009: 147). No other kind of source can do this.

The recordings are freely available online, so readers can listen to the extracts that I have discussed: https://www.auschwitz-prozess.de/. This site, curated by the Fritz Bauer Institute, Frankfurt, also contains useful background material and lists of the witnesses and other trial participants. The main trial archive, consisting of the official records of the pretrial investigation and open trial, correspondence, and other materials, such as financial records, has also been digitized and is openly available through the website of the Hessen State Archive, Wiesbaden. I have also used archive material from the Hessen Justice Ministry, held in Wiesbaden, the Central Office in Ludwigsburg, and the important holdings of the Fritz Bauer Institute, especially relating to press cuttings.

The story of the creation and rediscovery of the recordings has been told on a number of occasions, and I have nothing new to add to the accounts in the histories of the trial by Devin Pendas and Rebecca Wittmann. There is a very useful recent account by the archivist of the Fritz Bauer Institute, Johannes Beermann-Schön, that takes the story up to the digitization of the sources

(Beermann-Schön 2020). A brief summary will be useful here to give some context to the sources that I am using.

The trial archive—consisting of the official trial files and the recordings of the testimony—was awarded UNESCO World Documentary Heritage status in 2017, ensuring that it shifts from closed trial archive to open archive of memory. The recordings of the testimony were preserved only through the active intervention of committed political actors, in particular Hermann Langbein and the then Hessen Justice Minister Lauritz Lauritzen. At the time of the First Frankfurt trial, the German Code of Criminal Procedure (*Strafprozessordnung*, often abbreviated to StPO) did not require verbatim transcripts or even summaries of evidence in open court: judges and lay jurors were expected to formulate their verdict from notes taken by themselves and the limited formal protocol taken by the official court recorder (*Berichterstatter*): the latter noted important statements as requested by the judges and ensured that the correct order of proceedings was recorded, for example, recording that defense councils were present for all the accused at each session and logging the swearing in of witnesses and interpreters. The text produced by the official recorder is preserved in the trial archive, but other notes are not. This procedure preserved the absolute autonomy of the trial judges and the sense of a trial as a uniquely unrepeatable live encounter of voices and ensured that the trial could not be re-legislated on the basis of simply reading the documents. The law was changed in 1965, with courts now required to keep summarized records of the content of witnesses' statements, though not verbatim transcripts.

Nevertheless, at a time when magnetic tape recording was becoming both practical and affordable, German jurists began to discuss whether tape recordings could be used to supplement or replace the work of the *Berichterstatter*. From the mid-1950s, recordings began to be made of large trials, in particular, complex cases of fraud: they could be made only with the explicit consent of the witness and on the understanding that they were wiped after the final verdict. Since the Frankfurt trial was clearly going to be a huge undertaking (the term "Mammut-Verfahren" [mammoth proceedings] was coined for such large trials), both Judge Hofmeyer and Fritz Bauer were in favor of recordings being made, receiving the go-ahead from the Federal Court of Justice in February 1964 (Beermann-Schön 2020: 92). It is likely that Bauer had already formulated the idea of preserving the recordings of the evidence, given the international resonance of the filmed testimony at the Eichmann trial, but the federal court's decision defined the tape recordings as equivalent to the judges' notes, rather than the official transcript, ensuring that they could not be preserved in the trial archive.

There are recordings of 324 of the 360 witnesses: Beermann-Schön has established that in two cases the recorder had a fault, three witnesses refused permission, and six recordings were wiped afterward, either because the court had neglected to ask permission or the witness had requested this afterward. The reason for the absence of the other recordings could not be established (Beermann-Schön 2020: 98).

There are no recordings of interpreted testimony from before the court's move to the newly built Gallus complex at the beginning of April 1964. For the move, a new recording apparatus had to be installed for recording on BASF tapes of the kind that were commonly used by amateurs. As Beermann-Schön has indicated, this shows that the court did not prioritize sound quality at this stage (Beermann-Schön 2020: 96). A complex apparatus, consisting of a mixing desk, twenty microphones, and five speakers, had to be installed; the tape recorder was hidden behind the curtain, but the mixing desk with its operator Heinz Fickert was always visible. Fickert was present for the whole trial, changing the tapes and switching individual microphones on and off at the direction of Judge Hofmeyer.

The impetus for the tapes' preservation came from Hermann Langbein: after having a request to Hofmeyer for preservation and access to the tapes turned down, he had more success with Justice Minister Lauritzen, who issued a decree in September 1965 declaring that the historical value of the recordings necessitated their preservation (Beermann-Schön 2020: 101). This did not solve the problem of where and how to store the 103 tapes that could not be included in the main trial archive but had somehow to be preserved: eventually they were handed over to the office of the president of the Frankfurt District Court, where they lay forgotten for more than twenty years.

A further trial of an Auschwitz perpetrator, in 1987, led to the tapes' reemergence: a defense council of the former SS man Ernst-August König recalled the existence of the recordings, and they were eventually found after an extensive search. In 1989, they were finally given to the Hessen State Archive in Wiesbaden, where they were first used by the documentary filmmakers Rolf Bickel and Dietrich Wagner for a film marking the thirtieth anniversary of the trial (Bickel and Wagner 1993). After its founding in 1995, the Fritz Bauer Institute established a collaboration with the archive and the German Broadcasting Archive to digitize the recordings and make them accessible. The recordings were transferred from tape to CD-ROMs, and the publication history of the recordings began with the approximately 100 hours of testimony on the DVD-ROM collection (*Der Auschwitz-Prozess: Tonbandmitschnitte, Protokolle, Dokumente [DVD-ROM]* 2007).

This initial collection contained only a third of the recordings, but the openly streamable full set was online for the fiftieth anniversary of the trial in 2013. As Beermann-Schön has observed of the recordings, "The tapes only survived the march of time through a string of coincidences and the initiative and interventions of individuals" (2020: 107). When considering the status of the recordings as sources, it is important to bear this history in mind. The recordings have an ambivalent status: they are still not part of the official trial archive, though they are the central element in a broader "archive of the First Frankfurt Auschwitz Trial" that now has UNESCO status and is a locus of international memory discourse well beyond the specifically German legal issues that were negotiated in court.

This institutional history should remind us of the precarity of testimony and the fact that the vast majority of survivors' speech about their experiences is evanescent, vanishing in the moment of its articulation. Also, there is no testimony that is not structured by its context and no response to testimony that is not affected by context and sources: our access to these witnesses' words is of a very different quality to that of the audience listening in court. In court, the interplay of voices occurs between embodied speech and its amplification, with the ritual of switching between microphones structuring the communication by drawing attention to the judge's authoritative role in managing turn-taking behavior and ensuring that only one person speaks at any given moment.

Our experience of these testimonies is also affected by the distribution of the microphones: we have a different spatial experience to those in the courtroom, meaning that interpreting what is happening is sometimes difficult. Voices and sounds occurring at different distances from microphones can produce misleading hierarchies of significance but can also give us access to events that may have passed unnoticed at the time. As in the case of George Preston and Franz Schuh that I cited at the beginning of the introduction, the placing of the microphone allows us to hear Schuh's struggles in the foreground while Preston shouts in the background.

One of the fascinating aspects of this trial is the tension-filled intimacy of the relationship between witness and interpreter: they have to define a relationship with each other as the testimony proceeds, which may operate along a spectrum between trust and mistrust and collaboration and conflict. This situation is produced by their physical proximity in the courtroom and the fact that they are speaking into a single microphone placed on their table. This means that their voices are associated with each other through closeness and the means of technical reproduction, and their vocal interaction occurs before their voices are amplified: this is not the case when the interpreter renders the words of other participants. The electronic apparatus enforces a physical and vocal intimacy between witness and interpreter.

Historians of the trial have made extensive use of the documents from the pretrial investigation in order to reconstruct the legal issues and the efforts of the prosecutors to contact witnesses from across the world. This material is of less relevance to my study, but important discussions of these sources from a historical, source-critical perspective, what they contain, how they are structured, and what is excluded, can be found in work by Katharina Stengel, Julia Wagner, and Rebecca Wittmann (Stengel 2022: 30–2; Wagner 2010; Wittmann 2002). The new status of the "Frankfurt trial archive"—the official trial archive plus the recordings and the material curated by the Fritz Bauer Institute plus the documentation for the UNESCO—should not mislead us into thinking it is complete or self-contained. The official trial archive is structured by the need of a powerful institution to insist on the regularity of the proceedings and to place them within the legitimizing institutional memory of the legal system: its inclusions and exclusions reflect this need. Wagner has pointed to the absence of documentation about the prosecution's financial and political struggles or the emotional burden of the investigation, though interviews with Hermann Langbein, Gerhard Wiese, and Joachim Kügler from the early 2000s give us some insight (Wagner 2010: 347; Wojak and Meinl, 2003: 285–332).

The archive of the pretrial investigation is a rich source of autobiographical narratives and testimony, many made by people from a multitude of different victim groups, many of whom rarely if ever spoke about their experiences beyond their own communities, but is structured around the needs of the investigation: the voices of victims are therefore not absent but serve a purpose that is not fully their own. For a study interested in reconstructing the court as a workplace for translators, we find a certain amount of vital evidence, in particular for the agreed rates of pay, but there is much missing. The archive contains invaluable *Kostenbände* (financial records) that document the expenses paid to individuals since the judicial system was subject to financial oversight, but why certain rates were set, why one interpreter or translator receives more than another for similar work, is hard to reconstruct: we can extrapolate to an extent from the legal structure, but we have no concrete evidence for why a certain decision was made.

There is also no record—or at least only occasional fragmentary hints—of why certain translators and interpreters were preferred over others or how difficulties in locating qualified individuals were resolved. I discuss the evidence that we do have in Chapters 3 and 9, but it is clear that a significant amount of negotiation was carried out verbally, leaving no record, apart from the occasional reference to a previous telephone call, for example. So reconstructing how translators and interpreters negotiated issues of qualification, pay rates, and insider–outsider status has to rely on the fragmentary evidence that we possess.

It is clear, therefore, that translation and interpreting are not a concern that the institution needs to document thoroughly: the people who made this extraordinary, multilingual proceeding possible are absent from the archive, except in very specific circumstances. Effectively, the job of the sworn translator is to sign off on the final moment of a process that has produced a text that can function as a substitute original. For this reason, there is no need for careful documentation of translation processes as the institutional structure that supports the sworn translator's work makes all the preceding processes irrelevant and unnecessary to document in the archive. Thus, the archive makes invisible the very thing that enables it to exist.

The Frankfurt Courtroom

Since this project is about interactions in context, I read the recordings of testimony as evidence for such interactions rather than analyzing them for evidence about Auschwitz or the crimes of the perpetrators. I am directly concerned with the experiences of the witnesses in giving testimony in that moment rather than with their experience of the camp itself. It will therefore be useful to provide some context for readers who may be unfamiliar with West German judicial proceedings and the setup of the courtroom. Fuller accounts are provided by Devin Pendas and Rebecca Wittmann in their histories of the trial; since I am not concerned here with the legal and procedural issues, and am focusing my attention on the recordings of testimony, I will only provide a brief summary.

The court in question is a *Schwurgericht*, a jury court of the Federal State of Hessen empowered to try the most serious criminal offenses. There have been some reforms to the German Code of Criminal Procedure since the 1960s, but in essence, the proceedings are divided into three phases: *Voruntersuchung*, *Zwischenverfahren*, and *Hauptverhandlung*. The preliminary investigation, or *Voruntersuchung*, is conducted by the prosecutor's office in collaboration with the police, and it may lead to an investigation overseen by a judge (in our case, Judge Heinz Düx, who had a long record in supporting the prosecution of Nazi crimes and who pushed for the court to visit Auschwitz). This phase produced a rich and extensive archive of witness testimony in many forms, along with revealing statements by perpetrators and their supporters, international correspondence and other documents, much of which is still to be explored by scholars. Katharina Stengel has discussed in detail the range of material produced in this phase from a source-critical perspective (Stengel 2022: 26–33). The immense complexity and international nature of the trial has left an extensive archive full of open and hidden translation processes: I only consider a small fraction in Chapter 6, on the pretrial phase.

At the end of this stage, the case may be dropped, or the prosecutor's office may produce a formal indictment (*Anklageschrift*). The Frankfurt indictment, finalized in April 1963, runs to more than 500 pages in the critical source edition and contains substantial citations of witness statements against the accused: it hides the traces of extensive translation and interpreting activity, much of which is now impossible to reconstruct (Gross et al. 2013: 105–520). Once the indictment has been entered, the proceedings move to a second phase, the *Zwischenverfahren*, in which the court considers whether to open proceedings and, if so, whether to amend the charges as set out in the indictment. If the trial is to go ahead, the court issues an order to convene (*Eröffnungsbeschluss*) that contains the charges and that shapes the public phase of the trial. Alongside the public prosecutors, the victims of a crime are able to participate in a prosecution through a *Nebenklage*, in which they are represented by their own councils, can give their own testimony, and question the accused.

A number of the witnesses whom we hear thus have a different status in the trial, and their representatives are able to pursue different lines of questioning. *Nebenkläger* from the German Democratic Republic (GDR) were represented by Friedrich Karl Kaul, and those from the rest of the world, including West Germany, were represented by Henry Ormond and Christian Raabe. Two of the East German *Nebenkläger* gave testimony in the main trial, and seven of the others: only three of them (Aron Bejlin, Milton Buki, and Mieczysław Kieta) spoke a language other than German. Buki, who spoke Yiddish, will be mentioned several times in this study. When we come to the public phase, with which this study is mostly concerned, and which lasted from December 20, 1963 to August 20, 1965, the witness testimony that we hear on the recordings is given in the context of a long previous negotiation over law, memory, and meaning, and the questioning is structured around the issues set out in the trial indictment and order to convene. Each witness has already given testimony to the investigators at least once and possibly several times in different forms (and potentially different languages).

By contrast with proceedings in an adversarial system, the presiding judge leads the questioning, with the other judges and lay people on the panel having the same right to ask questions, though in practice they do this very rarely. The function of the jury is different from the Anglo-American system: the verdict is reached by a panel of three professional judges and six lay jurors, all of whom have equal say. The dramaturgy of the trial is not structured around a clash of contrasting narratives, with the judge presiding over it in a supposedly elevated position, but—in theory at least—the presiding judge leads a gradual process of uncovering the truth through questioning and challenging evidence. The judge is, however, not a prosecutor but a neutral party obliged to apply the law to the evidence. Prosecution and defense do play a vital role in questioning witnesses, objecting to lines of enquiry, and, in the case of the defense, supporting the rights of their clients but are less prominent than in an adversarial trial. On the recordings, we most often hear the lightly Hessian-accented voice of Presiding Judge Hans Hofmeyer. Further information about all the participants in the trial, as well as the chronology of the proceedings, can be found on the website of the Fritz Bauer Institute: https://www.auschwitz-prozess.de/materialien/.

The testimony given by the survivor-witnesses comes after an initial stage in which the defendants are questioned on their biographies and on the charges against them. The phase in which witnesses give evidence and are cross-questioned, and the defendants are confronted with the evidence against them, was by far the longest part of the main trial, lasting from February 24, 1964 to May 3, 1965. The questioning of witnesses takes the same form: they are asked to confirm their personal details and then are asked to give a chronological account of their deportation, arrival, and experiences in the camp. Their life beforehand or after liberation plays no role unless it is directly relevant to the evidence, for example, in establishing how the witness knows the defendant. So when witnesses try to include other kinds of information in their statements, they are always pushing against this structure: at times, they are given leeway to talk as they wish, but at others they can be brought up short abruptly.

Questioning concentrates on the areas of interest for the charges against the defendants, and witnesses may be asked multiple times to clarify and explain specific details, by the judge or by prosecution and defense councils. Toward the end of the testimony, defendants can be confronted with this evidence and have the opportunity to make statements or ask their own questions. At times, the witness will be asked to stand and approach the defendants in order to identify them. The interpreter has to manage the communication in this situation in which a formalized question-answer structure can shift to more complex cross-questioning and moments of conflict and confusion.

The courtroom is set up in such a way as to emphasize the discursive authority of the judge and the isolation of the witness. The recently completed "Gallus" complex provided a large room with a stage and theatre curtain, in front of which sat the panel of judges and lay magistrates, alongside the court reporter, archivist, and other personnel, including in this case the sound engineer. Facing the stage to the left is a very large bank of defendants and their councils, several rows deep, with desks and several microphones. To the right, against the wall, sits the row of public prosecutors, and next to them the representatives of the *Nebenklage*. On the same wall hang two very large maps, showing the Auschwitz 1 and Birkenau complexes: witnesses are often asked to orientate themselves on these maps, describing where specific things happened. The plans show the camp complex at a late stage of its development, but the court had developed enough knowledge to be able to reconstruct the camp topography throughout its history. At the back of the room sit the spectators and press, and police officers stand at strategic points as a visual representation of the authority of the state.

The individual being questioned sits at a small table in front of, and beneath, the judges; the isolation and intensity of focus, as well as the performance of discursive authority, is embodied in this choice.

Participants

The voice we hear most often on the tape is that of Presiding Judge Hans Hofmeyer, who leads the questioning. Occasionally, we hear the voices of other judges asking follow-up or clarifying questions. It is important to distinguish between the voices of the state prosecutors Hanns Großmann, Georg Friedrich Vogel, Joachim Kügler, and Gerhard Wiese from the representatives of the *Nebenklage* Henry Ormond, Christian Raabe, and Friedrich Karl Kaul: all are prosecuting the accused but have different legal status, which is reflected in the way they conduct business. Ormond, for example, encourages the witnesses he has summoned to talk more about the aftereffects of their experiences, and Kaul—as the only legal representative from East Germany—is concerned to turn the trial into an indictment of the IG Farben concern and thus of the West German capitalist system (Weinke 2002: 236–57).

Of the defense, the most active speaker is Hans Laternser, who had made a name for himself as a defense council in Nuremberg: while the other representatives (twenty-two in total) for the most part did the expected job of offering legal defense, Laternser's aggressive manner and his frequent questioning of the legitimacy of the proceedings gained a certain notoriety. He shared a taste for flamboyant melodrama with Kaul, and their (for a listener) often rather childish exchanges are a lowlight of the trial. Eva-Maria Kalz has written illuminatingly on the behavior of the defense in the trial (Kalz 2020). We occasionally hear other defense councils: of interest for this project are those who share a language background with some of the witnesses from Eastern Europe (see Chapter 9).

The political—and geopolitical—aspects of the trial and the attitudes of prosecution and defense are fascinating, but there is no space to discuss them in full here. Readers are referred in particular to Annette Weinke's study on the Cold War context of post-Holocaust trials in West and East Germany (Weinke 2002). The brief summary set out here should help to account for some of the language use and communicative strategies that we will encounter on the recordings.

Language, Translation, and Transcription Method

For the analytical chapters of this study it has been necessary to work with a transcription method that allows the interactions in court to be analyzed while also being legible and accessible to a nonspecialist reader. This section sets out how I have approached this task and gives information about the transcription system I have used. One of the extraordinary things about the archive of the First Frankfurt Trial is the fact that all the recordings have been fully transcribed in a substantial project; as of time of writing, the transcripts are all available on the website of the trial archive alongside the recordings. Taken together, the recordings and transcripts are an invaluable resource that is only gradually being explored by scholars.

The transcripts themselves are not available in translation, but they do record the different languages used in court as well as giving a sense of the interactions between the participants. However, they are designed to create clarity about meaning and for easy readability and searchability and so represent a specific form of compromise that allows them to be used as historical sources. For a linguistic, interaction-based study such as this, a different form of transcription is necessary that will bring out other features of the exchanges in court.

I have therefore opted for a different kind of compromise, which makes visible elements of the exchanges that are important for understanding the relationships between the participants and the dynamics of the interpreting without (hopefully) being so technically detailed as to be inaccessible for the reader. My transcriptions are orthographic; that is, they are based on the "standard" orthography of the languages spoken in the courtroom rather than attempting to render pronunciations phonetically unless this is necessary to illustrate a point about linguistic hybridity. This means that elements of the linguistic variety of the courtroom that are not the subject of this study are not recorded; for example, there are significant dialect variations in the Polish and German spoken in court, as well as distinctions of class and education. The German spoken by some of the accused reflects their background in German-speaking areas of Central and Eastern Europe, especially Silesia or Transylvania: the linguistic and cultural variety of these regions and the multilingualism of many of the inhabitants play an important role in the trial. The *hessisch* elements of Judge Hans Hofmeyer's speech also remind us that the relationship in Germany between regional linguistic features and an ideology of "standard" or "educated" language is different from that found, for example, in the UK. There would be more to say about these linguistic issues of class and regional identities at the trial than I have space for here.

I have simplified the transcription using standard orthographies in order to make space for a more complex transcription of the exchanges between the participants, which are the main object of this study. My transcription adopts simplified elements of the method employed in conversation analysis in English and German without taking over the analytical methodology for my study (Hutchby and Wooffitt 2008; Brinker and Sager 2010). I divide the extract into numbered steps, which allows me to note overlaps, interruptions, simultaneous speech, and features like background noises where they are relevant. I use a small number of symbols to denote features like pauses and emphasis without being absolutely precise about length of pauses or quality of intonation, as this would fill the transcripts with information that is not relevant for my analysis: the reader is encouraged to listen to the extract in order to get a fuller impression.

After some deliberation, I have often included punctuation based on standard rules and patterns of written language: this makes for easier reading, clarifies meaning, and supports my specific analysis, although it also imposes structures and rhythms that do not grasp the complexity of spoken language. Commas mostly indicate a short pause, so I have only used the marker + to indicate a longer or irregular pause.

+	pause
Italics	strong emphasis
:	elongated vowel
= =	marks expressions like =aha= and =eh=. =eh= is used here as a compromise form to cover a range of similar articulations (=ähm= =um=)
(...)	incomprehensible utterance
[ ]	my insertion or commentary; ... indicates omitted passage

There are issues with this system, which the reader should bear in mind. Standard orthographies and written punctuation systems are not neutral reflections of linguistic practice but are bound up with structures of social power and privilege, which are also manifested in the courtroom in specific ways. Speech that appears to depart from these "rules" can be considered a sign of linguistic deficit or inadequacy, which has important consequences for a witness and for the ethical choices that an interpreter has to make. This issue is particularly acute for the many witnesses whose testimony is characterized by bilingualism or multilingualism or linguistic hybridity; in these cases, I have made choices about how to present their speech that help to illustrate the decisions that the interpreters are making.

With Yiddish speech, I have chosen to use the YIVO transliteration system rather than accepting the system used for the transcripts of the recordings, which is based on German orthography. This establishes a clear demarcation between German and Yiddish. The court recognized Yiddish officially as a separate language requiring an interpreter, but there are times during exchanges when participants appear to treat it more as a variant of German that can be easily understood, and there are occasional disparaging comments, especially from the defense. Establishing the distinction is therefore important if we are to prioritize the perspective of the witnesses.

Nevertheless, it is not always possible to decide whether a witness is intending to speak German or Yiddish; witnesses often try to speak German in the courtroom in order to communicate directly, and there can be interference from their other languages. I have for the most part not tried to "correct" this issue because linguistic hybridity is a compelling feature of many survivors' speech. It appears to be determined by a combination of factors: the way the prisoners spoke with each other in the camp, the education of the witnesses and their understanding of German before deportation to Auschwitz, their linguistic and migration biographies before and after liberation, and the concrete linguistic conditions of the courtroom. It is not always possible to determine which factor is the most important at any moment, so I have refrained from trying to disentangle these levels, instead concentrating on the moment of communication itself and how the interpreters negotiate it.

Finally, on the question of translations: since the original speech of the witnesses and interpreters is key, I have always quoted them in the original languages, providing an indicative English translation. The translation is designed to illustrate the issues that I am discussing, in order to help orient the reader, rather than rendering all potential nuances of style, meaning, or voice. For all other texts, such as historical or critical works or other archive materials, I have simply given a translation.

The example below will illustrate this transcription method. It comes from a moment in the testimony of the Polish-Jewish *Sonderkommando* survivor Simon Gotland on July 27, 1964, 49 minutes into the recording. Gotland is being asked to establish whether the accused Stefan Baretzki participated in selections on the Birkenau "ramp" and to provide a description that identifies him securely. The three participants here are Gotland, the Presiding Judge Hans Hofmeyer, and the Polish-German interpreter Wera Kapkajew.

Gotland speaks in a hybrid of Polish, Yiddish, French, and German; Polish and Yiddish are the languages he grew up with, and he has acquired French as a migrant worker in France in the 1930s and again after 1945. He tries to speak German in court, but his other languages interfere, and Kapkajew tries to persuade him to stick with Polish so she can work. Gotland speaks a German that does not follow standard grammar ("er komme" for "er kam"), and I have transcribed this based on repeated listening to the recording. Step 2 shows that Gotland and Kapkajew are speaking simultaneously. The + in step 5 indicates a slightly longer pause but cannot provide an interpretation: the pause may or may not be meaningful for Gotland but is not taken up in Kapkajew's turn, in step 6, when she is trying to sum up what he has said.

Finally, step 3 gives us an indication of why transliteration is not ethically neutral. The word "tiger" used by Gotland is not Polish—this would be "tygrys"—but either German or Yiddish. It is not possible to decide which language is interfering here or whether it is even meaningful to make a distinction. I have transcribed this word with a small "t," which would indicate Yiddish, in order to contrast with Kapkajew's use of the German word "Tiger" to translate it. I thus suggest that Gotland is referring to the way Yiddish-speaking prisoners referred to Baretzki, but this is simply an interpretation with no definitive evidence to back it up.

My English translation gives an idea of the content of the exchange while indicating the languages spoken, as far as this can be established. I do not try to find equivalents for Gotland's nonstandard grammar. The translation is intended to be used alongside the original and the recording, and anything of significance for the interaction with the interpreter will be discussed in the text. I explore Gotland's testimony in more detail in Chapter 12.

1. Hofmeyer:	nun =eh= wie ist er denn auf die Rampe gekommen? Ist er da mit dem Fahrrad gekommen oder zu Fuß?
2. Gotland:	er komme er komme
Kapkajew:	niech pan słucha
3. Gotland:	on przyszedł jak *tiger*
4. Gotland:	(…) przyszedł
Kapkajew:	*niech pan słucha pytanie!* Jak on przychodził przyjeżdżał na rampę? Rowerem czy na piechotę?
5. Gotland:	nie + piechotą wiedziałem
6. Kapkajew:	er ging zu Fuß, wie ich gesehen habe, wie ein Tiger

1. Hofmeyer:	[German] Now =eh= how did he come to the Ramp? Did he come by bike or on foot?
2. Gotland:	[German] He came he came
Kapkajew:	[Polish] Listen to
3. Gotland:	[Polish] He came like a [Yiddish/German] *tiger*
4. Gotland:	[Polish] (…) he came
Kapkajew:	[Polish] *Listen to the question*! How did he come[1] to the Ramp? By bike or on foot?
5. Gotland:	[Polish] No + he came on foot I saw
6. Kapkajew:	[German] He came on foot, as I saw it, like a tiger

Part III

Interpreting in the Frankfurt Courtroom

6

Interpreting during the Pretrial Investigation

In this chapter, I discuss the work of interpreters who made the trial possible, working during the pretrial investigation. This will not be a comprehensive history of the investigation since my main focus is on the recordings and the way that testimony is cocreated in court. The archive resources do not provide enough material to analyze the processes of ethical decision-making, but there are several key issues that I will address here that will help to contextualize the courtroom exchanges. In the course of the pretrial investigation it became increasingly clear that a successful prosecution would depend on survivor testimony from well beyond Germany: this was going to be an international event attracting international attention that would be unpredictable and hard to steer.

I concentrate here on the interpreting of survivors' voices during questioning to the extent that it can be reconstructed in the documents. The holdings of the trial archive give an impression of the immense contribution of written translators to the preparation of the trial: for example, the translation of documents from other trials, such as the Bergen-Belsen trials held in the British Zone in 1945, trials held by the Soviet authorities, and especially the trials of Auschwitz personnel held in Poland, played an important role in preparing the Frankfurt indictment and would make for a rewarding study of institutional translation practices. The translation of correspondence with foreign judicial authorities and victims' organizations, of witness statements taken abroad, or often very moving letters from survivors themselves, are vital for the investigation and the preparation of the indictment. Other modes of interpreting, such as liaison interpreting or language brokering by relatives or fellow survivors, play a significant role but are rarely documented; we should, however, assume that they are happening constantly. The question of power and insider status—who is empowered and trusted to translate in what circumstances—is as influential here as it is within all institutions. The contribution of these written translators and interpreters to the investigation is unfortunately beyond the scope of this study.

As we observe the investigation proceeding through the archive, we see an awareness developing of the linguistic and cultural variety of victim populations who suffered at Auschwitz and the necessity of finding ways of contacting them, gaining their trust, and collecting their testimonies. For much of its fundamental knowledge about the operation of the camp complex at different times, the prosecution did rely on the testimony of German-speaking former political prisoners, but this was never going to be sufficient, and the testimony of large numbers of Polish political prisoners was also necessary. The story of the deepening collaboration between the court, the Hessen Justice Ministry, the Polish authorities, and especially the Auschwitz-Birkenau State Museum is fascinating in its own right and has been told by a number of scholars (alongside the works by Pendas, Stengel, Weinke, and Wittmann, see Gańczak 2022).

This Polish-German collaboration, though underpinned by good personal relationships, operated at a level of relations between postwar nation-states; the testimony of former resisters, including Jewish prisoners who identified themselves first and foremost as resisters, tended to be securely tied to a national, and thus linguistic, identity. But to get to grips with specific areas of the camp's activity, and to define and describe them as crimes in terms of the legal code, many different kinds of survivor voices were necessary: those who could give evidence on the killing of prisoners with phenol injections, the arrival of transports at the Birkenau "ramp" in spring 1944 and the selections for immediate killing in the gas chambers, the fate of the so-called Gipsy Camp, or the work of the *Sonderkommandos* were scattered throughout the world in places where Jewish survivors had settled after the war. The multilingualism of many of these survivors and the frequent hybridity of their speech were a challenge for the interpreters at the trial, but the trial was made possible in the first place by the efforts of multiple translators making different types of text in many different languages available for use as evidence.

As so often, much of the evidence for translation processes is absent from the archive: once the process is complete, the stamp confirming the authenticity of the translation means that the translated text can count as a replacement original and can be drawn into the set of texts that are available for use as evidence. Those individuals who are responsible for authentication mark the end of the process with their name and stamp with which they claim personal responsibility for the correctness (*Richtigkeit*) of the translation, but other translators are very often anonymous or absent from the archive.

The sheer amount of translation activity that supports the proceedings is impossible to quantify: translated documents and correspondence with different levels of institutional status are received, sent, commissioned, and exchanged on a daily basis, including languages that are ultimately not heard spoken at the trial (Hebrew in particular, but also Spanish, Danish, Norwegian, and Swedish). If anything made clear to the court the international and multicultural impact of the Holocaust, then it is this constant translation activity: the Holocaust becomes visible through translation.

To what extent can witness voices in foreign languages be trusted? How does one trust witness accounts that are formulated in collaboration with others or in languages that the witness is not fluent in? Which translators can be trusted by the institution, and how is trust secured? The purpose of a translator with the power to authenticate a text is to make translation disappear, to replace a text with the text derived from it, and to establish it as a testimony that can be ascribed to the named witness, whatever the original language; the complex relationship between the two texts is now irrelevant and is not the court's problem. The translators are engaged in a process that helps to create testimony and witnesses; their specific task is to ensure that the sheer variety of languages and forms of expression in which survivors talk and write about their experiences becomes legible as a German concern. The tension between the transnationalism, variety, and hybridity of testimony and the necessity to translate everything into a specific form of German discourse is one of the defining features of the Frankfurt trial.

Many translators contribute to the complex process of making testimony available, which means formulating them in a specific kind of Standard German. This is a double-edged achievement: witness statements, often formulated in collaborative, multilingual, or hybrid contexts, may go through multiple layers of translation and mediation in order to become testimony in ways that are recognized by the court. For example, in June 1963, W. Paluszewski of the Israeli police, who conducted many interviews with survivors for the court, interviewed the survivor Jakub Silberstein, originally from Tomaszów Mazowiecki; at the end of his statement, Silberstein confirms, "I have given my statement partially in German, Yiddish and Hebrew. The transcript was made in German and I understood the contents very well" ("Vernehmung Jakub Silberstein," 3.6.1963, 37638/89, 17259). This is a good illustration of how the hybrid, collaborative speech of survivors and migrants is overwritten and made available as testimony. The archive documents disguise this process, but it has to be negotiated in public during the main trial. The provision of translations by the court's foreign partners, and the willingness of many individual survivors to go to great lengths to write in German where possible, is a tribute to their determination to support the court's work in pursuit of justice at a moment when the West German authorities seem to be taking it seriously.

If interpreting works "well"—in other words efficiently, in the court's terms—then interpreters are effectively invisible in a trial archive. Where necessary, they support a witness giving testimony or a defendant being questioned during the investigation, and once the questioning is over and an agreed transcript in Standard German has been made, the interpreter stamps and signs off on it along with the other participants. Everything that has come before, including any negotiation or conflict over language or understanding, vanishes from the official record. What remains in the memories of the participants is a different issue: the informal conversations of the court personnel about the witnesses, the witnesses' feelings about what has happened, and informal assessments of the interpreters' work are not recorded but may become important at a later stage.

The official task of the interpreters is to assist in the process of transforming the variety and individuality of survivor's speech into consistent, usable witness statements in Standard German. The first-person narrative of these statements masks a process of collaboration and compulsion, linguistic standardization, and clarification that applies in a "normal" (non-interpreted) interaction, with intralingual interpreting adding extra layers: there is no means of access to a "pure," unmediated form of testimony here, as the testimony is created in the communicative interaction itself. These transcripts of testimony are a specific text genre created for a specific purpose, and we should not expect to be able to "hear the voice" of the witness here.

There are, of course, issues of power, coercion, and discursive dominance in the production of these testimonies, but the witnesses sign off on them, and in this specific and special case there is a sense of shared desire to identify evidence and formulate it in a way that supports the indictment. So, in signing off on them, survivors also sign off on their cocreated status as witnesses in the court's sense.

In order to understand questions of interpreting, there is no sense in comparing the testimonies made by witnesses at the pretrial investigation with the recordings of their testimony in open court. In any case, this form of reading is part of the armory of the court—witnesses can be challenged on discrepancies—and my analysis examines how communication and relationships work in context rather than trying to reconstruct a purer testimony or point out contradictions.

In this chapter, I will concentrate on a small number of moments where issues arise with interpreting that illustrate the concerns of this study: insider–outsider status, relationships of trust between the participants, and questions of power and language ideologies. The smooth running of the evidence-gathering phase relies on anticipating the extent of the requirements of non-German speakers and ensuring that interpreting causes a minimum of disruption to the "normal" proceedings; trying to tame and normalize the extraordinary is a feature of much of the activity of the legal authorities. An awareness develops quickly that the process will necessarily be long and drawn out, and there are complications connected with inviting witnesses from abroad and finding times that suit them.

The prosecutors spent significant time and resources in trying to arrange for a group of survivors from Romania to travel for interviewing in Vienna: writing to the investigating judge Heinz Düx, who traveled to Vienna in the summer of 1962 to interview this group, a court official suggests that they should allow a whole day for each witness, "since the interviews using an interpreter will take longer" (Letter from Oberlandgerichtsrat Fiedler to Heinz Düx, June 28, 1962, 37638/70, 12819–20).

Another issue is deciding what language pair will be required: this causes significant problems for many of the multilingual witnesses as their background and ways of speaking are not reducible to a single national language. For example, many of the survivors who came from Romania to give testimony against Victor Capesius were bilingual in Hungarian and Romanian and often had German characterized by fluency or at least some ability in a regional variant, but that did not always extend to being able to respond to Standard German legal language. In this situation, the obligation to select one language was a political matter reflecting complex questions of identity: a survivor gives testimony against Capesius through an interpreter in a situation in which all three of them are from the same multilingual region. In some of these testimonies we feel the shock at the Nazi assault on such hybrid identities in moments when prisoners arriving on the Hungarian transports in 1944 encounter the Hungarian and Romanian-speaking Capesius on the Birkenau "Ramp."

Many witnesses who spoke with an interpreter in open court had originally claimed to know enough German to be able to dispense with their services. The transcripts contain a statement confirming in the name of the witness that he or she is able to understand and answer questions in German and so does not require an interpreter. There is a striking example in the case of Ignacy Golik, whose pride in speaking German in open court I cited in the introduction. Golik came from Warsaw to Frankfurt in October 1959 to make his statement to the prosecutors Vogel and Kügler. At the beginning of his testimony, the transcript states, "[At school] I learned the basics of German. In later years I studied further independently, meaning that I can now speak German fluently. I am now able to follow my questioning easily without an interpreter" (October 13, 1959, 37638/16, 2388).

The journalist Golik is proud of his ability to speak directly to his German interlocutors, though his testimony in open court shows that he did need support from an interpreter. We have therefore to imagine that the smoothly expressed transcript of his statement disguises a more complex process of negotiation over language and meaning. But it is important to him to use German as a matter of principle. We are reminded here also just how many of the witnesses from Central and Eastern Europe would have learned German at school, whether or not they lived in areas with significant German-speaking populations: the survivor-witnesses' desire to use their German, however hesitantly, to communicate directly with their listeners, is one of the fascinating features of this trial and gives it its specific linguistic "flavor."

An important function of statements such as Golik's is to ensure that any issues with understanding are laid at the door of the witness: he has claimed to be able to understand and has signed off on this transcript. Any difficulties in communication are no longer relevant, and the linguistic procedures of the justice system are affirmed.

In the early stages of the investigation the prosecutors interviewed a large number of Polish survivors who had settled in West Germany after the war: they were easy to find and could mostly speak German. The transcripts of their interviews tend not even to mention language as an issue: for this group of witnesses, German is taken for granted, and there is no need for them to confirm they have understood. We therefore have little idea how they actually spoke or expressed themselves (for example, Stanislaw Smulczynski, February 9, 1960, 37638/26, 4227–32; Aron Cukiermann, February 17, 1960, 37638/26, 4298–300).

Witnesses who came from Poland often spoke German for their pretrial questioning, but many then resorted to the support of an interpreter for their testimony in open court. For example, the Polish former political prisoner Erwin Bartel, who had been deported to Auschwitz in June 1941 and who had traveled to Frankfurt from Katowice in October 1959, made the following declaration: "I have a good command of German and am fully able to follow the questioning without any difficulty" (October 19, 1959, 37638/16, 2434). During his trial testimony on August 27, 1964, Bartel has the support of the interpreter Wera Kapkajew; he begins by speaking German, but as the nearly five-hour testimony proceeds, he relies more and more on her.

Interpreting patterns vary with witnesses with varying levels of fluency in German, but for many witnesses, speaking German in their questioning has a meaning beyond the practical question of "being understood." On occasion, the statements made by witnesses on their language competence reveal extra information that tells us something about the attitude they wish to display to the questioners. For example, Josef Glück, a Jewish survivor from Cluj who settled in Haifa after the war, insists on his ability to conduct the session without an interpreter: "In 1944 Clausenburg [=Cluj] belonged to the Hungarian state. Within my family German and Hungarian were spoken. I have enough of a command of German that I do not require the presence of an interpreter. Even today I still speak Hungarian and German with my family in Israel" (October 16, 1961, 37638/56, 10284).

Glück feels the need to declare why he is a Hungarian speaker despite the city now being in Romania: the court is, of course, aware of this and has interviewed many survivors from this region while building the case against Victor Capesius. The slightly awkward formality of the third sentence ("ich bin der deutschen Sprache so kundig, dass es einer Zuziehung eines Dolmetschers nicht bedarf") suggests that these are not Glück's original spoken words but a formulaic confirmation that the witness accepts responsibility for the success of the communication. The unnecessary information about Glück's family is the most interesting aspect: he confirms here not only that he has kept in touch with German, rather than rejecting it, but also that it is part of his intimate, emotional identity as a survivor: we can read this as a moving offer of reconciliation to a court that shares Glück's aim of seeking justice.

The Polish former political prisoner Stanisław Głowa, who came to Frankfurt on November 21 and 22, 1960, giving testimony about the murder of prisoners with lethal injections, makes this offer of reconciliation more explicit (see Stengel 2022: 200). He began his testimony with the support of the interpreter Wera Kapkajew; however, it had to be abandoned temporarily because Kapkajew had to leave. She was not able to attend the next day, but Głowa declares that he is able to follow the questioning.

The questioning concludes with a long statement by Głowa (37638/41, 7060–1), in which he declares his acknowledgment of the court's work and his desire for reconciliation:

> To conclude my questioning I would like to emphasize strongly that I have made this statement without hatred and that it is the pure truth in every point.
>
> In this context I would like to express my appreciation for the German institution that has brought the crimes of Auschwitz to atonement. Far greater than this, however, is my hope that this trial will lead to reconciliation between the German and Polish peoples.

> I have read the transcript through myself and have a good enough command of German that I have understood everything. What is recorded coincides precisely with the statement made by me.

This is a moving statement that demonstrates the goodwill of this witness and his willingness to work with the court to the end of justice, even without an interpreter. His willingness to speak German is a part of this project of reconciliation: collaborating with a German court in their language in pursuit of truthful testimony is a powerful gesture, but with his signature, Głowa accepts responsibility for the success of the communication. He seems uncertain about this, however, since there is an addendum after the signatures:

> Addendum: I would like to state again that I am able to read and understand German, but that I find speaking difficult.
>
> Aside from that, the details in my statement are so deeply impressed on my memory [so fest in mir verhaftet] that I will never forget them to the end of my life.

This statement seems to leave some unresolved issues hanging at the end of the session, that we are unable to reconstruct now, but the final declaration is designed to ensure that his interlocutors do not mistake "poor," nonstandard, or unclear expression for a sign of unclear memory.

This becomes an issue in Głowa's testimony in open court, on June 11, 1964. His courtroom testimony is very powerful and emotionally direct but there is a moment when he is challenged by contradictions. Głowa has been questioned on whether he was present when the accused Josef Klehr killed prisoners with lethal injections: in his pretrial testimony he had claimed that he was, but under questioning in court, some doubt has arisen. Prosecution counsel Kügler reminds Głowa that the interpreter had been absent for the second day of his questioning and draws his attention to the confirmation that he had understood everything: "It is true that an interpreter was not present when you made this statement … However, at the end of the transcript there is a comment that you understood everything thoroughly and that it was all correct" (155'). Doubt has crept into the testimony, and Głowa has to confirm that contradictions have not arisen because of his inadequate linguistic ability. The danger here is not that witnesses cannot express themselves but that the defense may use linguistic issues to pull apart the prosecution case.

In a letter to the Frankfurt prosecutor's office in July 1959, Hermann Langbein had confirmed that he has been locating Polish witnesses, such as Bartel, who have the "advantage" of speaking good German: "In addition you have the advantage that they can all speak German, so that an interpreter need only be present for difficult expressions" (Letter Langbein to Vogel and Kügler, July 26, 1959, 37638/12, 1643). Clearly there is no financial advantage to this—the interpreter is paid whether or not they speak a word—so it is clear that the presence of interpreters is seen as an obstacle. The interviews take longer with an interpreter, of course, but Langbein would not need to worry about this. A witness speaking imperfect German is seen as more useful than one whose testimony is translated, even by a skilled interpreter.

A letter from the lawyer Edward Kossoy, who had been identifying Greek Jews in Israel to give testimony, gives us an idea of the class and language ideologies involved in the search for witnesses. Writing in German, Kossoy comments, "The Greek Jews from Salonika are more than averagely credible witnesses, but are for the most part very uneducated [primitiv] and scarcely able to understand German" (Letter Edward Kossoy to Oberstaatsanwalt Wolf, October 15, 1959, 37638/16, 2418). One of the testimonies sent by Kossoy gives us an idea of the sheer complexity of the linguistic situation with many of the Jewish witnesses. The survivor Jakob Arroyo, originally from Greece but now settled in Tel Aviv, gave his testimony to Kossoy in November 1959. There is no indication of the original language of this testimony (presumably Hebrew), but Kossoy writes in German and may have translated the testimony into German himself, either as a written text or taken down directly from a spoken version: no translator is named, indicating that this is not a certified translation. Arroyo talks about the moment of his deportation in May 1943. A German civilian (not named) tells the gathered Jews that they are being relocated to work: he speaks German, but there is a rumor that he can speak Greek and Ladino. His words are translated by an interpreter:

> The interpreter translated his speech into Ladino [Spaniolisch]. Now, Ladino is a vernacular [Jargon] that it peculiar to the Greek Jews. We noticed that this interpreter spoke this vernacular fluently and idiomatically. Despite this, we all agreed that he could not have been from Salonika. We do not know where he was from. (37638/19, 2871)

There is a fascinating complexity to this linguistic situation: a German address is translated into Ladino, then this situation is described in Hebrew (presumably) before being translated into German for a court seeking evidence against German perpetrators. The figure of an interpreter who cannot quite be placed is very interesting: he has an ambiguous ethical status. He is not part of their community but speaks their language, so where does he belong? On the side of the perpetrators or the victims? It is also not clear exactly whose voice we hear in the explanation of Ladino: the word "now" ("nun" in German) gives it a spoken, colloquial flavor. Did the witness really say this in his statement, has Kossoy inserted it afterwards, or did they both agree that this might be necessary? These documents hint at a complex communication, gaining legitimacy from a claim to a spoken, authentic origin but withholding access to it.

Despite the preference for German-speaking witnesses, a successful prosecution was going to depend on the testimony of witnesses speaking a variety of languages, and the language situation was often complex. A witness interviewed by the Bavarian police is dismissed, partly because his German is so poor: "Anitzenko does live in Munich and is married to a local. But his German is very poor and he cannot read German" (June 7, 1960, 37638/35, 5947). Anitzenko cannot remember the names of any of the SS personnel and so is not considered to be a useful witness. There is no record of an interpreter being used, leaving one with the impression that Anitzenko's usefulness as a witness is also being assessed on the basis of his linguistic ability.

Other witness statements taken by the German police, rather than the Frankfurt prosecutors, show informal modes of interpreting based on trusted acquaintances. For his statement to the police in Lübeck, the Polish former political prisoner Franciszek Gorczyński asks for a friend, Johannes Golenia, to be present as interpreter: "G. speaks poor German and could not make himself understood correctly." This suggests that they had made an initial attempt without an interpreter present. Golenia, who is not a sworn interpreter, signs the following statement: "The questioning was translated by me, I confirm with my signature that the transcript is identical to my translation" (LKPA Lübeck, February 8, 1960, 37638/27, 4328).

Golenia here does not vouch for the accuracy of the translation but confirms the accuracy of the transcript of his translation: the translation itself is taken for granted, as is Golenia's presumed role in enabling, mediating, and organizing the conversation. The complex processes of "thin," bureaucratic trust that structure the court's work are not necessary here: personal, intimate trust is enough for this document to be confirmed as valid.

The Polish-Jewish survivor Simon Gotland—whose testimony I discuss in more detail in Chapter 12—gave his initial statement on September 4, 1962. Judge Düx had written to him in Paris on August 17 asking if he required an interpreter, and Gotland replied on August 22, stating, "I do not need an interpreter" (37638/72, 13276 and 13308). After the experience of giving testimony in open court, and the linguistic difficulties this caused him, which reflected negatively on the perception of him as a witness, he makes sure to bring a trusted interpreter with him. When questioned at the West German embassy in Paris in May 1963 for a different investigation, he brings a friend with him: "Since the witness has only a moderate command of German and speaks Yiddish, he brought a friend with him as interpreter, namely Herr Hermann LEWIN, stateless, born 1 April 1897 in Zaleszczyki (Galicia)" (37638/87, 16497).

As a fellow survivor with similar background—though we should note that Lewin is stateless, rather than a French citizen, as Gotland is—Lewin is trusted by Gotland to represent his words properly. Gotland is here being "questioned as witness for information," so his testimony does not have the status of evidence, and there is no need for a sworn interpreter in this situation: the quality of the interpreting is the responsibility of the witness. It is only the operation of structures of "thin" trust that permit a statement to become testimony for the court.

The Ukrainian survivor Volodymyr Martynec—one of the group of OUN activists who collaborated with the Nazis until they fell foul of Nazi geopolitics—writes from New Jersey in English stating that he is prepared to give testimony, but he would require a Ukrainian interpreter. In the end, he is unable to travel to Frankfurt, and so is interviewed at the West German Consulate in New York on March 17, 1965 in the presence of representatives of prosecution and defense. His questioning begins with his daughter Sofia as language broker, who is replaced in the afternoon by his wife Eufrozyna. At the end, the participants sign a joint declaration:

> Since the witness has only a limited command of German the questioning was carried out in Ukrainian and English with the assistance of first his daughter and then his wife. All three lawyers present declared that they were satisfied with the interpreting work of these two ladies, although they are not sworn interpreters. The consul signed below speaks English. (37638/94, 18569)

This is a characteristic situation of language brokering, with family members acting as trusted collaborators in migrants' encounters with official bodies, but what stands out here is the official confirmation of the quality of the interpreting. Sofia and Eufrozyna have coordinated and enabled a complex exchange between participants with different levels of ability in the three languages being spoken. The representatives of the Frankfurt court, balanced between prosecution and defense, declare themselves able to approve the interaction, despite the lack of professional qualifications of the "ladies": exactly how they were able to exercise quality control for the Ukrainian interpreting is not clear. Effectively, they declare here that it is "good enough," as all the parties have been working toward a shared aim. One layer is impossible to trace here: how and by whom the record of the exchange was rendered into German.

The prosecutor's office showed itself willing to accept improvisation in the employment of interpreters if it was necessary. The Transylvanian survivor Alfred Ehrenfeld, who had settled in Sweden after the war, presented difficulties for a number of reasons. Initially, the prosecutor's office wanted to arrange for him to be questioned at the West German embassy in Stockholm, and Ehrenfeld requested an interpreter: "The witness has asked for an interpreter to be present at his questioning as both he and we consider his command of German not to be adequate." The embassy staff clearly also felt that Ehrenfeld required an interpreter (May 5, 1962, 37638/67, 12280–1).

Shortly after this, the embassy contacted Düx to say that it did not have the resources to interview Ehrenfeld in its premises; the witness therefore had to come to Frankfurt, which he did on July 2, 1962, despite difficulties getting a visa ("Aktenvermerk Dr. Düx," May 14, 1962, 37638/67, 12333). His testimony in Frankfurt was supported by the Hungarian-German interpreter Rolf Dienesch, who had replaced the court's appointed interpreter Dr. Baer at the last minute: "The interpreter Rolf Dienesch also presented himself. An attempt had been made to contact the publicly certified Hungarian interpreter [handwritten comment in margin: Dr. Baer]. He was however unable to attend and referred us to his cousin, Herr Dienesch." Dienesch is sworn in during the testimony, enabling the statement to operate as testimony (37638/70, 12892). But it is clear that Dienesch has been accepted on the grounds of a personal recommendation rather than an application process, meaning that there is a certain flexibility in the criteria governing insider status, where necessary.

During Ehrenfeld's dramatic testimony, he accused Victor Capesius of selecting on the Ramp at Birkenau some Cluj business rivals for gassing: another example of the extraordinary personal intimacy of a genocide that is often imagined to be abstract and mechanical. Here, he is also confronted with Capesius: he has to identify him, and Capesius has to respond directly to the allegations. The confrontation of witness and accused is one of the most dramatic aspects of these pretrial testimonies, potentially traumatic for the survivor: the transcripts give us a certain impression of the drama and emotion of these encounters but couched in a sober language that seeks to record only different statements about the truth of an allegation.

The trial records do not allow us to reconstruct the interactions on these occasions, and the role of the interpreter is absent from the transcript.

Nevertheless, Dienesch's role must be decisive, as in all forms of consecutive interpreting: translating, reorganizing, and clarifying what has been said, mediating and managing the interaction, and dealing with any conflicts. These are moments when relationships of trust are negotiated and tested at many levels. Dienesch continues to work for the court and so must have performed in a way that gained institutional approval. Listening to Ehrenfeld's testimony in open court, however, we find that Dienesch has also developed a complex relationship with the witness: when speaking German, Ehrenfeld speaks clearly and confidently, but when speaking Hungarian for translation, he is quieter, speaking only for the interpreter. They are also disciplined by the presiding judge for conversing privately: Ehrenfeld has clearly found an ally in the interpreter and regards him as a source of support (August 17, 1964, 49'. The interaction is audible on the tape but is not recorded on the transcript).

On occasion, translators are brought in to act as interpreters on the basis of their status in the institution. For example, Elisabeth Grimmeisen, a long-standing employee of the Justice Ministry who we have seen taking on the translation of written testimonies from Polish, is employed to interpret for the questioning of Jan Sikorski on May 16, 1960. As an employer, the state prosecutor's office is willing to turn to trusted employees to do this work where necessary: qualifications in interpreting are not seen as necessary.

The statements at the end of the transcripts about language and communication practices in the court are often revealing about the working relationships that have developed. In this case, Sikorski confirms,

> I have been able to follow the questioning in German well and have also given my statements in German. On occasion, I did not understand an individual word or was not able to pronounce it in German; the interpreter who was present then translated.
>
> I have read through the transcript in German. In a small number of cases the interpreter translated something for me, when I did not understand it straight away. (37638/33, 5543)

His statement has a double function: Sikorski stresses how much he has understood himself and thus that his testimony was communicated directly in German; the presence of the interpreter as a person who was only rarely necessary helps to emphasize this point. Secondly, the bureaucracy is able to confirm that its language practices have produced no problems and that any misunderstandings or misstatements are the fault of the witness. So it produces authenticity in two different ways: the guarantee of direct, authentic speech and the bureaucratic production of a text that can be accepted as evidence.

The bureaucratic recording procedures are a way of ensuring that potentially complex or unruly issues of communication are defused before they can find their way into the files that the court will refer to. There are hints of complex issues, including in the last-minute employment of translators, in some of the transcripts. For example, for the questioning of Tadeusz Szewczyk, on May 16, 1960, an experienced interpreter appears to have been brought in to make the final confirmation.

Szewczyk has declared that he required an interpreter: "I do not speak German well and request that an interpreter is present. The student Janusz Kluźniak, resident in Frankfurt/Main … was brought in" (37638/33, 5587). Kluźniak is not described here as a sworn translator, so there is a limit to what he is able to do: at the end of the questioning the sworn translator Kapkajew is brought in to perform that final act of authentication, which Szewczyk confirms: "The transcript in German was translated for me by the sworn interpreter Frau Kapkajew … into Polish. The transcript is identical with my statement" (5600).

Kluźniak is employed on occasion by the court during the main proceedings, having sworn his interpreter's oath. He applied for work with the court in a letter of February 14, 1964, having been informed by a Polish journalist that the court required an interpreter, stressing his familiarity with the material: "I have many years of experience in the field of interpreting and am well informed about the subject of the Auschwitz trial since I worked for the pre-trial investigation during the questioning of witnesses and their identification of Dr. Victor Capesius" (37638/92, 17835).

He is now a state-certified interpreter and translator, meaning that he has finished his training and passed the state examination in Hessen (it seems he was still a student when he worked during the pretrial investigation). Despite his experience, he was only employed four times for interpreting from Polish in open court, when Wera Kapkajew was absent. What does it mean for a witness when one interpreter's work is considered more "professional" than another's?

Conclusion

This discussion has just scratched the surface of the linguistic and translation issues that characterized the pretrial phase, and most of the translation processes that contribute to producing the trial indictment and other documents are now impossible to reconstruct. But it is clear that this trial would have been impossible without the work of translators and interpreters and the willingness of survivors and their representatives to collaborate and compromise with the linguistic standards and procedures of the West German legal authorities.

Most of the detail I have discussed here is entirely normal practice in preparing a trial, but the sheer scale of the trial, the extraordinary nature of the evidence being recorded, and the linguistic diversity of the witnesses (as well as some of the perpetrators) ensure that "normal" procedures are tested to the limit. Trying to tame and normalize the extraordinary is a feature of much of the activity of the legal authorities. In terms of translation, the bureaucratic processes of authentication and approval are designed to nullify the disruptive potential of translation. Statements signed by translators, interpreters, and witnesses at the end of transcripts ensure that these individuals take responsibility for the success or failure of communication and understanding, thus protecting the court's own linguistic practices from challenge or question.

The many fields of tension that arise are what give this trial its specific character, very different to special tribunals created to deal with specific genocides: they tell us about insider–outsider status, relationships of trust between the participants, questions of power, and language ideologies, which have consequences for the interactions in the public phase of the trial.

If we think about the proceedings in terms of language and translation processes, we can perhaps characterize the linguistic culture of the trial as a dynamic process of exchange between a dominant Standard German legal discourse, as target or necessary final destination of translation processes, and a range of other languages, other forms of German, and hybrid speech being spoken and written across the world: each of these modes of speech bears a complex political, ideological, and emotional load. This is the "sound" of the First Frankfurt Auschwitz Trial. If we center these different modes of expression and translation processes rather than regarding them as peripheral, then we can acknowledge the richness of survivors' language use and their agency while never losing sight of the power structures within which they, along with the many translators and interpreters, had to work.

7

Public Commentary on Interpreting at the Trial

The testimony of Simon Gotland, who appeared in court on July 27, 1964, was described the next day in an unsigned article in the *Frankfurter Neue Presse* as a "language that no one understands":

> His hands clasped like claws around the back of the chair, the heavyset man sits facing the court as if he has to be ready at any second to jump up and flee. From time to time he glances around himself helplessly, apparently not understanding most of the questions posed in carefully chosen words by the many black-robed men. He is sometimes startled when his own torrent of words yells back at him in triple volume from the loudspeaker. And the more intensely the memories burst out of him, the less the other participants in the trial understand him; it is as if he is walled in.
>
> Simon Gotland's language seems for a moment to symbolize the fate of many Auschwitz prisoners. If they survived, they found themselves in a strange world, outwardly so intact and cultivated, in which there was no longer any room for the dark days, and hardly any possibility of articulating them in language. This was the experience of Simon Gotland, who appeared as a witness for the prosecution in the Auschwitz trial on Monday. He speaks in many languages that nevertheless reach no one. His Polish mother tongue is almost forgotten, since he left for Paris at a young age; today, no one can understand the mixture of the "German" that was common in the camps at the time and a kind of Yiddish, and French is still so difficult for him to speak that even the interpreter has no idea what to do with it.
>
> Gotland stumbles from one language to the next, becoming more confused the more effort he makes. With great effort, the Polish interpreter, who has to be summoned quickly, helps him get through the terrifying hours. (*Frankfurter Neue Presse* 1964)

This article is unusual in its detailed focus on a particular witness and his struggles to articulate his experiences; it also makes telling comments about the situation in which survivors found themselves after liberation. As I show in the final chapter, this view of Gotland downplays his agency as a witness and exaggerates the incomprehensibility of his speech, but it does put unusual emphasis on language and on the role of the interpreter in managing the situation. The French interpreter has to be replaced, and the Polish interpreter helps and supports him, not only by translating but also emotionally.

The article acknowledges the role of the interpreter in the dramaturgy of the testimony and suggests that part of the job consists in maintaining a relationship with the witness that allows him to speak and be understood. In an article on Gotland's testimony, Inge Deutschkron—who had survived the war in hiding in Berlin and reported on the trial for the German, Hebrew, and English press—makes a similar point:

> The witness Gotland, a dark-haired, simple man, caused translation difficulties with his mixture of Yiddish and French, unable as he was to make himself understood in German or in French. This problem was only solved when he was assigned an interpreter who translated from Polish. (Deutschkron 2018: 241)

In both these accounts, it is the witness who brings a problem to the court that has to be solved through the intervention of an interpreter; the *Frankfurter Neue Presse* article is unusual in that it shows a sensitivity to the linguistic situation in which many survivors found themselves, but this does not lead to any questioning of the court's procedures. The interpreter's job is to make the witness available so that the court can work.

On another occasion, a similar report by Walter Pfuhl—while attempting to be sympathetic—can't help but shade into clichés about a babbling Jewish speaker whose language is brought under control by the interpreter:

> German, Yiddish, Polish, all jumbled together, this is how the small, frail David Schmidt [*sic*: actually Dawid Szmidt] from Israel speaks … But the court can make neither head nor tail of his gibberish [Kauderwelsch], so the tried and tested Polish court interpreter is summoned, and the testimony gradually takes shape …
>
> The ritual of questions and answers, that had visibly put the nervous, emotional witness under pressure, is concluded. He leaps up, relieved, spots a friend whom he has not seen since their time in Auschwitz …
>
> Embracing, stammering in Yiddish, dissolving in tears of joy, the two of them leave the room, more staggering than walking. (Pfuhl 1964)

Not all reporters are interested in the witnesses or their language use beyond the factual content of the testimony: more often than not, they are focused on the perpetrators and their actions and so report Gotland's evidence in the German words of the interpreter. For reporting that relies on the direct authenticity of the witness's account, interpreting has to be ignored, as it potentially introduces a barrier.

Mention of interpreting is very rare in the extensive press reporting on the trial. For the most part, observers quote the interpreted words, clearing them up for consistency and Standard German grammar, sometimes editing for length or stitching together statements from different parts of the testimony to make greater impact. This is the procedure followed also by Hermann Langbein and his collaborators in their transcript of much of the trial proceedings and, a further step removed, by Peter Weiss in his "documentary" play *Die Ermittlung* (The Investigation). Radio documentaries and plays have also tended to ignore interpreting, as it takes time, may be unproductive in terms of the aims of the text, and can be frustrating to read or listen to. What this means is that the voices of witnesses who relied on interpreters are less likely to be acknowledged, and where they are, the complexity of the communication can be "cleaned up" in the construction of a voice that does not reflect the way the witness actually spoke.

On at least one occasion, this leads to a significant distortion of a witness's words. An article in the *Frankfurter Rundschau* in May 1964 contrasts the accused Oswald Kaduk's claims of Polish anti-German hatred with the conciliatory words of Józef Seweryn: "I would prefer to be able to be friends with everyone here!" (Mir wäre es auch lieber, ich könnte mit allen hier Freund sein! (*Frankfurter Rundschau* 1964b)). In fact, when we listen to the recording of his testimony (May 25, 1964, 160'), we find that Seweryn's words are directed at one of the defendants, Klaus Dylewski, and express regret at being obliged to give testimony. This is not a simple call for reconciliation: "I am unhappy today that we are both sitting here talking like this to one another. I would be happier if Dylewski were my friend" (Mnie jest dzisiaj przykro, że siedzimy obydwaj i jeden na drugiego mówi. Ja bym był bardziej zadowolony gdyby Dylewski był moim przyjacielem). The interpreter Wera Kapkajew, however, renders his words in a way that can be misconstrued as a more general appeal, by leaving out Dylewski's name: "I am very sorry that we have to sit like this today speaking against each other like this. I would much prefer for us to be friends" (Es tut mir sehr leid, dass wir heute so sitzen müssen und einer gegen den anderen was sagen müssen. Es wäre mir viel lieber, wenn wir Freunde sein könnten).

The way that witnesses are cited through translation is revealing about the language ideologies of press observers and the understanding of testimony that is being negotiated as the trial proceeds: direct, authentic, individual speech is validated, and anything that potentially muddies the communication has to be played down or edited out. Accounts that focus on the witnesses' language are rarer, but they provide a contrasting public discourse that acknowledges the situation of the speaking survivor and that the difficulty of communication may be the key to understanding. On occasion, this means making the interpreter visible as mediator, support, or simply part of the drama of the scene.

Reports that refer to interpreting tend either to comment on how the interpreter affects the proceedings or to use discussion of their work to reflect on questions of language. Accounts that acknowledge interpreters as active participants in the testimony situation sometimes complain about the length and tedium of an interpreted testimony. For example, writing in the *New York Times* about the testimony of Alexander Princz, who spoke Czech with the support of the interpreter Michael Benesch, Irving Marder describes the repetitiveness of consecutive interpreting as inducing a form of trance state:

> He replies unemotionally, confidently, volubly to the judge's questions. The interpreter renders the judge's German into Czech, Mr. Prinz's [*sic*] reply into German. As the afternoon wears on, one's attention tends to wander during the laborious translation sequence. Bits of dialog and fragments of sentences float up to the gallery as through a mist:
>
> Witness: "... I saw them hanged."
> Judge: "What was that?"
> Witness: "Hanged."
> Interpreter: "Hanged."
> Judge: "How did they do it?"
> Witness: "They put the rope around the neck, then the hangman pushed them off the platform."
>
> The voices fade into the mist and then emerge again. The witness has finished his testimony. (Marder 1964)

As a description of the experience of listening to a long testimony and an admission that intense concentration is not always possible, this is interesting, but it puts the blame clearly on the interpreting for interrupting the flow and interest and creating distance to the proceedings.

Rarely, the interpreter is acknowledged as an active participant in the communication. Bernd Neumann's reports occasionally do this: his remarkable reporting conveys a sense of the drama of the trial from a position of sympathy, clear political commitment, and understanding of the importance of precise language. Here, citing the words of the Czechoslovak Sonderkommando survivor Filip Müller through the interpreter Erwin Jarolim, he qualifies the idea of quoting a witness "literally," ensuring that the reader understands the testimony has been mediated by the interpreter:

> [Oberscharführer Moll] took the child away from the mother, carried it away, I saw this in Crematorium IV, where there were two large pits. He threw the children into the boiling fat of these people. Then he went up to his "servant," a Frenchman, a lightweight boxing champion, and said in these words: "I can now eat well. (These are the words of the interpreter.) I have done my duty". (Naumann 1964)[1]

Müller's characterization of Moll's voice, his coldness and cynicism, is important for the impact of this piece. The phrase "in these words" (in the original, "wörtlich") seems to produce a need to clarify that Moll's statement comes to us in a translation of Müller's Czech: a good example of linguistic integrity on the part of the writer.

Writing about the same day's testimony in the *Frankfurter Rundschau*, Peter Miska structures a report dealing with the power of Müller's testimony around the fact of interpreting. The report opens by acknowledging the presence of the interpreter translating an answer to Judge Hofmeyer's question about the pits in which bodies were burnt: " 'There were two large pits,' Müller replies in Czech. Next to him, the interpreter translates." At the end of the article, after setting out in sympathetic terms Müller's harrowing testimony—including a number of direct quotations—Miska returns to language: " 'Please,' says Presiding Judge Hofmeyer, 'repeat after me: I swear it, so help me God.' The Czech Filip Müller says in German: 'I swear it, so help me God' " (Miska 1964).

Occasionally an interpreter is acknowledged as an active participant in the drama of a scene. Here, Stefan Boratyński finds the courage to make a criticism of the defense for challenging the integrity of his testimony after he was seen conferring with another witness. The inclusion of an unnamed Kapkajew in the description of this scene emphasizes the witness's caution in making this potentially face-threatening challenge: "At this point, the interpreter asked whether the Polish witness Stefan Boratyński, with the permission of the court, might be permitted to say something else" (Strothmann 1964). This brief moment acknowledges implicitly that she and the witness have been conferring privately: the politeness formulae that she uses emphasize the risk of this situation for the witness.

In an account focusing on witnesses' difficulty in formulating their memories of Auschwitz and providing answers in the form required by the court, Felix Rexhausen shows how Kapkajew supports a witness who is struggling with his emotions. Neither witness nor interpreter is named here: the story is designed to illustrate a general point about the witnesses' inability to follow a trial: "The witnesses are often simple people, who would have difficulty understanding the mechanisms even of a normal trial." So they often assume that questions from the defense are "malicious, full of hostility against them":

> One witness [Szmidt] was supposed to show the defense council a photograph; when he takes it, the interpreter remarks that the witness is afraid he will not get it back. When the Presiding Judge attempts to reassure him, he replies: "I'm a stranger here, I don't know how things work" [Ich kenn' mich hier nicht aus].

The interpreter explains the problem to the court, speaking for the witness. This prompts comments from Rexhausen praising Judge Hofmeyer for his calm handling of the situation: "The Presiding Judge, Hans Hofmeyer, assists the witness where possible. He is calm, patient, takes pains to remain entirely objective, controls this courtroom effortlessly with his mild-tempered seriousness" (Rexhausen 1964). This article is a good illustration of the way that interpreters' emotional support work for the witnesses also serves to reproduce the power hierarchies in the courtroom: the problem is caused by the witness's ignorance.

Translation issues tend only to be made explicit when they serve the dramatic structure of the report. A report in *Die Welt* from May 15, 1964, records the unnamed Kapkajew hesitating over a translation in the testimony of Jan Pilecki: "'The bunker of the Political Department had a bad reputation [einen schlechten Ruf],' translates the interpreter. She corrects herself quickly: 'a gruesome reputation [einen grausigen Ruf]'" (*Die Welt* 1964). This small moment dramatizes the testimony, giving the impression of an interpreter searching for appropriate language alongside the witness (Pilecki had in fact used the Polish word "ponury"—gloomy, bleak—and the word Kapkajew actually used in court is "grausam" (cruel), which is easy to mishear as "grausig").

Reports on the dramatic testimony of George Preston use the translation of his outburst at the defendant Emil Bednarek for dramatic effect. At the end of his testimony on March 4, 1965, Preston shouts at Bednarek, causing the interpreter

Franz Schuh to lose control of the situation. I have already commented on this exchange in the introduction, but it is notable that the press reporting on this scene adds to Schuh's translation. Preston shouts at Bednarek that he has grown fat, but two articles quote Schuh's translation as "you fat pig" (du fettes Schwein). On the recording, there is no evidence of Preston having said the word "pig" or Schuh the word "Schwein," so the reporters—perhaps based on conversations in the audience afterward—have added this extra layer of drama. Preston tended to use the German word "Schwein" when quoting SS men's words, so it is possible that they have picked it up from this (*Christ und Welt* 1965; *Neue Presse* 1965).

Public Commentary on Wera Kapkajew's Work

Beyond these rare acknowledgments of the work of interpreters, press commentary concentrates on the person of Wera Kapkajew; she is also the only interpreter mentioned in person in memoirs and comments made by other participants in the trial. This material—limited in scope though it is—allows us to explore how attitudes toward interpreting and the interpreter intersect with thinking about Holocaust witnessing and the responsibilities of the listener: what does the person of the interpreter come to represent in this situation?

In January 1965, the *Frankfurter Rundschau* published a substantial interview with her by Uwe-Jens Petersen, which talks about her work and comments on her celebrity:

> Anyone who a year ago … watched the first Polish witnesses in the Auschwitz Trial appearing before the court may well have noticed a woman coming in, delicate in a black outfit. The witnesses and the woman had to state their name, place of origin and profession, and we learned that "she" is Wera Kapkajew, an interpreter, resident in Frankfurt. Since then the number of Polish as well as Russian witnesses has become legion—and Frau Kapkajew translated articulately into German, so that the words spoken in foreign sounds came to life in our language: the fear, a thousand times over, the horror. Auschwitz, the cry of terror echoing from naked brick walls. Wera Kapkajew not only translates word for word, but also the moods. All the way up to anger. All the way down to tears. (Petersen 1965: 264)

The headline dubs her "the interpreter of horrors" ("die Dolmetscherin des Grauens"), identifying her person clearly not with the court or the legal system but with the material she has to translate and the experiences of the witnesses. There is more to her role here than simply translating evidence, but she mediates the experience of Auschwitz and the feelings connected with it to an audience well beyond the courtroom. The comments are a strange mixture of acknowledging her professionalism and expertise and characterizing her as a focus for the emotional experience of listening to a witness's voice. Once an interpreter becomes visible, then much discursive energy needs to be expended on making her transparent: this explains the emphasis on her ability to imitate the witnesses so that her voice merges with theirs. This enables listeners to establish a direct, authentic, and emotional connection with the witnesses without worrying about complex questions of mediation or the construction of sources.

Kapkajew here becomes a proxy for the experience of listening to the witness: the listener's feelings about what he is hearing are projected onto her voice and body. Petersen's emotional response to the testimony comes at the expense of listening to the content of the statements: Kapkajew translates "moods" ("Stimmungen") and is able to transmit a sense of the impossibility of speech. Despite Petersen's obvious political sympathy for the witnesses, the view of language and testifying on display here is problematic: the witnesses speak "in foreign/strange/alien sounds" ("in fremden Lauten"), which gives the impression of barely human speech coming from an alien world. The witnesses' experiences "come alive" "in our language": languages represent different worlds of experience rather than potentially overlapping or shared areas of contact and communication. The interpreter, then, bridges an otherwise unbridgeable gap between the experience and the listener.

The emotional language and emphasis on experience and voicing serve to reassure us that translation is not a problem to be concerned about: Petersen preserves the sense of the gap between the listener's understanding and the witnesses' experience while positioning the interpreter as an assurance that the listener can still access the experience. Her voice and body short-circuit the gap, meaning that concrete issues of translation, expression, and professional practice need not disturb the listener's impression of authenticity and immediacy.

In *Die Welt* in May 1965, Walter Pfuhl writes strikingly about how the fragmentary witness statements eventually came together to conjure up the reality of Auschwitz (showing that, at least in this case, the intentions of Fritz Bauer had been fulfilled, beyond simply bringing the prosecutions):

> Even so, the testimonies brought enough to light. From a thousand fragmentary sentences, from words that the witness could only stammer and sob, but which were mercilessly amplified by the loudspeaker, a picture of the reality of Auschwitz came together.

Kapkajew comes to represent the observer's empathy with the witnesses, becoming a channel for emotion:

> The delicate interpreter who had to translate the testimonies of sixty Polish witnesses and who could see their faces from up close, speaks without any hesitation what many are feeling: she will continue to live with these people [mit diesen Menschen weiterleben], whether she wants to or not. (Pfuhl 1965)

We gain the impression that the fascination of these male writers with her appearance, skill, and emotional facility is a way of gaining permission to express strong emotions about the witnesses: to feel empathy while avoiding the danger of identification or of getting too close to the darkness of their stories. That these comments are not an adequate description of her actual interpreting practice will become clear in the course of this study.

Another commentator takes this fascination with Kapkajew's person further: one might say, too far to be comfortable. A *Frankfurter Rundschau* author, who signed himself "RK", writes up an interview with her in December 1964, maintaining that he had attended the testimony of Josef Bodek simply because a colleague had recommended observing Kapkajew ("'You have to love her!' … It is a love that arises from high respect for a phenomenal interpreter"). After giving some biographical details that stress how she is at home in three different cultures ("Kulturkreise"), RK puts her linguistic fluency down to her cultivation and love for literature ("Tolstoy is her God"). She learned German from the poetry of Rilke and (the pro-Nazi aesthete) Rudolf Binding, and admires Hermann Hesse but not the new authors, "Grass and the rest of them."

RK describes them showing their mutual sympathy through playful literary references and then makes a sharp turn to interpreting:

> We nod and understand each other. We toss the ball back and forth, a few hints are enough, the response is immediate. Now I understand how it is that translation and interpreting come to her so brilliantly and fluently. "You have to give yourself up completely to what you're doing," she says.

The article ends with a comment on Kapkajew's claim to have contracted a phlegmon through the emotional load of the work. There is a moment of extreme discomfort for the reader here as the action of rolling her sleeve up and showing a scar is too reminiscent of the actions of survivors who showed their tattoos in court:

> She pushes up her sleeve and shows me tiny scars at her elbow. "One month ago I contracted a phlegmon, just out of nowhere. Phlegmon is a typical

> concentration camp sickness. I had simply identified with Auschwitz too much".
> (RK 1964)

Kapkajew has clearly decided to talk about her phlegmon in this way as part of her professional, public self-positioning, but it is notable that the cited words in this article are far less cautious and nuanced than her statement to the Dutch television interviewer, where she was very careful to avoid saying that she "identified" with survivors. Whether this represents her actual words to RK is impossible to say, but the contrast is striking. RK also creates a sense of cultural affinity through shared love for a specific conservative-bourgeois interpretation of German literary tradition: the genealogy Goethe-Rilke-Hesse-Binding reveals a restorative literary alignment characteristic of a mid-twentieth-century German conservatism that slipped easily into support for the Nazis and then easily into the world of the early Federal Republic. This may explain the sense of discomfort at the "new literature" that is beginning to challenge the postwar consensus.

One thing that commentators on Kapkajew's work agree on is that she voices the witnesses rather than simply translating the content of their words: "Wera is a woman who enjoyed the unanimous praise of both press and audience: she translates the witness statements fluently but precisely. Yes, she is even, to a certain extent, able to translate the feelings of these people too" (*Frankfurter Rundschau* 1964a). Hermann Langbein, the Austrian political prisoner and former general secretary of the International Auschwitz Committee, whose efforts were instrumental in locating many of the witnesses and persuading them to testify, comments on what he views as Kapkajew's uncanny ability to inhabit the voices of the witnesses:

> Frau Kapkajew's translations were very accurate and fluent, but not only that, she has the gift of reproducing the tone of voice and nuances in a way that gives the listener the impression of hearing the witness himself speak. After the last Polish witness had been questioned, the Presiding Judge gave her warm words of thanks for her assistance. (Langbein 1995: 16–17)

A commentator for the Dutch news program *Achter het Nieuws* formulates it like this: "The survivors were able to relate all these terrible things thanks to the interpreter Wera Kapkajew, who slipped into the skin of 80 Polish witnesses" (Wage 1965). The last surviving member of the prosecution team, Gerhard Wiese, remembered Kapkajew in an interview he gave to Polish journalists in 2019:

> The witnesses, whether from Poland, Russia, or Israel, found themselves in Germany for the first time, heard the German language, and had to revive in their testimony things that they had wanted to forget. Their reactions varied. Some spoke briefly and concisely, as they had when giving previous statements, others could not hold back their sobbing, and we had to interrupt the hearing. A translator from Polish and Russian, Wera Kapkajew, was helpful. She not only translated the statements but adjusted her voice to best reflect what the witness said. (Domagała-Pereira and Dudek 2019)

Here, Wiese connects Kapkajew's skills to the difficulties that survivors experienced arriving in Germany and reliving their trauma: her perceived ability to ventriloquize is a solution to this problem, enabling the court to understand what the witnesses are expressing in their testimony. She conveys both the difficulty of giving testimony and the factual content of the statement. It is notable that Wiese views the process of giving testimony as "reviving" (ożywić) the experience, a view that has consequences for the role and ethical responsibilities of the interpreter, as well as the listener: if an interpreter imitates the voice and manner of the witness, then we as listeners are able to share the experience.

Bernd Naumann lavished praise on Kapkajew in an article from November 1964, though his aim seems to be directed more at criticizing the quality of the Czech interpreters than at discussing Kapkajew's practice specifically:

> The next witness statement … showed what an outstanding role was being played by the Polish and Russian interpreter Frau Kapkajew. Her translation skills, rapid and able to deal in a virtuosic way with long passages, become all the more obvious when compared to other interpreters who translate for the Czechoslovak witnesses. Up to now, there has been no Czech interpreter who even approaches Frau Kapkajew's ability, despite the fact that one of them was a university language specialist. (Naumann 2013: 19)

One commentary that does look beyond either vague comments on "skill" or "fluency" or ideas of voicing or emotional identification comes from the East German prosecutor Friedrich Karl Kaul. The prosecution team, though based in the West German state of Hessen, included representation from the German Democratic Republic as counsel for the *Nebenkläger* (civil plaintiffs) resident in the GDR. Kaul was a well-known personality in both German states: a Jewish lawyer who had fled the Third Reich after being interned in a concentration camp in 1935, Kaul had joined the German Communist Party in 1945, settling in East Berlin, but had succeeded in being admitted to legal practice in both

East and West. He participated in a number of high-profile political trials in West Germany, ensuring that they could be instrumentalized for propaganda purposes by the East German government.

In his memoir of the trial, Kaul provides a rare description of the dynamics of the interpreting situation, acknowledging that the witnesses' words are not heard directly: his depiction of the interaction between the participants during the testimony of the Polish witness Stefan Boratyński creates a sense of the human drama of the situation. He even acknowledges—with a certain sense of irony—her justification in interrupting him when he is in full flow: "The nimble interpreter interrupts me with a sign of her raised hand. Deftly, and without the slightest hesitation, she translates what I have been saying."

Kaul uses vocabulary suggesting quick-wittedness and flexibility ("flink," "gewandt," "wendig," suggesting deftness, skill, agility, nimbleness, and versatility) and often shows how the instructions of the court to the witness are transmitted through her: "The interpreter instructs the witness in what is required of him." In one dramatic sequence, she is shown to follow the witness toward the defendants, where he is to identify Robert Mulka, the former adjutant of the camp commander Rudolf Höß:

> Suddenly, Boratyński's slim body jerks. He stops before the accused Mulka, points at him, speaks some Polish words. The interpreter, who had followed him, turns to the judges' desk and translates: "This is the adjutant of Commandant Höß." (Dobrawa 2013: 77–8)

Here, the key moment of eyewitness identification is relayed through the interpreter: Boratyński speaks incomprehensibly while looking at the accused, and it is Kapkajew who relays the information to the court. In other words, she acts as a mediator between the worlds of the witness and the court and also as a person who makes the testimony possible in the first place. It is notable that Kaul has no compunction in drawing attention to the role of the interpreter in determining the pace and structure of the testimony: here, interpreting is in the service of factual truth rather than emotional experience, and so the interpreter's structuring role can be acknowledged.

In these commentaries, Kapkajew often becomes a focus for ways of thinking about the emotional experience of listening to victim testimony; there is a sense of fascination with her art and skill and the way she performs the role but without questioning the possibility of accessing the experience of the witness. The witnesses are viewed as fundamentally passive or inarticulate, and she enables the testimony to take place, thereby bridging a gap that is not just linguistic. Descriptions by writers like Walter Pfuhl of the witnesses as helplessly stammering in a way that has to be ordered in court downplays their agency in telling their stories: Kapkajew plays a gatekeeper role here, one that she seems to have supported in the statements she makes to the press. She works very hard on gaining thick trust with members of the press as well as the witnesses and the court: it is an extremely successful professional strategy.

The commentaries on interpreting all share one common feature: communication difficulties are a problem caused by the witnesses, and the role of the interpreters is to solve this problem. Even writers who are sympathetic and sensitive to the situation of the survivors and their language use—as in the article on Simon Gotland that I cited at the beginning of this section—locate the problem within the individual witness and the legacy of their time in Auschwitz. The linguistic practices and power structures of the court are not questioned in these accounts, and the interpreters' task is to reproduce power by "solving" the problem of witnesses' language use. Empathetic engagement with the witnesses is a double-edged sword: supporting the witness while reproducing the court's power structure. That this focus on emotion, empathy, and ventriloquism does not do justice to the full complexity of the interpreters' responses to their task will become clear in the rest of his study.

8

Institutional Norms and Expectations

The rest of this study explores the work of the interpreters in the public phase of the trial from different angles in order to give an impression of the interactions between interpreters, witnesses, and other participants and to explore the conditions under which survivors gave testimony to their experiences. The hundreds of hours of recorded testimony make it necessary to be highly selective in the choice of material; it will not be possible to give anything like a comprehensive picture of interpreting activity at the trial. For this reason, I have chosen a small number of themes to explore in detail, working with examples taken from a number of different testimonies that are relevant to the themes of this study. There is no aspiration here to cover all possible angles on this material but to make a selection that helps to illustrate the ethical choices that interpreters are confronted with in their interactions with survivors. These short extracts are, of course, still fragments from much longer recordings that only reveal their full range of meanings when listened to as part of the full testimony and within the longer interaction between the participants.

Since each witness is different, with personality, background, and experiences affecting how they respond to the challenging situation they find themselves in, and with different intentions for their testimony, which overlap or clash with the intentions of the prosecution in complex ways, it is hard to make meaningful generalizations. Nevertheless, the examples I set out here focus on questions of power, trust, control, ethical decision-making, and linguistic hybridity, all of which present significant challenges for the interpreters. The focus of these chapters shifts from the institutional view of the roles and obligations of the interpreters toward the witnesses and their interactions with the interpreters. In each case, I concentrate on moments where interpreting, power hierarchies, language use, or (mis-)communication become visible and need to be negotiated between the participants: what does this mean for the activity of giving testimony?

A brief introduction will describe the dynamics of interpreting in the courtroom, the regular rhythms and rituals of the formal interactions, in order to give a picture of the concrete situation and the context for the work of interpreting. The rest of this chapter then sets out the conceptions of translation that structure the court's work and the expectations placed on the interpreters by court officials. It will show how normative, institutional expectations are put into practice during the live exchanges and how the court monitors and assesses the interpreters, exercising discipline when boundaries have been crossed. It will consider potential clashes between different conceptions of the nature and meaning of testimony and will explore questions of power from the court's perspective, showing its differential treatment of interpreters depending on the levels of institutional trust that they have accumulated.

The trial opened on December 20, 1963, in the Römer—the Frankfurt city hall in the Old City—but was displaced on April 3, 1964, to the newly built Gallus complex; the scale of the proceedings and the public and media interest overwhelmed the physical confines of a normal courtroom. The theatre in which the trial was conducted was a very large, open space dominated at one end by a high proscenium arch and stage curtain: as metaphors for the theatricality of legal proceedings go, it is impressive but simplistic. The closed safety curtain before which the judges sat does seem to hint at the mystery of the "real business" of the court—the process of judgment—that happens away from the public after the evidence has been gathered and negotiated.

On the stage in front of the curtain sat the panel of three professional judges and six lay jurymen and women, alongside clerks, an archivist responsible for the documents required for the day's proceedings, and a sound engineer responsible for the tape recording. On the left, from the point of view of the spectator, sat the accused and their councils in rows behind small desks, flanked by police officers. Along the wall to the right sat the prosecution team and the representatives of the *Nebenklage* (civil litigants). Behind them hung two very large plans, one of the Auschwitz Main Camp and one of Birkenau.

The presence of these large plans means that an image of the camp complex loomed over the proceedings at all times, allowing connections to be made between the spoken discourse and the visual aid. Thanks to the work of the historians, the court had a good grasp of the chronological development of the camp, which it could test or confirm using the testimony of witnesses, but the schematic overviews only represent a snapshot of a specific moment in the camp's history, meaning that witnesses are not always able to orient themselves using them. More importantly, a bird's eye view of the camp complex is not a victim's perspective but a perpetrator's and planner's view and therefore not "objective": for many witnesses, it is not possible to align their own memories and internalized experiences with the lines and shapes on the plan.

For some witnesses—chiefly former political prisoners, whose positions within the camp had allowed them to gather detailed information, or witnesses from Poland for whom the spaces of the camp were familiar from postwar trials, commemorations, and political discourse—this was easier. But, as Stengel has pointed out, those Jewish witnesses who had survived the Hungarian transports in the spring of 1944 or survivors who had settled in Western countries, where knowledge about Auschwitz was limited, often had real difficulty orientating themselves. Witnesses are regularly asked to use a pointer to indicate on these plans where specific things occurred or which blocks they lived in; one of the tasks of the interpreter is to guide them through this often-tricky procedure, producing a sharp change in the role of interpreter for the duration.

The rest of the space was taken up with the large audience of observers, family members, and journalists. On the recordings, we often hear them in the background, shifting, reacting, commenting, and occasionally attracting an outburst from Presiding Judge Hofmeyer, who calls individuals to order in an attempt to preserve the dignity of the court. Even though the audience is "silent" in the sense that they have no discourse to contribute to the trial, their continued presence is vital for the public validity of the proceedings, and it is clear that many of the trial participants are also speaking to the public: some witnesses and defendants formulate parts of their statements with the audience in mind, as on occasion do the more flamboyant members of the prosecution and defense, in particular Friedrich Karl Kaul and Hans Laternser.

On warm days, the large windows of the theatre are open, and one can often hear traffic, footsteps, voices, and occasionally the sound of boisterous children coming out of school. The public proceedings are on display to the world in specific ways: the strictly hierarchical spatial order works with the court's ritualized linguistic practices to reproduce its authority and the legitimacy of its criteria for making judgments, and the openness of the performance is a vital part of this order. The plans on the wall ensure that the court's view of the past is ordered in specific ways that support the finding of evidence.

Witness statements all follow the same basic structure (I do not consider the questioning of the defendants here, as it is not relevant to the work of the interpreters). At the beginning, the witness is asked to confirm personal details: name, age, profession, and marital status. They also have to confirm that they are related neither by descent nor by marriage ("nicht verwandt und nicht verschwägert") with any of the accused, a moment that sometimes produces reactions of horror or amusement on the part of the witnesses. The judge also asks whether they are willing to have their testimony recorded "in order to support the court's memory" ("zur Stützung des Gedächtnisses des Gerichts"), and the next section begins with a standard question about when the witness arrived at Auschwitz and why they were deported: the Jewish and Sinti survivors normally give the standard answer "for reasons of race" ("aus rassischen Gründen"), while others confirm they were imprisoned for political reasons. Testimonies tend to focus on the period spent at Auschwitz, though the civil litigants are encouraged by their representatives to talk about the postliberation consequences of their experiences.

Testimonies can be very long, as the legal code requires witnesses to be able to speak for as long as they wish, though it often becomes clear that the court believes there is nothing further to be gained from continuing the questioning. The first part of the testimony, led by the presiding judge, gives the witness space to tell those aspects of their story that are relevant to the indictment: this usually repeats, expands, or varies narratives and evidence that they have already presented during the pretrial investigation. Following this, the mode of questioning changes, and the judges, prosecution, and defense ask more challenging questions about the evidence, can question discrepancies between the testimony given previously and what they have just heard, and can make challenges on procedural grounds. The witness may be asked to identify the accused, and the accused can be challenged on the evidence against them; the accused can also ask questions of the witnesses and make statements in their own interests. Finally, the witness swears an oath and is let go; the oath is required for the validity of the evidence, and in some cases, the presiding judge may decide that the witness has provided nothing of relevance, and so they may be let go without the oath.

The linguistic rituals and spatial organization of the courtroom are designed to control and structure the dramatic exchange and clash of voices, sifting what is useful from what is extraneous: there is a continual tension between the court's need for authentic, unmediated speech and the requirement to keep it under control. Because of the size of the room, there are microphones in front of each potential speaker, meaning that the voices can be both recorded clearly and amplified in court. This does not disrupt the immediacy of the voices like the equipment of simultaneous interpreting, but it means that speakers have to move toward microphones if they are to be heard properly. Thus, conversations between interpreter and witness are not always heard by all in court but are present as "private" and thus unsanctioned speech at the margins of the official discourse.

This spatial arrangement produces a point of focus, namely the small table at which the witnesses sit to give their testimony. It is below the panel of judges, with the ranks of defendants to the left, the prosecution and the plans to the right, and the audience behind. It is intimidating, but at the same time powerful, if a witness is confident enough to exploit the situation. The interpreter sits at the same table: this is the key difference with many other international post-genocide tribunals. The communication between witness and interpreter is direct and intimate, allowing a relationship to develop and for both of them to display complex, shifting attitudes toward the situation.

The expected model for interpreting is consecutive: all voices have to be heard in their specific quality by all participants. Interpreters are not asked to summarize witness statements but to translate "word for word": the same stricture does not seem to apply to other forms of speech, however. Interpreters are never pulled up short for not translating questions to the witness word for word but only for failing to render the witnesses' speech authentically. Witnesses are the only participants in the trial for whom it is not obligatory that they understand everything that is said, but they are the ones who have most at stake in terms of their testimony and the consequences of being believed or not. Witnesses are often desperate to understand what is happening around them, how their testimony is being received, and what the accused are saying about them.

Interpreters thus sometimes ask permission to translate or summarize what is happening in court or make explicit the fact that they have asked the witness clarifying questions before translating the answer; making explicit that they are doing this is a way of stretching the conventions without challenging them. But they do not always draw attention to their practice in this way, and significant aspects of the testimony and the relationship between interpreter and witness are negotiated "under the radar" of the court, with the court either not realizing or turning a blind eye. Judge Hofmeyer often exercises his authority by shutting down such exchanges but on other occasions allows them to continue. It is notable that an interpreter with a significant resource of institutional trust, such as Wera Kapkajew or Michael Benesch, is able to "get away with" more background conversation with witnesses than other interpreters.

A further complication with consecutive interpreting—and a dramatically visible feature of this trial—is that it is never a simple process of transmitting meaning between parties who understand nothing of what is said by the other. Even in the case of two mutually entirely incomprehensible languages, meaning always leaks past the interpreter in the form of gesture, intonation, hesitation, and other paralinguistic elements which are interpreted or misinterpreted by the hearers before translation can happen and which affect how the translated words are received when they do arrive. In the Frankfurt courtroom there is no testimony given in a language that none of the other participants understand, at least partially, or believe they understand.

The multilingualism of the early Federal Republic—a society that had recently absorbed millions of German-speaking refugees from Poland, Czechoslovakia, Hungary, Romania, and other territories—meant that there was a large pool of qualified lawyers who either spoke or understood the languages of the witnesses' countries of origin. Education and, often, working relationships with the Allied authorities meant that most shared a certain standard of English, French, and Russian for East German representatives like Kaul. Members of the court also assume that they understand Dutch and—with dramatic consequences for some witnesses—Yiddish.

Almost all the non-German witnesses have a certain level of German, on a continuum from fluency and confidence in legal language to a few words of camp language or remembered from school. Witnesses from the countries of the former Austro-Hungarian Empire often have a high degree of fluency, as do a number of Polish witnesses, depending on their region of origin or level of education. This means that the interpreters' work is being constantly monitored by both the witnesses and court personnel; they have to deal with challenges and corrections, as well as with moments where other participants take over the communicative role of interpreter. Much of the witnesses' language is to some extent hybrid: elements of German introduced into non-German speech in an attempt to speak directly to the court, non-native German with interference from other languages, non-native English or French with interference from other languages, or a mixture of two or more languages in various proportions. Witnesses' speech often reflects their multilingual background, the language of the prisoners, their experiences as migrants, their intentions in court, and their reactions to the progress of the communication.

The interpreters are confronted with a range of problems arising from this situation: their work depends on the illusion of a separation between languages that they are qualified to bridge, and they tend to expend a lot of effort in organizing this complex communication, assessing what and how to translate, upholding the linguistic separation, and ensuring that the witness sticks to one of their languages. The specific "sound" of this trial arises from a back-and-forth movement between witnesses' non-German, multilingual, or hybrid speech and the authoritative legal Standard German discourse of the court. The interpreters are intimately and inextricably implicated in the power relations of this situation, and their work has consequences for judgments about the "competence" of the witnesses and their ability to be heard as truth-tellers in their own voice.

In this courtroom, interpreting involves performing the role in such a way as to uphold the inadequate institutional model of consecutive interpreting ("just translate word for word") while finding ways of making it work in practice without going so far as to attract sanction from the judge; it involves deciding when to take a lead role in organizing exchanges between the participants and when to take a back seat, when to offer advice and expertise and when to say silent; it involves making ethical choices about how to represent the witness and their testimony and what stance to take up not only toward descriptions of extreme violence and suffering but also toward challenges to the testimony. It involves developing relationships of trust (or mistrust) with all participants and deciding when to take a risk and exploit that trust in order to achieve an aim. It involves deciding who to protect: the witness, the institution, or oneself.

Institutional Norms and Behaviors

Toward the end of the testimony of the Soviet doctor Aleksandr Lebedev, on 1 October 1964 (201'), the defense attempted to undermine his evidence with a suggestion of political bias and collusion with other witnesses. In a ritualized exchange that is a standard part of the proceedings, but which caused some amusement in the audience, the defense councils Joschko and Laternser read out a series of questions designed to implicate Lebedev in a politically motivated conspiracy against the court; in each case, Presiding Judge Hofmeyer declares the question inadmissible, meaning it cannot be put to the witness or entered in the record. It also means it may not be translated, so when Wera Kapkajew asks Hofmeyer whether she can translate a hostile question about Lebedev's other activities while in Frankfurt ("Darf ich das übersetzen?" May I translate this?), she receives the sharp reply, "Nein, Sie dürfen es nicht übersetzen" (No, you may not translate it).

This prohibition serves several purposes: to separate speech that may be used in evidence from speech that may not; to control the interactions and demonstrate the limits of acceptable language and behavior; and to reproduce in public the judge's authority over these distinctions. For the defense, this is not a failure, as they have spoken the "forbidden" language in public and have obliged the judge to make the prohibition visible, providing ammunition for potential allegations of bias and mistrial. All of this is part of the regular discursive theatre of a trial, but the prohibition on translation has significant consequences for the witnesses: it makes clear that they are not of central concern, and they often react with disbelief at being excluded from these exchanges. They provide testimony whose meaning and significance are negotiated by others.

An interpreter has a choice to make here: to keep quiet and exclude the witness; to explain that the witness does not need to understand; to explain what is happening "under the radar"; to request action from the court to remedy the situation; and to challenge or reject entirely the legitimacy of the court's procedures. The last option is effectively out of the question, as no interpreter would sacrifice their professional standing in this way, but it is always visible as a possibility. Each option implies an ethical choice arising from a complex understanding of the situation and the need to display an attitude toward the participants, their status, and their needs.

During Lebedev's testimony, Friedrich Karl Kaul objects to the prohibition, indicating that it may breach a principle of equal treatment (one that is normally applied to the defendant rather than the witness): "He needs to be questioned in exactly the same way as a witness who can understand German. So I insist that the proceedings are translated into his native language" (October 1, 1964, 326'). Once Hofmeyer has given the court's decision on which questions are admissible, council for the *Nebenklage* Ormond raises a point of order, asking that the ruling should be translated for the witness. Hofmeyer refuses: "Why should he get translations of questions that are not ruled in order?" (355').

Hofmeyer wants to avoid conflict and move the proceedings on: the questions that are not admitted are irrelevant for the witness, as his role is only to provide testimony in response to specific, permitted questions. Once this principle has been established, however, Hofmeyer is able to exercise power in a more "generous" way, showing some sympathy for Lebedev's feelings and desire to follow how his testimony is being negotiated. As soon as this flexibility is shown, Kapkajew exploits the situation in order to explain more than she has been asked to, including the content of the questions. In other words, she does translate some of the information that had been prohibited (356'):

1. Hofmeyer:	Nun, also, Frau Dolmetscher, sagen Sie dem Zeugen informatorisch, dass einige Fragen der Verteidigung nicht zugelassen worden sind.

2. Kapkajew:	Было поставлено адвокатом несколько вопросов. Первый был вопрос-комплекс, именно о Лангбайне, второй другого характера, и Суд признал их, как вопросы политического содержания, как не имеющие отношения к делу, и отклонил эти вопросы. Вы теперь отвечаете на те вопросы, которые связаны только с Лангбайном, поэтому Суд попросил Лангбайна удалиться на это время. Ich habe sogar übersetzt, dass Sie angeordnet haben, dass Herr Langbein den Sitzungssaal verlässt.

1. Hofmeyer:	[German] So, madam interpreter[1], pass the information on to the witness that some of the questions asked by the defense have been ruled out of order.
2. Kapkajew:	[Russian] Several questions were put by counsel. The first was a question-complex specifically about Langbein, the second was of a different nature, and the Court ruled that they are questions of political content, thus irrelevant to the case, and dismissed those questions. You are now answering those questions that relate only to Langbein, so the Court has asked Langbein to withdraw at this time. [German, to Hofmeyer] I have even translated the fact that you instructed Mr. Langbein to leave the courtroom.

Hofmeyer allows this to happen, even though it must be clear that more is being said to the witness than intended. Judge Hofmeyer has the discursive power not only to include and exclude, to reward and to sanction, but also to be flexible in the interests of the smooth running of the proceedings. An interpreter who has accumulated a reservoir of institutional trust can occasionally exploit this in order to make a choice in favor of the witness without overtly challenging the power hierarchy. In another example, Kapkajew acts on behalf of the witness Henryk Porębski (September 18, 1964, 175'), who has been trying to follow the accused Josef Klehr's objections to aspects of his testimony:

1. Porębski:	Jak, jak, jak?
2. Kapkajew:	Wie soll ich +
3. Hofmeyer:	Nein, brauchen Sie ihm nicht zu sagen
4. Porębski:	Jak?
5. Hofmeyer:	Also übersetzen Sie ihm: Der Angeklagte Klehr weist darauf hin, dass das Frauenlager erst Anfang 1943 desinfiziert worden sei.

1. Porębski:	[Polish] What, what, what?
2. Kapkajew:	[German] How should I +
3. Hofmeyer:	[German] No, you don't need to tell him
4. Porębski:	[Polish] What?
5. Hofmeyer:	[German] So, translate for him: The accused Klehr indicates that the women's camp was not disinfected before the beginning of 1943.

Porębski's insistence on being included is supported here by Kapkajew's choice of question: she doesn't ask "May I translate," which would invite a prohibition that closes the exchange, but begins the question "*How* should I translate," which leaves the exchange open. Hofmeyer's prohibition is more weakly expressed, and he makes a concession to Porębski's position, inviting Kapkajew to summarize Klehr's statement. It does not need to be translated "word for word," indicating that the witness does not possess a status requiring access to the quality of the accused's voice or the full statement beyond what he can deduce from listening. Thus, this small incident exposes a certain hierarchy in the modes of interpreting that specific participants have a right to: the accused and the court have the right to full access to the witness's voice, but not vice versa.

Hofmeyer's concession here is interesting: showing sympathy with the difficult emotional situation of the witness, he also shows that he has the power to be flexible and make exceptions; both witness and interpreter have achieved a short-term goal, but it has necessitated expending energy, risking face, and exploiting trust. This example illustrates on a small scale how discursive power can operate from the perspective of the institution: the presiding judge—who is of course acting according to a prescribed set of rules but who has considerable power and discretion in how they are put into practice—controls the discourse and interactions and polices the boundaries of behavior, imposing sanctions where necessary and defining what can be "heard" in the court's terms.

From the perspective of the court, interpreting is an inconvenient but necessary evil; the procedures for managing interpreters are designed to make language issues disappear, to become inaudible in the terms of the court's discourse. The court requires a text in German; evidence in other languages is not admissible. Interpreters are not there to "solve" the problem of language—this would require the court to restructure its proceedings from the perspective of the witness—but to defuse it.

In the rest of this section, I discuss a small number of examples that illustrate how the court deals with problems raised by interpreting in order to reestablish order.

Formal issues need to be resolved before any testimony can be valid. The court must ensure that the interpreter is sworn in: in most cases, they are able to make reference to the professional oath that they have sworn on their original swearing-in as court interpreter. The oath does not need to be repeated but they have to confirm this, even where the flow of testimony is interrupted. So, thirty minutes into the testimony of Magda Szabó on August 24, 1964, the witness, who has been speaking German, switches to Romanian for the first time, in the middle of a sentence, in order to clarify an issue that she cannot explain otherwise. She is talking about forced labor on the banks of the Vistula river: "Wissen Sie, das Fluss war so: + între, stiti, a fost =uh= o cotitura" (You know, the river was like this + in between, you know, there was =uh= a turn).

Before she can continue, the interpreter Rolf Dienesch has to be sworn in before he can work (Hofmeyer: "Moment, bevor wir hier den Herrn Dolmetscher einschalten, müssten wir ihn noch vereidigen." Just a moment, before we call on the interpreter, we need to swear him in, 32'). The court relies on a spoken testimony text in German: nothing else can be admitted, so the procedure of confirming the interpreter's oath is required. The swearing-in of the interpreter transforms them from a translator into a creator of a new original, which replaces the source. Only when this has been confirmed can the witness continue.

Defense counsel Laternser makes explicit that the interpreter is not just a conduit for the witness but the creator of an original text. During the testimony of Witold Dowgint-Nieciuński (January 29, 1965, 170'), he interrupts Kapkajew's attempts to translate the witness's answers to questions that the defense has objected to. A question is only answered when the German text has been produced:

1. Laternser:	ich widerspreche dieser Frage
2. Laternser: Kapkajew:	die gestellt worden ist er hat ja *geantwortet*
3. Prosecution council Raabe:	sie ist ja beantwortet, die Frage
4. Kapkajew: Laternser:	darf ich bitte noch die ist dann beantwortet + die Gerichtssprache ist *Deutsch* + wenn übersetzt ist
5. Kapkajew:	ja ich kann ja noch nicht anfangen
6. Laternser:	ja ja sicher + ich widerspreche ja der Frage
7. Kapkajew (to herself):	nicht der Frage sondern der Antwort

1. Laternser:	I object to this question
2. Laternser: Kapkajew:	that has just been asked But he has *answered* it
3. Prosecution council Raabe:	It has been answered, the question
4. Kapkajew: Laternser:	Please may I just It is only answered + the language of the court is *German* + when it has been translated
5. Kapkajew:	Yes I haven't been able to start yet
6. Laternser:	Yes yes of course + I've objected to the question
7. Kapkajew (to herself):	Not to the question, but to the answer

This exchange is characterized by repeated use of the German emphatic particle "ja," which is employed in colloquial speech to show that the speaker believes what they say to be obviously true, often in response to a challenge. It is a good example of how Kapkajew's language use in court reflects her confidence in her own position and status: she challenges Laternser directly and participates in a discussion of procedure. At the end of the exchange, however, she is reduced to sotto voce sarcasm in a critique of Laterner's tactics: it is an admission of defeat in this case, showing her awareness that open challenges to authority are not possible, whatever her privileged status as an interpreter.

The interpreter's subordinate position within the power hierarchy often becomes clear, even for an experienced, trusted individual like Wera Kapkajew, who likes to intervene in conversations between the judges and other officials. During the testimony of Leon Uchwat (September 10, 1964, 87'), she tries to get permission to interpret for the witness an exchange between Hofmeyer and defense counsel Stolting but is rebuffed:

1. Kapkajew:	Darf ich bitte übersetzen?
2. Stolting:	Ich spreche augenblicklich mit dem Herrn Vorsitzenden, Frau Kapkajew.
3. Kapkajew:	Ich wollte ja nun *übersetzen*
4. Hofmeyer:	[to Stolting]: Bitte schön, jetzt weiter.

1. Kapkajew:	May I translate, please?
2. Stolting:	I'm talking to the Presiding Judge right now, Frau Kapkajew.
3. Kapkajew:	But I just wanted to *translate*.
4. Hofmeyer:	[to Stolting]: Please, carry on.

Moments like this demonstrate the limits of interpreters' ability to ensure that witnesses are able to follow the proceedings: they not only make clear interpreters' subordinate status but also show the witnesses that the proceedings are not at heart about them and their experiences. The feeling of exclusion from the core business of the court, especially if they have made a long trip and have summoned the courage to speak about violence and loss, is a frequent source of frustration, and witnesses attempt to compensate for it by finding other ways to have their voices heard.

One of the most moving aspects of this trial is listening to witnesses trying to speak directly to the court—and thus to the public—in German rather than through an interpreter. They also seem to perceive the interpreter as a barrier rather than an enabler, and, as Katharina Stengel has shown, Hermann Langbein encouraged witnesses to speak German wherever possible (Stengel 2012: 517). There are many examples of striking, courageous, individual voices speaking the language of the court in different forms, registers, and degrees of hybridization with other languages.

I return to this issue in more detail later, but we should note here that it is in the interests of the court to create a clear separation between languages and to ensure that the witness is identified with one of them. From the perspective of a court requiring clear, precise, and understandable testimony, this is vital—a spoken text in one language is replaced with a text in Standard German—but from a perspective that is more interested in the voices of the survivors in their individuality than in the legal issues, the expressiveness of their speech is compelling and revealing of the complexity of survivor biographies.

The court regards interpreters as a solution to a problem that is seen to arise from witnesses not being able to express themselves clearly. Judge Hofmeyer intervenes during the testimony of the Czech witness Vladimír Hanák (November 13, 1964, 57') in the middle of his German narration about arriving prisoners being forced into a truck to be driven to the Birkenau gas chambers:

1. Hanák:	ein SS-Mann schimpfte sagte "glauben Sie dass + bekommen Sie noch ein neues Wagen? alle müssen + antreten" also man musste so pressen dass die Leute haben gerufen in allen Sprachen "um Gottes Willen Hilfe! + Pomož! + haben wenig Platz!" und man machte es so + zwei drei schicken + und die Leute das waren tot + schon in halb Stunde ohne Luft
2. Hofmeyer:	Also Herr Zeuge + Sie würden uns einen Gefallen tun wenn Sie tschechisch sprechen würden
3. Hanák:	Gut
4. Hofmeyer:	dann haben wir durch den Dolmetscher die einwandfreie Übertragung

1. Hanák:	An SS man cursed said "do you think that + you'll get a new truck? Everyone has to + line up" so we had to squeeze together so tight that the people shouted in every language "For God's sake help! + Pomož! + we have no room!" and they did it + sending two or three + and the people they were dead + already in half an hour without air
2. Hofmeyer:	So Mr. Witness + you would do us a favor if you would speak Czech
3. Hanák:	Fine
4. Hofmeyer:	Then we will have the correct version from the interpreter

The precise detail of the narrative is not clear in Hanák's German narration, but it gives a dramatic impression of the confusion of the situation and the different voices shouting against each other. Once the interpreter Michael Benesch becomes more involved, Hanák reacts by becoming less expansive and dramatic in his narration, simply providing short answers to direct questions. In fact, the questioning does not return to the incident that Hanák was describing, so it is lost.

By contrast, Hofmeyer speaks supportively to certain witnesses, encouraging them to speak German when they have been unable to offer specific answers to a particular line of questioning. Here, for example, Magda Szabó (August 24, 1964, 17') is trying to describe the process of selection on arrival at Birkenau:

1. Szabó:	die Offizieren haben ja die + die + diese + =oh= Sortierung gemacht
2. Szabó:	Oder wie ich soll das sagen
Hofmeyer:	Ja
3. Hofmeyer:	Geben Sie acht
4. Szabó:	Ja
5. Hofmeyer:	+ =eh= wenn Sie uns nicht richtig =eh= sich ausdrücken können
6. Szabó:	Ja
Hofmeyer:	in der deutschen Sprache, und es wäre Ihnen leichter, das in rumänisch zu sagen können Sie es auch + oder in ungarisch sagen, können Sie es auch in ungarisch sagen + es wird uns dann übertragen werden +
7. Hofmeyer:	Nur für den Fall
Szabó:	Wenn Sie denken, wenn Sie das verstehen
8. Szabó:	was ich sagen kann, dann
Hofmeyer:	ja ich verstehe es schon

1.	Szabó:	So the officers made the + the + this + =oh= selection
2.	Szabó:	Or how should I say it
	Hofmeyer:	Yes
3.	Hofmeyer:	Wait a moment
4.	Szabó:	Yes
5.	Hofmeyer:	+ =eh= if you can't =eh= express yourself correctly
6.	Szabó:	Yes
	Hofmeyer:	in German, and you would find it easier to say it in Romanian you could also + or say it in Hungarian, you could say it in Hungarian + it'll then be translated for us +
7.	Hofmeyer:	Just in case
	Szabó:	If you think, if you understand
8.	Szabó:	what I can say, then
	Hofmeyer:	yes, I do understand it

Szabó is able to assert herself here and continues in German but becomes rather curt in her answers as if Hofmeyer's comment has damaged her confidence. Other witnesses internalize the discipline and correct themselves when they stray into German (e.g., Józef Seweryn, May 22, 964, 4': "Teppiche und verschiedene solche Sachen + aha + przepraszam") ([German] Rugs and different thinks like that + aha + [Polish] excuse me).

Power is negotiated in various ways during a testimony: from the perspective of the court it is necessary for all participants to understand the rules, the required rhythms and turn-taking patterns, and the roles they have been assigned. When things are working well—in the sense that the court can work without having to worry about language issues—much of the labor of power is delegated to the interpreter, who takes responsibility for the smooth running of a testimony, organizing the discourse in such a way that problems are resolved before they reach the surface of the text.

Some witnesses are better able to adopt the discursive positioning necessary for the smooth functioning of consecutive interpreting: they speak in short blocks, consisting of units of sense or individual narrative moments, pausing and waiting for the interpreting. Those with experience of giving testimony in multilingual trials—in particular, many of the witnesses from Eastern Bloc countries—tend to understand these rules better. They interrupt the flow of their narrative in order to make themselves heard by the court, meaning that their testimonies consist of highly illuminated moments of concentrated language rather than a cohesive, flowing narrative: this can be very powerful, even though it feels unnatural and goes against the intention of many witnesses to simply tell their story. However, even the most practiced witness experiences moments where the compulsion to narrate conflicts with the restricted rhythms imposed by the questioning and interpreting: interventions by Judge Hofmeyer and others tell us a lot about institutional attitudes toward witnesses and interpreting.

Helen Goldmann, who gave testimony in English on September 3, 1964, with the support of the interpreter Regina Schmidt-Ott, finds it difficult to adapt to the requirements of consecutive interpreting. While trying to tell the emotional story of the separation from her mother and baby sister, she has to be interrupted in order for the interpreter to work: she understands German well enough to believe that she can answer the questions without having them translated and speaks over the interpreter, using the question as a springboard to tell the story in her own way.

This is a key moment in which the prosecution has to impose its own genre of testimony on a witness who wants to speak in a different way: she wants to talk about her loss, while the court requires her to identify the defendants. Here, it is prosecution counsel Raabe—representing the civil litigants—who intervenes, as her testimony is not providing the required evidence (10'):

1. Raabe:	Verzeihen Sie, Herr Vorsitzender. Dürfte ich nur eins drauf =eh= Wenn Sie vielleicht die Zeugin drauf hinweisen würden, dass sie die Dolmetscherin doch wirklich zu Ende übersetzen lässt. Denn es stellt sich heraus, dass sie, die Dolmetscherin, übersetzt korrekt, aber sie versteht anscheinend doch Ihre Fragen nicht direkt, wenn sie sie nicht übersetzen lässt
2. Hofmeyer: Goldmann:	ja please
3. Raabe:	denn dadurch kommen diese Missverständnisse
4. Hofmeyer: Goldmann: Kaul:	gut please diese Frage ist nämlich nicht richtig über + nicht richtig beantwortet worden
5. Schmidt-Ott: Hofmeyer:	ja =mm= bitte
6. Schmidt-Ott:	you're =eh= begged to wait until I have translated the German questions
7. Goldmann:	okay, I'm sorry, yes

1. Raabe:	[German] Forgive me, Your Honour. Might I just say one =eh= If you would indicate to the witness that she really should let the interpreter finish translating. Because it turns out that she, the interpreter, is translating correctly, but she doesn't understand your questions properly if she doesn't let her finish translating
2. Hofmeyer: Goldmann:	[German] yes [English] please
3. Raabe:	[German] because that is where these misunderstandings come from
4. Hofmeyer: Goldmann: Kaul:	[German] fine [English] please [German] This question wasn't correctly trans- + answered
5. Schmidt-Ott: Hofmeyer:	[German] yes =mm= [German] please
6. Schmidt-Ott:	[English] you're =eh= begged to wait until I have translated the German questions
7. Goldmann:	[English] okay, I'm sorry, yes

Here, responsibility for a "failed" communication is laid at the door of the witness and the complex interpreting situation. It is not clear exactly what Goldmann is trying to say with her repeated plea to be heard, but it is obvious she is unhappy and feels that she does not have the opportunity to defend the value of her testimony in this situation.

One might expect such moments to always occur when witnesses are describing their most emotional or traumatic experiences, but in fact it is often when they are trying to rush through detail they consider irrelevant in order to contextualize the narration of a more significant event. During the testimony of Zdzisław Mikołajski (September 25, 1964, 127') the witness begins to accelerate in his narration about Hans Stark: this is not so much an emotional outburst as a sign that the witness is not interested in talking about the details that interest the court. Hofmeyer intervenes, "Nun mal langsam. Mal langsam. Das muss erst mal die Frau Kapkajew übersetzen" (Now slowly. Just slowly. Frau Kapkajew needs to translate it first).

During Witold Dowgint-Nieciuński's narration of his abuse at the hands of Kaduk (January 29, 1965, 43'), Hofmeyer intervenes more sharply: "Mal stop" (Just stop). In this case, the witness is accelerating his narration in order to get through the background to an incident in which he was beaten; this information is vital for the court but not for the witness. It is notable here that Kapkajew tries immediately to alleviate the brusqueness of Hofmeyer's intervention by addressing the witness with a very polite formulation: "Może chwileczkę, dobrze? Pan będzie łaskaw" (Could you give me a moment, please. Please be so good). Kapkajew here takes on the role of passing on the command in a way that is less threatening to the witness while still upholding the judge's discursive power.

Later in Dowgint-Nieciuński's testimony (198'), he is unable or unwilling to conform to the required patterns, and Kapkajew assumes the authority of the judge in order to silence him. Hofmeyer is becoming impatient with the witness's insistence on talking rapidly and interrupting the other participants without allowing time for interpreting:

1. Hofmeyer:	Dürfte ich vielleicht auch mal
2. Hofmeyer:	einen Augenblick was sagen? (...)
Dowgint-Nieciuński:	To jest, bo przecież, proszę chciałem wyjaśnić sądowi, że nie można
3. Kapkajew:	Pscht!
4. Hofmeyer:	Es ist aussichtslos

1. Hofmeyer:	[German] Could I perhaps
2. Hofmeyer:	say something for a moment too? (...)
Dowgint-Nieciuński:	[Polish] That is, because after all, I wanted to explain to the court, that it's not possible
3. Kapkajew:	Shh!
4. Hofmeyer:	[German] It's pointless

Hofmeyer's sarcasm and Kapkajew's unusually harsh tone here indicate that Dowgint-Nieciuński is now considered a "bad" witness: once the court's attitude has become explicit, the interpreter needs to make a choice about which side to come down on.

A further issue that leads to some negotiation over the ethical positioning of the interpreter is the requirement for interpreting in the first person. The court has a strict requirement for testimony in the first person and for translators to reproduce the perspective of the witness. Hofmeyer and other officials often take action to enforce this rule, as in this example from the testimony of Abraham de la Penha (March 26, 1965, 2'), who speaks Dutch and German, with the interpreter Erika Diedrich:

1. de la Penha:	Ja, dat kan ik niet zeggen + maar we waren ongeveer, want we zijn gelijk met een Hongaars transport gekomen, zo ongeveer 5.000 mensen
2. Diedrich:	Er könnt es nicht genau sagen, denn sie sind zusammen mit einem ungarischen Transport eingetroffen. Aber er schätzt =eh= dass sie ungefähr: so: 5.000 Menschen waren
3. Unbekannte Stimme:	(…)
4. Hofmeyer:	Ja + also =mmhm= Frau Dolmetscherin, ich möchte Sie bitten, das, was der Zeuge sagt, wörtlich uns so zu übersetzen, wie er es sagt, also nicht zusammenfassen, sondern genau mit den Worten des Zeugen uns das zu übersetzen. Sie sagen also =mm= ungefähr, glauben Sie, hätte dieser Transport wie viele Menschen umfasst?
5. de la Penha:	Tezamen met + zwei Transporte, ne? ungefähr 5.000

1. de la Penha:	[Dutch] Yes, I can't say + but we were about, because we came right along with a Hungarian transport, about 5,000 people
2. Diedrich:	[German] He couldn't say exactly, as they arrived together with a Hungarian transport. But he estimates =eh= that there were perhaps: about: 5000 people
3. Unidentified voice:	(…)
4. Hofmeyer:	[German] Yes + so =mmhm= madam interpreter, I would ask you to translate what the witness says word for word, as he says it, so not to summarize but translate for us exactly in the words of the witness. So you say =mm= about, you believe, how many people was this transport made up of?
5. De la Penha:	[Dutch] Together with + [German] two transports, right? About 5000

Hofmeyer demonstrates in turn four the direct switch between his address to the interpreter and to the witness ("Sie sagen also …" So you say) that restores the discursive order and the assigned role of the interpreter: he appears to be responding to a comment by another participant that is not clearly audible on the tape. Diedrich's tone is very cautious, with certain features of her speech weakening de la Penha's testimony: using the subjunctive form "könnt," for example, or extending the words "ungefähr" and "so" to express uncertainty. These features appear to reflect the interpreter's own nervousness and uncertainty since the witness is confident and clear about what he does and does not know.

The witness's response in the next turn is very interesting: he seems aware that there is an issue with the interpreting and switches to German in his response, excluding the interpreter.

The third-person requirement is a complex area for interpreters in court, requiring careful negotiation over relationships with the witness and with the institutional power structures. Sandra Hale has suggested that shifts to third-person discourse often reflect a sense of loss of control in the interaction, in particular for lawyers putting questions to witnesses: "It is common for lawyers to resort to the third person (for example, 'can you ask him') when they lose control or when they want to reprimand the witness. They either expect the interpreter to fix the situation or reprimand the witness, rather than do it themselves" (Hale 2007: 201).

So for a court official to switch to third-person style in an interpreted exchange is a sign that they wish to pass on responsibility for repairing the problem to the interpreter: where a witness is considered problematic, conversation is carried on about them, rather than with them, or questions are posed indirectly, positioning the interpreter differently. Thus, it is a power play obliging the interpreter to take up a position on the side of the court.

In the case of Diedrich, however, there are other possibilities. Interpreters often shift to third person themselves, either because they have not internalized the court's rules due to inexperience, but sometimes in order to explain or protect a witness. Directly voicing a speaker is a skill that has to be learned, and it entails taking on responsibility for the way the witness sounds and the impression they make as a speaker and source of knowledge. Shifting to the third person makes explicit the perspective of the interpreter rather than disguising it. When the interpreter takes up a stance of "explaining" the witness, we shift into complex ethical territory: they may be refusing responsibility for what is said or working to protect the witness against challenge or loss of face. Motivation is hard to establish, of course, but we can explore the effect of the shift to third person and back and try to understand how witnesses are or are not able to make themselves heard in this situation.

The small number of examples that I have set out here demonstrate some of the ways in which interpreters are involved in establishing and enforcing the court's linguistic behavioral norms. I will explore others in the next chapter, but the issues discussed here—rules about what may and may not be translated, the rhythms of consecutive interpreting, and the consistent use of third-person discourse—are relevant for how witnesses can be heard and for the ethical self-positioning of the interpreters. Each of these specific demands, in the context of a post-genocide trial, places interpreters in a position where they have to make ethical choices and position themselves within the power structure.

The presence of interpreters adds an extra layer of complexity to the exercise of discursive power in the courtroom; the far higher than normal stakes for survivor-witnesses at a post-genocide trial mean that the small, normal linguistic rituals of the trial can take on an intense emotional significance. Power is exercised by including and excluding, making visible or invisible, defining witnesses as good or bad, and exercising discipline or imposing sanctions. The ability to exercise leniency or flexibility in specific situations is another option in the exercise of power in the interests of the smooth running of proceedings.

For the most part, witnesses perceive it to be in their interests to internalize the court's rituals in order to achieve the aims they share with the court, namely to achieve justice: witnesses who do not conform can be assessed as "bad" or "inadequate," a potential source of deep injury for a survivor who has a story to tell. Interpreters have to negotiate this challenging set of requirements, ensuring that the rules are followed so that they can work: they are co-opted to establish discursive power—or reestablish it when there has been a conflict—but they are often able to intervene on behalf of witnesses if they are willing to compromise.

Discursive power operates in the courtroom through prohibitions and the internalization of legitimizing rituals. As Cornelia Vismann has suggested, the visibility of the prohibition and of what has been prohibited is vital for this process of sorting unruly speech into a discourse that can be used by the court to exercise judgment (Vismann 2019: 50). So there is a "shadow" text running alongside the text that the court will use: it is audible to all present, and often visible in terms of gesture, movement, and interactions, but it is fleeting, containing moments of emotion, conflict, negotiation, and many other interactions that are of no relevance to the verdict but are essential to our understanding of how testimony can be made in this situation. Chapter 9 develops these ideas, exploring how the different participants in the courtroom exchanges monitor, support, and challenge the work of the interpreters.

9

Challenges and Monitoring

The work of the interpreters is under constant monitoring from all sides in the courtroom; the monitoring is detailed and critical, carried out by individuals who have potentially competing perspectives and interests. The work is thus complex and pressurized, and interpreters are confronted with situations in which they have to negotiate competing interests and forms of professional trust. The interpreters all have a stake in the success of the interactions, as their institutional status, professional standing, and sense of the political or ethical value of their work depend on it. But the question of what is meant by a successful interaction, whose interests it favors, and who needs to make the greatest compromises to ensure it is complex. In this section, I explore some of the ways that the other actors in the courtroom monitor the work of the interpreters, contrasting institutional forms of control with witnesses' attempts to ensure that their interests are represented and their voices heard. Interpreters are having to negotiate different forms of trust in their interactions, sometimes having to play off accrued institutional trust against the relationships that are developing with the witnesses as they work.

Given the lack of specific training in court interpreting and limited institutional understanding of the emotional strain and ethical complexity of the work, the moments of critical monitoring of interpreters' work contribute to the discourse around the "professionalization" of court interpreting and discussion of appropriate qualifications. There is a moment when the court has to replace the interpreter Ottmar Schamschulla with Michael Benesch that reveals significant issues to do with professionalism and objectivity. Conflicts over interpreting come to a head during a sequence of testimonies by witnesses from Czechoslovakia in November 1964, when the prosecution begins to express doubts about Schamschulla's qualification for the work. During the testimony of Alois Vašut (November 5, 1964, 4'), Schamschulla takes criticism from the prosecutor Vogel for interpreting in the third person: up to this point, he has either used the first person or avoided personal pronouns in his renderings, but when a moment arrives when Vašut expresses his desire to bear witness, Schamschulla shifts his perspective.

When Hofmeyer asks when the witness first got to know any of the accused, he establishes that he did not know any of them before he witnessed Kaduk killing a prisoner:

1. Hofmeyer:	Und haben Sie während dieser Zeit schon einen dieser Angeklagten kennengelernt?
2. Schamschulla:	A seznámil jste se v tu dobu s některým zde + obžalovaným?
3. Vašut:	Neseznámil, jenom v tom případě, kdy jsem viděl tu událost, o které budu svědčit.
4. Schamschulla:	Noch nicht, erst zu der Zeit, als er die + das Ereignis erlebte, worüber er Zeugnis ablegen will.
5. Hofmeyer:	Und wann war das, bitte?
6. Vogel:	Herr Dolmetscher, ich bitte in der Ichform zu übersetzen, ja?

1. Hofmeyer:	[German] And did you get to know any of the accused at this time?
2. Schamschulla:	[Czech] And did you get to know at this time any of the + defendants here?
3. Vašut:	[Czech] I didn't, only on that occasion when I saw the event that I am going to testify about.
4. Schamschulla:	[German] Not yet, only at the time, when he experienced the + event that he wants to testify about.
5. Hofmeyer:	[German] And when was that, please?
6. Vogel:	[German] Mr. interpreter, I would ask you to translate in the first person, all right?

Vogel's intervention makes clear that it is not only the judge who is empowered to enforce the required standards for interpreting: the prosecution has a clear interest in clarity and direct access to the voice of the witness. Schamschulla appears to have retreated from first-person interpreting at a moment where the witness is making clear that the testimony belongs to him.

After this intervention, Schamschulla employs the first person more consistently, but problems continue, and he later (21') takes the blame for a breakdown in communication with the witness. The witness has identified the accused Kaduk but has not made clear that he knows exactly who he is to the satisfaction of the court:

1. Hofmeyer:	Na ja, es ist anscheinend nicht möglich, dem Zeugen das klarzumachen, was ich von ihm wissen will.
2. Hofmeyer: Ormond:	Ich will wissen, ob Ich habe erhebliche Bedenken, Herr Vorsitzender, ob der Dolmetscher in der Lage ist, wirklich die Fragen und die Antworten hier zu verstehen und gerichtlich zu übersetzen.
3. Schamschulla:	Bitte, ich muss =eh= wenn ich hierzu etwas sagen darf =eh= einwenden, dass ich natürlich die Gerichtssprache in diesem Sinne nicht beherrsche, da ich eben kein Gerichtsdolmetscher bin. Aber ich bemühe mich, das nach bestem
4. Schamschulla: Hofmeyer:	Gewissen Ja + Nun = eh= dann fragen Sie doch bitte einmal, als wen er denn diesen Mann zu erkennen glaubt, auf den er da gedeutet hat. Wer soll das denn sein? Soll das Kaduk sein?

1. Hofmeyer:	Oh well, it is apparently not possible to make clear to the witness what I want from him.
2. Hofmeyer: Ormond:	I want to know whether I have some genuine doubts, Your Honour, whether the interpreter is able to really understand the questions and answers here and to translate them in a legal sense.
3. Schamschulla:	Please, I must =eh= if I may say something about this, that of course I do now know the legal language in this sense, as I'm not a court interpreter. But I am making the effort in all good
4. Schamschulla: Hofmeyer:	conscience Yes + now =eh= then ask again who he claims to recognize in the man he pointed to. Who does he claim this is? Is it Kaduk?

Schamschulla explains his errors with his lack of legal qualifications but refers to the wording of the oath to support his claim of conscientiousness ("nach bestem Gewissen"). Ormond has concluded from the translated answer that the translation is inadequate rather than the formulation of the question.

A key moment in this exchange, however, is Schamschulla's response to Hofmeyer's initial impatience with the witness, which sees the judge switch to third-person address at the beginning of this extract (which he typically does when problems arise or he is becoming impatient). The interpreter expands Vašut's curt answer (step 3) considerably, strengthening his statement and protecting his reputation as a witness. The situation is therefore more complex than the critique of the interpreting implies: Schamschulla tries to protect Vašut from challenge but ends up taking the blame for the miscommunication.

The next day, during the testimony of Ota Fabián (November 6, 1964, 14') the court's poor opinion of Schamschulla's work culminates in his replacement. Fabian has been speaking quickly, without pauses for interpreting, and Hofmeyer has had to intervene on behalf of the interpreter, who has not been able to assert a structuring influence over the interactions. Defense counsel Joschko, a Czech speaker, intervenes to question the accuracy of the translation, and Hofmeyer is concerned that questions are not being answered properly. Christian Raabe of the *Nebenklage* then demands directly the replacement of the interpreter, and the subsequent exchange gives us a good idea of what the court wants from interpreting and how it prefers witnesses to act under the conditions of consecutive interpreting.

1. Raabe:	Herr Vorsitzender, ich bitte Sie, den Dolmetscher abzuberufen. Es geht so nicht weiter. In jedem, bei jedem Satz korrigiert ihn der Zeuge. Ich bitte auch den Herrn Dolmetscher, mir das nicht übelzunehmen, aber es geht ja hier schließlich um das Schicksal von =eh= auch von diesen Angeklagten. Wir können doch hier nicht so verhandeln, dass + dass wir laufend das aushandeln müssen, was hier nun gesagt worden ist. Ich glaube + also ich rüge die weitere =eh= Verwendung des Herrn Dolmetschers und bitte das zu Protokoll zu nehmen und bitte ihn abzuberufen.
2. Schamschulla:	Darf ich hierzu nur noch + eine Bemerkung machen?
3. Hofmeyer:	Ja.
4. Schamschulla:	Ich habe es gestern schon getan und gesagt, dass ich kein Gerichtsdolmetscher bin
5. Schamschulla: Hofmeyer:	dass ich überhaupt an sich =mm=
6. Schamschulla:	dass die Tätigkeit eines Dolmetschers und die
7. Schamschulla: Hofmeyer:	Tätigkeit eines Sprachlehrers doch sehr verschieden sind voneinander =mm=
8. Schamschulla: Hofmeyer:	dass die Technik des Dolmetschens doch sehr anders ist als =mm= =mm=
9. Schamschulla: Hofmeyer:	die Technik Ja, das ist uns bekannt, Herr Doktor =eh=

10. Hofmeyer:	und es ist natürlich ein Unterschied, ob man wissenschaftlich arbeitet oder ob man hier als =eh= simultan übersetzen muss. Nun =eh= wenn das Gericht damit einverstanden ist, können wir ja mal den Herrn *Benesch* vorrufen, ja? Ja? Herr Doktor Schamschulla, wollen Sie vielleicht mal hinten Platz nehmen. Wollen wir mal den Herrn Benesch vorrufen. Vielleicht kann er das.

1. Raabe:	Your Honour, I request that you dismiss the interpreter. It can't go on like this. In every, with every sentence the witness corrects him. I would like to ask the interpreter not to be offended, but we are dealing here after all with the fates of =eh= these accused. We can't carry on with proceedings when + when we constantly have to negotiate what is being said here. I believe + so I object to any further assignment of the interpreter and ask for this to be recorded in the transcript and for him to be dismissed.
2. Schamschulla:	May I just make + an observation here?
3. Hofmeyer:	Yes.
4. Schamschulla:	I did this already yesterday and said that I am not a court interpreter
5. Schamschulla: Hofmeyer:	that I am as such =mm=
6. Schamschulla:	that the work of an interpreter and the
7. Schamschulla: Hofmeyer:	work of a language teacher are very different from each other =mm=
8. Schamschulla: Hofmeyer:	that the skills of the interpreter are very different from =mm= =mm=
9. Schamschulla: Hofmeyer:	the skills Yes, we are aware of this, Doctor =eh=
10. Hofmeyer:	and it of course makes a difference whether one works as a scholar or as =eh= has to translate simultaneously here. Now =eh= if the court is in agreement, we can call Herr Benesch, yes? Yes? Herr Dr. Schamschulla, please take a seat at the back. Let us call Herr Benesch. Perhaps he can do it.

Both Schamschulla and Benesch are university-level teachers, and so equally qualified, but Benesch quickly establishes the trust of the court in contrast with Schamschulla. He is also able to interpret for Slovak-speaking witnesses, an issue that the court had not prepared for. Raabe's statement—"We can't carry on with proceedings when we constantly have to negotiate what is being said here"—indicates impatience with the attention being drawn to questions of interpreting. The success of an exchange is the responsibility of the interpreter, and he must be replaced if there are problems: Schamschulla's acknowledgment that he is out of his depth in this situation ensures that no criticism can be leveled at the court.

Benesch must take the full oath and is given extra instruction by Hofmeyer on the correct mode of interpreting. There follows (16') a telling interjection by the defense, proposing that witnesses are asked to speak in shorter blocks: Joschko asks for shorter sentences, while Hofmeyer suggests sentence-by-sentence translation. He has clearly built up an impression of the Czech and Polish witnesses that they tend to speak in fragments of sentences, which in itself causes problems.

1. Hofmeyer:	Herr Benesch, nehmen Sie bitte Platz. Und nun + wollen wir uns an den Zeugen noch einmal + Ich bitte Sie also, was wir fragen, wörtlich zu übersetzen, und was der Zeuge Ihnen antwortet, ebenfalls wörtlich uns wieder zu übersetzen, ja? + Und zwar in der direkten Sprache.
2. Joschko:	Entschuldigung, vielleicht darf ich kurz anregen, dass vielleicht nicht so viel übersetzt wird, sondern in kurzen
3. Joschko: Hofmeyer:	kürzeren Sätzen, ja. Satz für Satz, ja.
4. Joschko: Hofmeyer:	Ganz kurz. Ja + ja
5. Hofmeyer:	Nun ist es manchmal etwas schwer, weil sehr viele Halbsätze gebraucht werden, grade von den tschechischen und polnischen Zeugen. Aber immerhin, Sie wissen, worauf es ankommt, ja? Nicht zu lange Passagen lassen, sondern immer jeweils nach Beendigung eines Satzes diesen Satz übersetzen, ja?

1. Hofmeyer:	Herr Benesch, please take a seat. And now + let us turn to the witness again + I would ask you to translate word for word what *we* say, and to translate for us also word for word what the witness answers to you, all right? + And in direct speech.
2. Joschko:	Excuse me, perhaps I can also suggest that perhaps not so much is translated, but in short
3. Joschko: Hofmeyer:	shorter sentences, yes? Sentence for sentence, yes.
4. Joschko: Hofmeyer:	Very short. Yes + yes
5. Hofmeyer:	Now it is sometimes somewhat difficult, as a lot of half sentences are being used, particularly by the Czech and Polish witnesses. But anyway, you know what is important here, yes? Don't wait for passages that are too long, but always translate a sentence after the end of the sentence, yes?

Thus, for communication to succeed under the conditions of consecutive interpreting, the onus is on the witnesses to discipline their speech and on the interpreters to follow specific patterns. Schamschulla has accepted a severe sanction—loss of employment—and the court has developed a view of certain kinds of witnesses as problematic in their language use: Czech and Polish speakers, who, in Hofmeyer's view, tend to speak in short, incomplete sentences.

Once the court has "solved" the problem of interpreting from Czech, it begins to accept things where we might think that there is cause for doubt. Benesch interprets for the Slovak-speaking witness Ján Weis on November 5, 1964, after Schamschulla has been challenged by Kaul on the quality of his work. Schamschulla informs the court that Weis is speaking Slovak, not Czech ("Der Zeuge spricht slowakisch. Das ist nicht identisch mit tschechisch. Darauf möchte ich hier hinweizen." The witness is speaking Slovak. That is not the same as Czech. I would like to draw attention to this); Kaul apologizes for his criticism, trying to soften it ("Ich möchte dem Herrn Dolmetscher nicht zu nahe treten." I mean no offense to the interpreter), but Hofmeyer intervenes to say that he has already called for a substitute interpreter (November 6, 1964, 12').

Benesch interprets during the afternoon session, during which Weis tells the story of his father's murder by lethal injection at the hands of Klehr. Weis's narration is quiet but intense, told in short statements, and both Benesch and Hofmeyer are clearly moved by it; Benesch interprets calmly in a monotone without attempting to express emotion in his voice. At the end of this narration (36'), Hofmeyer asks Benesch how he feels the interpreting from Slovak is going:

1. Hofmeyer:	Herr Dolmetscher, wie werden Sie fertig mit der Sprache? Geht es?
2. Benesch:	Wenn es Sie nicht stört, dass ich mir öfter eine Antwort wiederholen lasse, wenn ich nicht sicher bin.
3. Hofmeyer:	Also ich möchte sagen, dass wir eigentlich dabei bleiben sollen. Daß ich keine Bedenken habe gegen die Art der Verdolmetschung + Dann möchte ich Sie bitten, es weiter zu machen.

1. Hofmeyer:	Herr Dolmetscher, how are you getting on with the language? Is it working?
2. Benesch:	If it doesn't bother you that I often have to ask for an answer to be repeated, if I'm not sure.
3. Hofmeyer:	So I'd like to say that we should stick with this. That I have no objections to this kind of interpreting + Then I'd like to ask you to carry on.

Hofmeyer is here willing to rely on Benesch's own judgment about the quality of his interpreting from Slovak, even though Benesch himself quietly suggests some doubts. After the experience with Schamschulla, Hofmeyer seems happy to accept a lot on trust without explicit monitoring of performance: the judge has the power to establish institutional trust on the basis of an impression gained from a quick comparison of two interpreters' performance. An interpreter can spend years building up a reservoir of institutional trust, but a judge can produce it in an instant when it is convenient.

Challenges to interpreters are often partisan: challenges by the prosecution are countered by the defense and vice versa. So, for example, during the testimony of Rudolf Rybka on October 19, 1964 (57'), the interpreting of Erwin Jarolim is repeatedly challenged by prosecution counsel Raabe. The following two extracts also demonstrate the different forms of informal monitoring that interpreters' work is subject to:

1. Rybka:	Když kdokoliv přijížděl, jestli přijížděl SS Obersturmbannführer Caesar nebo jestli přijížděl někdo jiný, Aumeier, Palitzsch nebo Kommandant Höß, tak vždycky naši kamarádi, z Harmense Hühnerfarm telefonovali k nám: Pozor, jede k vám +
2. Rybka:	někdo.
Jarolim:	Ganz gleich, wer zu uns nach Harmense kam, die Kameraden aus der Hühnerfarm haben angerufen und haben gesagt:Achtung, es kommt zu Ihnen Besuch.
3. Hofmeyer:	Ja + ja, es kommt Besuch. Nun =um= kam der Besuch ja
4. Raabe:	Verzeihen Sie, Herr Vorsitzender, aber der Herr Dolmetscher hat, glaube ich, nur die Hälfte uns eben übersetzt. Zumindest habe ich eine ganze Reihe von Namen gehört, die ich jetzt von dem Herrn Dolmetscher nicht mehr
5. Raabe:	gehört habe.
Hofmeyer:	Sie haben recht

1. Rybka:	[Czech] Whenever anyone arrived, whether it was SS Obersturmbannführer Caesar or someone else arrived, Aumeier, Palitsch or Commandant Höß, our friends called us from the Harmense chicken farm: Watch out, someone is coming
2. Rybka:	to you.
Jarolim:	[German] No matter who came to us in Harmense, the comrades from the chicken farm called and said: Watch out, you're getting a visit.

3. Hofmeyer:	[German] yes + yes, the visitor comes. Now =um= the visitor came
4. Raabe:	[German] Forgive me, Your Honour, but the interpreter has only, I think, translated half of it for us. At least, I heard quite a number of names that from the interpreter
5. Raabe:	I didn't hear.
Hofmeyer:	[German] You are right.

Raabe has been listening to the list of names provided by Rybka and rightly notes that Jarolim has not repeated them. This shows, incidentally, how carefully the trial participants listen to the voices of witnesses whose language they do not understand: aspects of meaning reach listeners before the translation is made. Shortly after this (69'), Raabe reports that members of the audience, who have been following the interpreting, have informed him that there are errors:

> Herr Vorsitzender, ich bedaure, aber ich habe Bedenken gegen die weitere Vernehmung dieses Zeugen in Anwesenheit dieses Dolmetschers. Mir wurde von Zuhörern gesagt, dass die Übersetzung nicht korrekt gewesen sei in entscheidenden Punkten. Und ich bitte, die Möglichkeit zu prüfen, ob man die Vernehmung nicht mit einem anderen Dolmetscher fortsetzen kann.
>
> Your Honor, I regret to say that I have concerns about the further questioning of this witness in the presence of this interpreter. I have been told by people in the public that the translation was incorrect in decisive aspects. And I request that you consider the possibility of continuing the questioning with another interpreter.

Two defense counsels, Jugl and Joschko, both of whom understand Czech, demur. Jugl can find nothing to object to: "Ich verfolge die Übersetzung. Das stimmt nicht. Sie ist bis jetzt zumindest nicht falsch gewesen. Ich habe nichts festgestellt" (I am following the translation. That is not true. Up to now it has at least not been incorrect. I haven't noticed anything). Joschko points to some small details (Jarolim has forgotten to mention the name of a prisoner who identified Mulka to the witness at the time) but is also satisfied: "Aber sonst ist es im großen und ganzen dem Sinne nach übersetzt … Also *dem Sinne nach* stimmt es überein bis auf Einzelheiten" (But otherwise for the most part the sense has been translated … Beside some details, the sense is correct). Raabe then withdraws his objection in order not to hold up the questioning.

The interpreter's work is being monitored by prosecution, defense, judge, and (unnamed) spectators, who feel entitled to address courtroom personnel with their concerns. We are reminded here of the multilingual nature of the early Federal Republic, with large numbers of speakers of Czech, Polish, Romanian, and Hungarian present and actively interested in a trial in which their history is also at stake: the active involvement of people in the audience is remarkable here. Not only do interpreters have to deal with this constant, informal, inconsistent, and unstructured monitoring, but they also find themselves in the middle of disputes about procedure and fairness between prosecution and defense. It is notable that the dispute is framed in terms of attitudes toward desired translation strategies: the defense is happy with a translation of the "sense," whereas the prosecution wants what it thinks of as word-for-word fidelity because of the danger of missing vital details.

On occasion, interpreters feel entitled to hit back at criticism, though this tends only to be those who have gained a secure status in the courtroom: Kapkajew and Benesch, for example, feel empowered to respond to criticism from defense and prosecution. During the testimony of Ladislav Polednik (November 12, 1964, 69'), defense counsel Stolting interrupts the translation of a longer passage, about where and when Polednik saw prisoners being beaten, as he believes that the answer is evasive. Benesch retorts that he should wait to hear the whole answer, in an aggressive tone that suggests his confidence in the interpreter's role of structuring elements of the communication and ensuring that the witness is heard ("Herr Rechtsanwalt, ich übersetze die volle Antwort, ich nehme an, es ist in Ihrem Sinne." Sir, I am translating the full answer, I assume that you are in favor). Stolting accepts defeat in this instance.

Kapkajew employs similar strategies in order to establish her status in the courtroom as someone whose competence should not be questioned lightly. She is especially determined in pushing back against questioning from the defense, as in this example during the testimony of Henryk Porębski on September 18, 1964 (183'). The testimony concludes with a discussion about identifying the accused Baretzki on a photograph. There is a lot of cross talk at this stage, with Hofmeyer trying to pin down Baretzki's evasive answers and defense counsel Gerhardt emphasizing the uncertainty of identification. This rather loud exchange drowns out the witness's attempts to contribute: he speaks quietly and uncertainly, relying on the interpreter to relay his comments at an audible volume. At one point, he offers the suggestion that there may have been confusion over SS men with similar names, a point which the defense wants to clarify:

1. Gerhard:	Frau Dolmetscherin, sagte der Zeuge zu Ihnen im Augenblick
2. Gerhard: Kapkajew:	dass es dort zwei ähnlich klingende Namen gab? Ja?
3. Kapkajew:	Ja.
4. Kapkajew: Gerhard:	Ich habe das doch übersetzt Ja, ich habe das nicht gehört, ist doch
5. Gerhard: Kapkajew:	das ist doch sehr wichtig für uns Ich habe das doch übersetzt
6. Gerhard: Kapkajew:	Ja nein, ich habe das nicht gehört Ich habe es ja laut genug gesagt
7. Gerhard:	Nun Entschuldigung.

1. Gerhard:	Madam interpreter, did the witness just say to you
2. Gerhard: Kapkajew:	that there were two similar sounding names there? Yes?
3. Kapkajew:	*Yes.*
4. Kapkajew: Gerhard:	I did *translate* it. Yes, I didn't *hear* it, it is
5. Gerhard: Kapkajew:	That is very important for us, after all. But I *did* translate it.
6. Gerhard: Kapkajew:	Yes no, I didn't hear it. I said it loud enough.
7. Gerhard:	Well I beg your pardon.

This moment of simultaneous, competitive talk is a small power struggle between Kapkajew and Gerhardt, in which Kapkajew sets out to defend her competence as a participant who is able to define truth and falsehood in specific areas: the witness has retreated entirely into the background in an exchange that is about defending professional trust.

There are, however, also times when she feels obliged to accept responsibility for failures in communication, even when the miscommunication does not arise from her mistake. In the following example, the witness Mieczysław Kieta (August 31, 1964, 24') is giving evidence against the accused Klehr and has just explained how his father had been led away to be killed in Birkenau. He speaks slowly and deliberately, and the exchange is subdued in mood, with little overlapping, after the story he has just told:

1. Kieta:	To nie było moje pierwsze spotkanie z Klehrem.
2. Kapkajew:	Das war nicht mein erstes Treffen mit dem Klehr. . . .
3. Hofmeyer:	Darf ich mal unterbrechen? Sie haben eben übersetzt: Das war nicht mein erstes Zusammentreffen.
4. Kapkajew:	Ja.
5. Hofmeyer:	Sollte das nicht heißen: mein einziges Zusammentreffen?
6. Kieta: Kapkajew:	Tak To nie było moje pierwsze?
7. Kieta:	Jedyne
8. Kapkajew:	Ach, nie miał +
9. Kieta: Kapkajew:	Jedyne Gut, das war nicht mein einziges Zusammentreffen [muttering] pierwsze (...)

1. Kieta:	[Polish] That was not my first meeting with Klehr.
2. Kapkajew:	[German] That was not my first meeting with Klehr. . . .
3. Hofmeyer:	[German] May I interrupt? You just translated: That was not my *first* meeting.
4. Kapkajew:	Yes.
5. Hofmeyer:	Should that not be: my *only* meeting?
6. Kieta: Kapkajew:	[Polish] Yes [Polish] That was not my *first*?
7. Kieta:	[Polish] Only
8. Kapkajew:	[Polish] Ah, he didn't +
9. Kieta: Kapkajew:	[Polish] Only [German] Fine, that was not my *only* meeting [muttering, Polish] first (...)

Here, Kapkajew accepts responsibility for the error despite having translated correctly in the first place. Hofmeyer has pointed out that Kieta's answer was illogical and checked this detail (which is significant to back up the security of the witness's identification of Klehr) via the interpreter. Kieta can clearly understand the German exchanges and steps in to answer Hofmeyer's question before the translation. At the end, we hear Kapkajew muttering: the only audible word is "pierwsze" (first), and we can assume that she is reassuring herself that Kieta initially said this rather than "jedyne" (only).

Another strategy available to the interpreter is to stress her obligation to neutrality as a way of ensuring that she does not carry blame for misunderstandings. In the case of Henryk Porębski, both prosecution and defense are finding it difficult to pin the witness down to answering concrete questions about identifying the accused. Porębski is a witness who prefers to narrate incidents rather than giving direct answers. At one point the prosecution council Kaul exclaims, "Die deutsche Sprache ist ja wahrhaft nicht so schwer" (The German language is really not that hard, 107'), which suggests, perhaps unwittingly, that the problem lies with the interpreting. Kapkajew begins to share the frustration and clearly needs to clarify that she is not responsible for the difficulties. Eventually, during an exchange with Kaul about the witness's failure to answer questions, Kapkajew feels she has to assert her own professional neutrality: "Herr Rechtsanwalt, ich übersetze ja nur" (Prosecution council, all I'm doing is translating, 133'). Later, she stops interpreting in order to comment on this issue: "Entschuldigen Sie, dass ich nicht übersetze … Er versteht immer wieder nicht die Frage" (Excuse me for not translating … He keeps misunderstanding the question, 153').

Given the extent to which the interpreters intervene in, clarify, and restructure the witnesses' speech and their role in organizing the exchanges, this retreat into the sphere of neutrality may seem strange, but it shows how powerful the ideology of neutrality is and the determining role it plays in the court's attitude to interpreting. It provides a final refuge in case of challenge: Kapkajew is effectively reminding the court of the oath she has sworn and the trust they have placed in her professionalism. She is, after all, "just translating." The result, of course, is that Kieta is considered a problematic witness, and his desired way of narrating his testimony attracts a negative judgment.

These small but important negotiations over responsibility and error are about the power to assign blame to individuals and the interpreters' need to maintain face and reputation for competence while also making compromises that ensure smooth communication and, sometimes, to protect other participants from challenge. Kapkajew and Benesch find ways of pursuing their strategic interests in this complex situation of monitoring by participants with differing interests: the court is content with their work, for different reasons, which means they can afford to act flexibly in interpreting and to hit back at challenges from other participants.

Moments of challenge are often characterized by a shift to the third person: witnesses are talked about rather than being addressed directly via the interpreter, which can cause anxiety. In these moments, it becomes clear that the trial is fundamentally not concerned with the survivors and their experiences but that other things are being negotiated over their heads. A witness who is already anxious about testifying can be thrown off kilter by challenges to interpreting. For example, Helen Goldmann, who had traveled from Miami to testify on September 3, 1964, becomes confused during a dispute about the work of the interpreter Regina Schmidt-Ott, who is challenged by the prosecution.

Goldmann has been describing in English her deportation on one of the Hungarian transports in May 1944; she has been finding it difficult to answer questions about the arrival at Birkenau or of the SS men who met their train. At one point, she explains her lack of detailed recall as a result of her fear: "I was too scared to look. Because I was very scared" (4'). It may also be that she is anxious about her inability to answer very precise questions, and so her fear is also a commentary on the situation in the courtroom: she does not have the secure knowledge that the political prisoners had been able to gather and has no experience of giving testimony in court. She therefore reacts defensively at the challenge to the translation by the prosecution, assuming that her testimony is being questioned. Here (5'), Kügler claims that the interpreting has failed to clarify details that could allow the identification of the accused Dr. Lucas, who is alleged to have selected for death prisoners arriving at the "ramp" in Birkenau:

1. Kügler:	Herr Vorsitzender, ich bedaure, einwerfen zu müssen, ich glaube nicht, dass =eh= bei der Schwierigkeit der Materie die Übersetzung ausreicht +
2. Kügler: Schmidt-Ott:	Es fehlt also =eh= an den verschiedensten Dingen. He means =eh= the translation is not exact.
3. Goldmann:	Pardon?
4. Ormond:	(...) Sehr gutes Englisch.
5. Schmidt-Ott:	They say my English is not sufficient =eh= for this =eh= very difficult
6. Schmidt-Ott: Kügler:	translation. Also ich habe ich habe Bedenken bei der bei der äußerst schwierigen Frage, die hier =eh= geprüft werden soll, ob der Angeklagte Doktor Lucas die Selektion vorgenommen hat oder nicht.
7. Kügler: Voice: Schmidt-Ott:	Also ich habe (...) Well, they say, my translation is not sufficient, because =eh eh =

8. Schmidt-Ott:	they (…) question whether Doctor Lucas has been there on
Kügler:	Also ich habe ich habe nicht nicht jedes Mal =eh= eingewandt
9. Kügler:	wenn etwas nicht übersetzt worden ist
Goldmann:	I *know* he was there
10. Goldmann:	because I heard them
Kügler:	Einen Augenblick, bitte, einen Augenblick
11. Goldmann:	I was
Schmidt-Ott:	Well they say it's my translation.
12. Goldmann:	Oh.

1. Kügler:	[German] Your Honour, I regret having to intervene, I do not believe that =eh= the translation is adequate with this difficult material +
2. Kügler:	=eh= Many different things are missing
Schmidt-Ott:	[English] He means =eh= the translation is not exact.
3. Goldmann:	[English] Pardon?
4. Ormond:	[English] (…) Very good English
5. Schmidt-Ott:	[English] They say my English is not sufficient =eh= for this =eh= very difficult
6. Schmidt-Ott:	translation.
Kügler:	[German] So I have I have concerns given the given the extremely difficult question that is being =eh= tested here, whether the accused Dr. Lucas took part in the selection or not.
7. Kügler: Voice:	[German] So I have
Schmidt-Ott:	(…)
	[English] Well, they say, my translation is not sufficient, because =eh eh =
8. Schmidt-Ott:	they (…) question whether Doctor Lucas has been there on
Kügler:	[German] So I have I have not =eh= objected on each occasion
9. Kügler:	if something was not translated
Goldmann:	[English] I *know* he was there
10. Goldmann:	because I heard them
Kügler:	[German] One moment please, one moment
11. Goldmann:	[English] I was
Schmidt-Ott:	[English] Well they say it's my translation.
12. Goldmann:	Oh.

The complex crosstalk here, with Kügler addressing the judge, voices in the background, and Schmidt-Ott trying to clarify for a confused Goldmann what is happening, indicates that the proceedings have reached a crisis of trust that needs to be resolved. Goldmann believes her testimony is being questioned, and Schmidt-Ott has to reassure her that the issue is her own interpreting. This is a good example of the multisource challenges that interpreters often have to deal with simultaneously, organizing an exchange while taking criticism of their work.

As it happens, there has been little issue with Schmidt-Ott's translations up to this point: Kügler is here expressing his frustration at Goldmann's failure to provide the detail that the prosecution needs. Schmidt-Ott's situation is not helped during this testimony by the fact that her work is constantly under challenge from all sides; unusually, both prosecution and defense see strategic advantages in challenging her. For the most part, the challenges have little substance, but they are designed to cast enough doubt on the testimony that Goldmann's identification of the defendant Dr. Lucas cannot be seen as secure.

Goldmann sometimes has to be interrupted to allow Schmidt-Ott to finish translating: she often understands the questions in German or believes she understands them and wants to continue her narrative without waiting for her own words to be translated. The discipline of consecutive interpreting is difficult for her in this high-pressure situation where she is not able to maintain control over her narrative. She does not feel able to challenge the court, but the interpreter's status is such that she can challenge her over a mistranslation as a way of exercising some control. For example, she criticizes Schmidt-Ott's understanding of her statement as a way of pushing back against challenges to her testimony from other, more authoritative, parties in the courtroom. When questioned on a narrative about a blood test being sent away to Berlin before she could work in the kitchens, Goldmann questions the detail of Schmidt-Ott's understanding, alleging a false translation: "It didn't take a month, that's where you misunderstood me. I said a few weeks and you said four weeks, you see" (Goldmann 3.9.1964, 48'). These small details are immaterial to the case but they are vital for Goldmann's sense of control over her own testimony under the conditions of interpreting.

Toward the end of the testimony, the audience becomes involved, an extra layer of monitoring, but this time in support of the interpreter. Defense counsel Eggert suggests that Schmidt-Ott has not translated a specific line in the testimony, but we hear voices in the background shouting "doch, doch!" (Yes she did! 62'), which gives her the confidence to defend her practice.

The complex network of monitoring in support of conflicting interests puts pressure on the interpreter, especially here, as many of the participants are able to understand at least some of the English, and the witness reacts defensively to what she perceives (rightly) as attempts to doubt her testimony. Goldmann finds it difficult to adopt the discipline required for the interpreting situation; other survivors are able to use it to their advantage, but she becomes disconcerted and defensive. The only person in court whom she feels she can address directly is the interpreter: she adopts politeness formulae for this relationship ("Yes, ma'am"), but the interpreter is also the only participant whom Goldmann feels empowered to challenge directly. Moments like this may be small, but they tell us a lot about things that are unspoken in the courtroom, how witnesses can perceive what is happening around them, and how complex the work of the interpreters can be.

The second part of this chapter will explore how the witnesses themselves challenge the translation of their words. Every witness monitors the work of the interpreter carefully, however little they are able to understand German. There is no more important issue than trusting the interpreter to render their words precisely, honestly, and clearly, but some witnesses also see the interpreter as an interlocutor, advisor, or support. They employ elements of their linguistic repertoire to monitor, confirm, criticize, and intervene where they believe it is in their interests and where they feel empowered to do so. There are telling moments when these expectations clash with what the interpreter is doing or feels obliged to do: in this section, I look at examples where it is clear that the witness has been monitoring the translation and intervenes in their own interest.

Many witnesses—in particular the Polish former political prisoners—follow the translation of their words and vocalize approval: one frequently hears a witness say something like "tak jest" (that's right) after the interpreter has spoken. For example, the witness Wilhelm Prokop (June 18, 1964, 2') does this frequently throughout his testimony: as a Silesian, Prokop speaks and understands German well, but he is uncertain about using it in court:

1. Prokop:	Verzeihen Sie, ich möchte eventuell meine Aussage in polnischer Sprache =eh= aussagen, deswegen, weil es mir in der deutschen Sprache trotz alledem an Worten fehlt. Und ich =eh= fürchte, dass ich dann auf Umwegen meine Geständnis werde ab- ab- meine Aussage werde =eh=
2. Prokop: Hofmeyer:	machen müssen machen müssen
3. Prokop:	oder dass ein Wort missverstanden werden kann. Also ich würde sehr gern =eh= meine Aussagen in polnischer Sprache wiedergeben. Und falls =eh= + bei der Dolmetschung irgend etwas nicht so wiedergegeben wird, wie ich es meine, so behalte ich mir dann noch eine eine =eh= +

4. Hofmeyer:	eine Verbesserung vor
Prokop:	Verbesserung vor
Kapkajew:	(…)
5. Hofmeyer:	Ja.

1. Prokop:	Forgive me, I would if possible like to =eh= state my statement in Polish, because despite everything I lack some words in German. And I =eh= am afraid that I will be obliged to take diversions to make my confession =eh=
2. Prokop:	make my statement
Hofmeyer:	make my statement
3. Prokop:	or that a word may be misunderstood. So I would very much like to =eh= make my statement in Polish. And if =eh= + something does not come over in interpreting as I mean it in interpreting, I reserve the right to =eh +
4. Hofmeyer:	Make an improvement
Prokop:	an improvement
Kapkajew:	(…)
5. Hofmeyer:	Yes.

Prokop here declares that he will be monitoring and where necessary correcting the interpreting: he speaks German fluently in a high register, perhaps paying regard to the courtroom situation and thus performing a shared class identity, and stumbles only when expressing doubt about his language skills. He hesitates over some of the formal German verbs used in the legal context for giving testimony and confuses the word "statement" (*Aussage*) with "confession" (*Geständnis*). Hofmeyer's intervention lowers the register of the statement a little by using a more colloquial formulation (*machen* instead of the word *ablegen* that Prokop was seeking for the term "give a testimony"). Kapkajew offers what sounds like supportive words off microphone, accepting that he will be monitoring her work: this exchange allows Prokop to maintain control over the way his testimony is heard. He later says that he can discuss "less important" details in German—"Aber das sind ja schließlich weniger wichtige Sachen. Die kann ich noch in deutscher Sprache beantworten" (But after all these things are less important. I can still answer in German, 3')—and switches frequently between the languages.

Later in his testimony (32'), during an account of how the accused Capesius ordered his prisoner assistants to store medical items that had been brought to the camp by Jewish deportees, Prokop gets into an argument with the interpreter Kapkajew about the correct translation of the word "parter" (ground floor).

Kapkajew translates this correctly as "Erdgeschoss" (ground floor), but Prokop mishears it as "erster Stock" (first floor), becoming frustrated. A moment of conflict interrupts his narrative, and he takes his frustration out on Kapkajew before admitting his error: "Na parterze do stu diabłów!" (On the ground floor for God's sake!—literally "a hundred devils take it"). When Kapkajew corrects him ("Parter to jest po niemiecku Erdgeschoss," Parter means ground floor in German) he corrects himself and backs down ("No, w porzadku, dobrze, dobrze." Well, fine, good, good), and she ensures that the court knows whose mistake this is: "Der Zeuge hat sich geirrt" (The witness made a mistake).

Shortly afterward (33'), he takes a certain sarcastic pleasure in correcting a translation, perhaps reflecting a sense of shame or loss of face arising from the initial conflict:

1. Prokop:	Wiec tak, to myśmy te rzeczy tam oczywiście, nieprawdaż, do magazynu je złożyli, gdzie mieliśmy polecenie, je znowu osobno, oddzielnie ustawić do regalu.
2. Kapkajew:	Wir brachten also alle diese Medikamente ins SS-Lager. Und wir bekamen dann wieder ne Anweisung, sie alle genau in die Regale zu sortieren
3. Kapkajew: Prokop:	und Nie, nie, moja piękna pani
4. Prokop:	Nein, wir bekamen die Anweisung, die Medikamente gesondert von anderen Medikamenten abseits
5. Prokop: Kapkajew:	ins Regal zu stellen ins Regal

1. Prokop:	[Polish] So yes, then we put these things there, of course, ah no, we put them in the warehouse, where we'd had the instruction, separately, to put them separately on the shelf.[1]
2. Kapkajew:	[German] So we took all these medicines to the SS camp. And then we received another instruction to place them precisely on the shelf
3. Kapkajew: Prokop:	And [Polish] No, no, my lovely lady
4. Prokop:	[German] No, we received the instruction to place the medicines *separate* from the other medicines, apart,
5. Prokop: Kapkajew:	on the shelf on the shelf

The relationship between Prokop and Kapkajew continues to be tense, and he often does not take the time to pause for translation, meaning that she has to shift to simultaneous interpreting at times. Prokop shifts to German more and more, indicating frustration with the interpreting and a desire to speak directly—and often aggressively—to the court, especially the defense. He even makes fun of defense counsel Göllner's German when he makes a linguistic slip in asking whether Prokop had ever held a Zyklon-B can in his hands, causing some amusement in the audience (98'):

1. Göllner:	Haben Sie denn einmal mit eigenen Augen eine Zyklon-B-Dose in der Hand gehabt, entweder gefüllt oder leer?
2. Prokop:	Mit eigenen Augen kann man ja nichts in der Hand haben.

1. Göllner:	Did you hold with your own eyes a Zyklon-B can in your hand, whether full or empty?
2. Prokop:	You can't hold anything in your hand with your own eyes.

In Prokop's case, the monitoring of the interpreter's work becomes an expression of a more general mistrust of the court: Prokop has positioned Kapkajew as a representative of the institution and does his best to avoid having to speak through her. Other witnesses take up a more supportive attitude but are still keen to ensure that they are heard properly. Tadeusz Paczuła (April 30, 1964, 19'), who had worked in the Auschwitz I prisoner infirmary and was a witness who understands the vital importance of establishing lines of sight in his testimony and differentiating between things he saw and things he only heard, intervenes to correct a moment of imprecision in Kapkajew's version:

1. Paczuła:	I z tego bloku widziałem w nocy, jak prowadzono jeńców radzieckich.
2. Kapkajew:	Aus diesem Block habe ich einmal nachts gehört
3. Kapkajew: Paczuła:	wie die und gesehen
4. Kapkajew:	wie die sowjetischen Kriegsgefangenen geführt wurden
5. Paczuła: Kapkajew:	tak jest Ich habe sie auch
6. Kapkajew:	Gesehen
7. Paczuła:	gesehen gesehen

1. Paczuła:	[Polish] And from that block I saw at night the Soviet prisoners being led.
2. Kapkajew:	[German] From this block I heard once at night

3. Kapkajew: Paczuła:	The [German] and saw
4. Kapkajew:	[German] the Soviet prisoners of war being led
5. Paczuła: Kapkajew:	[Polish] That's right [German] I *also*
6. Kapkajew:	saw them
7. Paczuła:	[German] saw saw

The careful attention paid to interpreting by many witnesses is a tribute to the commitment to truth and to their thorough understanding of the requirements of courtroom testimony. It is vital to establish who gave instructions for killings of prisoners, and witnesses who are alive to this issue monitor the interpreting closely where they can. For example, Alfred Wóycicki (May 29, 1964, 10') makes sure that Kapkajew renders his words precisely when talking about who conducted an investigation into resistance activities and who announced death sentences for prisoners. The order was not given *by* the *Rapportführer* ("Nie przez rapportführera"), but when they were standing *before* the *Rapportführer* ("przed rapportführerem") the order was given by Maximilian Grabner of the Auschwitz Political Department: "Nie przez rapportführera tylko przed rapportführerem staliśmy, a odczytywał to nie rapportführer, tylko Grabner" (It wasn't given by the *Rapportführer*, but we stood before the *Rapportführer*, and it was not read out by the *Rapportführer* but by Grabner). Kapkajew then makes sure to correct the record, explaining the brief conversation in Polish between them: "Also das war eine kleine Verbesserung" (So that was a small correction).

When the witness-interpreter relationship is working well, the interpreter can make explicit the correction, informing the judge of the content of the exchange and ensuring that no face is lost. At times, she takes responsibility for errors, even when they originated with the witness, as during the testimony of Ignacy Golik (June 8, 1964, 25'):

1. Golik:	Po powrocie + z reguły taki samochód przywoził + jakieś rzeczy po ludziach gazowanych
2. Kapkajew:	Nach der Vergasung brachte jedesmal =eh= dieses Auto
3. Golik:	Nicht jedesmal + często
4. Kapkajew: Golik:	oft + Pan powiedział z reguły często
5. Kapkajew:	Also ich verbessere mich, oft =eh= die Sachen, irgendwelche Sachen mit.

1. Golik:	[Polish] When coming back + as a rule a car like this brought + some things from the people who had been gassed
2. Kapkajew:	[German] Each time after the gassing =eh= this car brought
3. Golik:	[German] Not each time + [Polish] often
4. Kapkajew: Golik:	[German] often + [Polish] You said as a rule [Polish] often
5. Kapkajew:	[German] So I correct myself, often brought = eh= the things, some things

Kapkajew has established enough institutional trust to be able to take responsibility for an error, for the sake of avoiding conflict with the witness, without casting doubt on her professionalism.

Kazimierz Smoleń (May 25 1964, 19'), a former political prisoner who had been director of the State Museum Auschwitz-Birkenau since 1955 and had been an important collaborator for the court since the beginning of the investigation, has a different approach to monitoring. He understands how important it is to differentiate between things he knows from first-hand experience and things that he is uncertain about, so he insists that Kapkajew does not increase the level of certainty in her translation, pulling her up even for seemingly trivial distinctions. For example, he interrupts her translation of the phrase "około czternaście Dienststelli obozowych" (around fourteen camp *Dienststellen*) insisting in German that she has missed the word "ungefähr" (around) and should insert it.

Witnesses' insistence on precision can lead them to react against an interpreter's tendency to use dramatic language in rendering a more neutral word: when talking about what he could hear of executions taking place, Tadeusz Hołuj (June 12, 1964, 7') corrects Kapkajew's rendering of "odgłosów egzekucji" (sounds of the execution) as "Detonation," insisting instead on the plainer "Geräusche" (sounds).

For many of these witnesses, it is clear that they are thinking of the legal situation when challenging the interpreter: they understand the importance of formulating their testimony in specific ways in order to achieve convictions for murder. So, for example, the Czech-speaking Pavel Bergmann (November 30, 1964, 113') insists on the specific nuance of his words when describing being beaten by the *Funktionshäftling* Danisch:

1. Bergmann:	Mě zbil například úplně zbytečné, a =eh= a jestli pan obhájce chce, tak mu řeknu, za jakých okolností
2. Benesch:	Er verprügelte mich einmal sehr, sehr schlimm. Und wenn der Herr Verteidiger es will

3. Benesch:	werde ich nähere
Bergmann:	Ne + schlimm. Nicht nur schlimm + zbytečné
4. Benesch:	=eh= völlig =eh=
5. Bergmann:	omylem + umsonst
Benesch:	Irrtümlich und umsonst, und wenn Sie wünschen, werde ich nähere Einzelheiten angeben

1. Bergmann:	[Czech] For instance, he beat me for no reason, and =eh= and if the counsel wishes, I will tell him under what circumstances
2. Benesch:	[German] He beat me once very very badly. And if the defense counsel wishes
3. Benesch:	[German] I will give more details
Bergmann:	[Czech] Not + [German] badly Not just badly + [Czech] for no reason
4. Benesch:	[German] =eh= completely =eh=
5. Bergmann:	[Czech] by mistake + [German] for no reason
Benesch:	[German] By mistake and for no reason, and if you wish I will provide more details

Bergmann knows that convictions can only be achieved by descriptions of "excessive" violence or violence carried out beyond "normal" instructions, so he insists on these changes: Benesch does not quite understand the nuance here, however.

Some witnesses seem to project their anxiety about testifying onto the relationship with the interpreter, meaning that the negotiation over interpreting takes on an overtly emotional significance. Rebecca Wittmann has referred to the testimony of the Polish former political prisoner Józef Kral (May 15 and 21, 1964) as "by far the most gruesome and devastating of any from witnesses at the trial" (Wittmann 2005: 155). During his account of his torture at the hands of Wilhelm Boger, Kral monitors the interpreter carefully, often insisting on his own versions when describing the most horrific acts of violence. Much of this testimony—with its precise description of the "Boger swing," the notorious torture apparatus—is hard to listen to. Kral appears to understand the requirements for consecutive interpreting: he speaks slowly, clearly, and in short sentences, pausing for interpreting rather than speaking in longer narrative stretches that a good interpreter can translate in full. Thus, his testimony consists of a long series of striking, individual images whose emotional power is clear even before the translation comes: as listeners, we are forced to pay attention to each individual moment and need to concentrate actively in order to construct the narrative in our minds.

Kral insists on being understood in a way that he has control over and becomes agitated if he perceives an inaccuracy. When talking about Boger's torture method (May 15, 1964, 29') he describes how prisoners would be hung up on a stake by their arms:

1.	Kral:	Tak na słupku wisiało się tylko 2 godziny, można było
2.	Kral: Kapkajew:	wisieć An so einem »Pfahl« konnte man nur zwei Stunden hängenbleiben
3.	Kral:	W innym wypadku mogło mogły uschnąć + mogły człowiekowi ręce usychać.
4.	Kapkajew:	=eh= Andernfalls konnten die Arme bei so einem Häftling abfallen
5.	Kral:	i uschnąć, uschnąć!
6.	Kral: Kapkajew:	krążenie krwi absterben
7.	Kapkajew:	Die Blutzirkulation wurde dann unterbrochen

1.	Kral:	[Polish] Yes, on the pole it was only possible to hang for 2 hours, you could
2.	Kral: Kapkajew:	hang [German] It was only possible to hang on a pole like that for two hours
3.	Kral:	[Polish] otherwise it could they could wither + the person's arms could wither
4.	Kapkajew:	[German] =eh= otherwise such a prisoner's arms could fall off
5.	Kral:	[Polish] and wither, wither!
6.	Kral: Kapkajew:	[Polish] the blood circulation [German] go numb
7.	Kapkajew:	[German] The blood circulation was then interrupted

Kral's agitation at Kapkajew's mistranslation is understandable here, as it gives an absurd image of the consequences of torture rather than an accurate one. The listeners can hear his intonation and can follow how this is being negotiated, so the interpreter begins to lose control of the interaction under the pressure of the emotional force of Kral's speech. Kral's extraordinary testimony is characterized by these small moments of tension, conflict, negotiation, challenge, and collaboration between witness and interpreter, and Kral's insistent monitoring and obvious doubts about the interpreting make Kapkajew's job difficult.

Kapkajew sometimes struggles to find adequate translations, indicating the pressure she is under from Kral's monitoring and the emotional intensity of the testimony. Here (May 15, 1964, 37'), she hesitates briefly over the word "zerwał" (broke), trying to find a way of rendering the image of a prisoner so contorted in pain that he breaks the "swing":

1. Kral:	Wróblewski zerwał huśtawkę
2. Kapkajew:	Wróblewski +
3. Kral:	*zerwał* tę huśtawkę, od bólu, *zerwał* tę huśtawkę
4. Kapkajew:	warf die »Schaukel« um vor Schmerzen

1. Kral:	[Polish] Wróblewski broke the swing
2. Kapkajew:	Wróblewski +
3. Kral:	[Polish] *broke* that swing, from pain, *broke* that swing
4. Kapkajew:	[German] knocked the swing over from pain

Kapkajew's version is interesting: she produces an image that perhaps seems more likely under the circumstances—tipping the swing over rather than breaking it. Kral insists so strongly on the word "zerwał," repeating it with an intense intonation that it is tempting to interpret this moment as the expression of a desire for the victim's pain to break the instrument of torture.

The tension between Kapkajew and Kral produces moments of confusion over face-saving. Discussing two prisoners, Janicki and Wróblewski, Kral confuses the names for a moment (36'). Janicki has been brutally tortured by Boger under the eyes of Kral and other prisoners and thrown into the corridor in front of them:

1. Kral:	Po około pół godzinie zabrano do przesłuchania Janickiego, przy otwartych przesłuchiwano, przyglądaliśmy się przy otwartych drzwiach
2. Kapkajew:	Nach einer halben Stunde wurde Janicki zum Verhör
3. Kapkajew: Kral:	geholt Nein, nie Janicki!
4. Kapkajew: Kral:	Nicht Janicki Wróblewski
5. Kapkajew:	Ah, ich hab mich + er hat sich geirrt. Wróblewski + wurde Wróblewski zum Verhör gebracht. Die Tür war offen, wir konnten zusehen

1. Kral:	[Polish] After about half an hour Janicki was taken for interrogation, he was interrogated with doors open, we observed it through the open doors
2. Kapkajew:	[German] After half an hour Janicki was taken for
3. Kapkajew: Kral:	interrogation [German] No [Polish] not Janicki!
4. Kapkajew: Kral:	[German] Not Janicki Wróblewski
5. Kapkajew:	[German] Ah, I made + he made a mistake. Wróblewski + it was Wróblewski who was taken for interrogation. The door was open, we could watch.

Kral's intonation and his shift to German are emphatic and feel like a challenge to Kapkajew, though it is unclear whether he has realized that the initial mistake was his. Kapkajew's first impulse is to take responsibility, as she has done during Golik's testimony, but in this case she feels no need to cover for Kral and so ensures it is clear who made the error.

This small number of fragments cannot do justice to the interactions in Kral's long and powerful testimony; the relationships develop in complex ways in the course of the questioning, and trust and mistrust are negotiated intensely along the way through challenges to interpreting and insistence on accuracy in the description of experiences of extreme violence. Kapkajew's interpreting performance has relevance for the different themes of this study: the intensity of Kral's telling and his insistence on control over the interpreting create ethical dilemmas for the interpreter that cannot be resolved by any institutional codes, rules, or simple direction to translate "word for word."

Conclusion

In this multilingual courtroom, the work of the interpreters is under constant monitoring from many different sides, all with competing interests. There is no testimony in which a language is spoken that can be understood only by witness and interpreter. The complexity of the linguistic situation in the courtroom and the number of people who are able to monitor what is being said create specific challenges. People from the multilingual territories of Central and Eastern Europe—survivors, accused, and court officials—encounter each other in the courtroom after the genocide and negotiate the events of the Holocaust through these shared languages. The languages of the Allied powers—English, French, and Russian—are also present and shared by many of the participants but play a smaller, less defining role than at Nuremberg. It is this specific constellation of multilingualism, with a complex history of power, conflict, hybridity, violence, and migration, that makes this trial characteristically (West) German.

It also means that the monitoring of interpreters' work is never only about "accuracy" or equivalence: "accuracy" cannot be considered a neutral term here. The monitoring is intense and constant and operates differently for each interpreter and language pair. It is also rather unstructured, with no set processes for checking and editing transcripts retrospectively, so all negotiations over language have to be concluded during the live proceedings. Some formal routines are available for prosecution and defense to challenge interpreting, and individuals make use of them regularly when they identify an interest in doing so. Their challenges are often partisan, whether or not they are justified in linguistic terms: the prosecution needs clarity in identifying individuals and connecting them with specific crimes, while the defense often uses challenges to produce a sense of doubt or mistrust in the testimony.

Specific allegations of bias are not a feature of these institutional challenges; they have more to do with negotiating professional standards, trust, and insider–outsider status. Judgments about an interpreter's trustworthiness in institutional terms can be made very quickly, and the presiding judge has the final power to make decisions about professional standards but also when to exercise flexibility in the name of convenience and the smooth running of proceedings. Ultimately, the aim of the complex procedures for establishing institutional trust—whether through longer-term processes of qualification, application, professionalism, and insider trust-building or in the heat of the communication itself—is to create a situation in which the court need no longer worry about language mediation and can rely on the interpreted German text as an original source for its judgment. The court's linguistic procedures are designed to crystallize out of a complex linguistic situation a clear model of original text and translation.

For the survivor-witnesses, however, very different issues are at stake. For witnesses, a challenge to the interpreting requires a high degree of confidence, or extreme pressure of emotion, as it is tantamount to a challenge to the institution and is a potentially face-threatening act. The majority of witnesses have an understanding of German on a spectrum from a few key terms of camp vocabulary to fluency: they regularly employ these resources, however limited, to monitor, approve, and occasionally object to translations. Their interventions tend to involve precise use of language in descriptions of things that are important for them to communicate; those with an understanding of legal procedure may try to ensure that the interpreting establishes the necessary degree of certainty, but others may simply push back against the frustration of not being able to narrate as they wish in the context of consecutive interpreting. Their interventions may also arise from defensiveness, a perceived need for face-saving, or shifting blame for errors in defense of their trustworthiness as witnesses under the pressure of questioning. Challenging the interpreter may be seen as a "safer" way of hitting back at challenges to their testimony: the interpreter may be perceived as part of the institution but as lower in the power hierarchy, and so criticism and challenge are seen as less risky.

The interpreter has to negotiate this complex situation, always concerned with demonstrating professionalism and trustworthiness, balancing competing interests and forms of trust, and making ethical choices about how to respond to challenges and threats to status moment by moment. Sanctions can range from the introduction of a formal correction routine that is resolved by mutual agreement to dismissal and loss of status as court interpreter. Interpreters such as Benesch or Kapkajew who establish a degree of institutional trust that allows them to respond flexibly to challenges and to defend their practice must constantly work at balancing the expectations of the different participants in the interaction: they confirm and reproduce the institutional power hierarchies while occasionally working in favor of the witnesses "below the radar."

10

Ethical Decision-Making and Relationships

The two previous chapters dealt with the expectations that the interpreters had to work with, whether in terms of institutional structures and professional standards or the constant monitoring of their work in the multilingual courtroom. I now move on to a closer look at aspects of the interactions between witnesses and interpreters: how do interpreters make ethical decisions about the way they represent the witnesses and their evidence to the court? What kind of relationship develops between interpreter and witness, and how do they deal with difficult issues and problems that arise? Was the relationship supportive, neutral, or conflictual?

We have already seen that the court is willing to let certain practices and forms of interaction pass, even though they may contravene a strict view of the limits of acceptable behavior on the part of the interpreters: how much leniency is granted depends on the extent that the court trusts the interpreter to ensure the smooth running of the proceedings. This chapter will show how interpreters understood the ethical requirements of their relationship with the witnesses, how much "deviant" behavior they were able to engage in in support of the witnesses, and whether this had positive or negative consequences.

On January 14, 1965, Milton Buki took the stand. Buki, a survivor of the Birkenau *Sonderkommando* with an extraordinary story to tell, was one of only two witnesses to testify purely in Yiddish. He works with the interpreter Moritz Grünblatt. I have chosen this example to begin the chapter as it shows an interpreter making a clear decision about how to represent the witness based on a strategic choice about the kind of relationship that will be necessary between them. As always, the session opens with the witness answering questions to authenticate his identity: name, age, marital status, profession, and place of residence. This includes the standard question, designed to certify that the witness is to giving testimony against a relative: "Sie sind nicht verwandt und nicht verschwägert mit den Angeklagten?" (You are not related, either by descent or by marriage, to any of the accused?)

Grünblatt renders this as "Ir zeyt nisht a koyrev fun al di angeklagte do?" (You are not a relative of all the accused over there?) Buki does not reply directly, instead exclaiming quietly "shanda," which the interpreter feels he has to explain: "Das wäre für ihn eine Schande, erklärt der Zeuge" (That would be a disgrace for him, the witness declares). What does interpreter Grünblatt have to translate here? The intention of the question is clear, and the exchange between the participants is formal and not out of the ordinary. But the judge's question about the relationship to the accused provokes the horrified, half-whispered answer "shanda," and the interpreter hastens to explain what it means. The similarity between the German word "Schande" and the Yiddish "shanda" allows a person who speaks German to believe that he has understood what is at stake here: it would be a disgrace for Mr. Buki if he were related to one of the defendants. So that is his problem, and the court can overlook it: Hofmeyer simply continues with the questioning.

But there is another possibility: interpreter Grünblatt translates the official German formula "verwandt oder verschwägert" with the more intimate word "koyrev" (relative), and Buki reacts with horror at the thought. It could also be that he finds the judge's question disgraceful, something outrageous, an insult against which he protests. The shame would lie with the court in this case, not with the victim. Grünblatt reacts quickly and defuses the situation by trying to make it clear to the court that he has not meant it that way. In trying to protect him and explain the problem, Grünblatt's careful verbal distancing from the witness shows that he is taking the court's side in the attempt to mediate between the parties. The horror of the Jewish witness is dismissed here since it challenges the court's procedures and reminds those present that this is not an ordinary trial.

Buki's statement continues, with Grünblatt attempting to mediate and explain the difficulties that the witness encounters. For example, when Hofmeyer asks Buki to look at the map of the camp and get his bearings (2'), Buki is overwhelmed and says something incomprehensible, and interpreter Grünblatt jumps in again and interprets his excessive demands for the court: "Der Zeuge erklärt, er ist sehr aufgeregt, und kann sich nicht zurechtfinden auf der Karte" (The witness explains that he is very nervous and cannot find his way around the map). This is probably about more than just Buki not being able to cope with the judge's complex spatial explanations. With his commanding overview of the spatial design of the camp and the functions of the various parts, Hofmeyer shares the view of the camp's builders, and Buki again experiences the victim's disorientation and fear. His perspective is suddenly confronted with the perspective of the perpetrators, a perspective that is considered objective and neutral in this court.

By explaining Buki's feelings to the judge, Grünblatt exceeds his role, but he apparently sees himself as a mediator who can speak on behalf of the witness and make him accessible to the court. Grünblatt takes a particular stance here; he wants to assist the witness, but by doing so he confirms the authority and perspective of the court and gives the impression that the problem lies with Buki, who is not in a position to think objectively. Judge Hofmeyer eventually expresses his growing impatience with Grünblatt's work and finally asks him to translate only "accurately" and in the first person (5'): "Wenn Sie die Freundlichkeit hätten, uns genau zu übersetzen, wie der Zeuge es sagt in der direkten Rede, nicht?" (If you would be so kind as to translate for us exactly as the witness says in direct speech, yes?). Hofmeyer's request to correct an attitude that is not conducive to the work of the court changes the relationship between witness and interpreter: the latter is no longer to be a supporter of the witness but a representative of the court; he is to neither protect the witness nor explain him to the court. In short, the Jewish interpreter should not assist the Jewish witness in a German court. Moments like this give us an impression of the incompatible worlds of experience that clash here.

Later (27), Buki makes clear to the court that he finds it hard to speak freely when giving an account of the work of the *Sonderkommandos* in Birkenau. For him, the ritualistic and distancing question-answer pattern provides a structure that allows him to speak at all about the worst aspects of his experience:

1. Hofmeyer:	Nun + Herr =um= Buki, wollen Sie uns doch einmal sagen, wie diese Vergasung und die nachfolgende Verbrennung vor sich ging. Wer hat die Leute dorthin gebracht? Wer hat ihnen was befohlen, und was haben die Leute dann getan? Wollen Sie uns das doch bitte mal schildern.
2. Buki:	=eh= beser beser volt gewezn tsu entfern oyf fragen, vayl ikh bin nisht instand fizish das tsu machen nokh gaystik, derfar vayl ikh bin zeyer afgeregt. Tsu redn derfray ist mir nisht =eh= kan ikh nisht. Af fragn kan ikh entfern.
3. Grünblatt:	Der Zeuge bittet, ihm Fragen zu stellen. Er ist wegen seiner Aufregung und physischer Erschöpfung nicht in der Lage, ausführlich zu berichten.

1. Hofmeyer:	[German] Now + Mr. =um= Buki, would you tell us again how this gassing and the burning that followed proceeded? Who took the people there? Who gave them orders and what did the people do then? Could you please describe that to us?
2. Buki:	[Yiddish] =eh= better better perhaps would be to answer questions, because I am not physically able to do that or mentally, because I am very nervous. Speaking freely for me isn't =eh= I can't do it. I can answer questions.
3. Grünblatt:	[German] The witness requests that you ask him questions. Because of his nervousness and physical exhaustion he is not able to report at length.

Chare and Williams have described this moment in terms of the witness's agency:

> "Here the court's parameters function as an emotional support for Buki … But it is also a format that he has chosen for himself. This process of negotiation takes away from the idea of a witness prevented from expressing his truth by terms dictated to him. Tailoring his speech to the needs of his audience is part of what allows him to testify. (Chare and Williams 2019: 119)

Grünblatt here continues to try to protect and explain the witness, resorting to third-person speech and providing an explanation for his psychological and physical state that Buki leaves ambiguous: Grünblatt assumes that Buki is "physically" and "mentally" unable to speak coherently because of exhaustion, which may be a reasonable assumption but is also not the only possibility. The experience of testifying may be producing physical symptoms, whether from the return of trauma or the stress of the testimony situation. We cannot know this, but Grünblatt's version again presents the problem as arising from the witness rather than the way the proceedings are conducted.

The structure of the communication and Grünblatt's and Buki's responses to it produce a paradoxical situation in which the interpreter's attempts to protect and explain the witness lead to the testimony becoming more impersonal, replacing an account of personal experience with a stylistic baldness that operates as a rhetoric of factuality as the court understands it. Here (11'), Buki is describing the killing of the previous *Sonderkommandos* and how the new arrivals had to clear up their clothing. His speech is calm in describing this incident, but the tempo increases in the second part of the extract: he starts speaking carefully and deliberately in German in step 1, shifting into Yiddish diction as the speed increases in step 4. I have tried to give a very limited impression of this in my transcription, but it can be no more than an interpretation:

1. Buki:	An dizem tage + [clears throat] wenn wir =eh= sind am 12. gekommen nach Auschwitz nach Birkenau un am 14. sind wir in Sonderkommando genumen geworen das ershte mal + wie ich glaube + haben die Sonderkommando gearbet am farbrenen di Sonderkommando fun before.[1]
2. Grünblatt:	Die erste Aufgabe des Sonderkommandos im Dezember 1942 war die Verbrennung der Leichen von den vorangegangenen
3. Grünblatt:	Sonderkommandos
Buki:	Vayl
4. Buki:	=eh= vayl wen mir zenen gekumen am platz iz =eh= gewezn in geshtrayfte =eh= geshtrayfte malbushim Kleidung un zenen gewen tseworfn af di felder. Zej zenen zikh funanandergelofn un azoy me hot zey
5. Buki:	oysgeshosn
Grünblatt:	Bei Ankunft des Zeugen mit seinem Transport lagen herum =eh= die gestreiften Anzüge der Häftlinge auf dem Platz.

1. Buki:	On this day + [clears throat] when we =eh= came to Auschwitz to Birkenau on the 12th and on the 14th we were taken into the Sonderkommando the first time + I think so + the Sonderkommando were working on burning the Sonderkommando from before.
2. Grünblatt:	The first task of the Sonderkommandos in December 1942 was burning the corpses of the previous
3. Grünblatt:	Sonderkommandos
Buki:	Because
4. Buki:	=eh= because when we came to the place they =eh= were in striped =eh= striped malbushim clothes and were thrown about on the fields. They scattered and so they were
5. Buki:	shot down
Grünblatt:	On the witness's arrival with his transport the =eh= striped outfits of the prisoners were lying about on the ground.

Grünblatt's technique here leads him to omit certain aspects of this account: Buki's speculation about whether this was the first time that the new *Sonderkommandos* had had to dispose of the corpses of the previous group and the image of the group scattering and being shot down. Grünblatt resolves a potential syntactic ambiguity in Buki's speech (who exactly was in the striped clothes?) by ignoring the problem.

A couple of interesting linguistic features of Buki's speech also go unnoticed: for example, his hesitation over expression that leads to interference from his English and his act of self-translation of the Hebrew-root word "malbushim" into the German "Kleidung" (step 4). Small details like this show the witness making compromises with the language of the court for the sake of being helpful to the interpreter and contributing to the success of the testimony. For this reason, we should be careful when talking about witnesses' testimony being "distorted" during these exchanges or assuming that they are not able to express themselves authentically: a witness like Buki is well aware of the institutional and discursive context of his testimony and understands what is needed for an effective testimony before this court. It is not the case that Buki is simply trying to give expression to his suffering, but he is more than capable of acting in accordance with the requirements of the situation.

Grünblatt's strategies demonstrate the ethical paradoxes of this situation: the third-person positioning shows a desire to explain, speak for, protect, and ultimately interpose himself before the witness in this difficult situation. Their shared identity as Jewish survivors may well be at the root of this behavior. Nevertheless, it leads to aspects of the testimony becoming lost, ambiguities being resolved, and a sense of personal experience fading into the background behind statements of fact. This may, of course, be in line with what Buki wants at this moment: he prefers to respond to question prompts rather than speak freely, and so we should be careful not to assume that his wishes are entirely at odds with what is happening. Nevertheless, the situation is fraught with difficulty for both interpreter and witness, who both appear to be faced with unresolvable dilemmas arising from the way the communication is structured and the nature of Buki's testimony.

These brief extracts introduce us to the complexity of the ethical decisions that interpreters are making moment by moment during these long witness statements. The rest of this chapter shows how different interpreters try to deal with these issues by adopting differing ethical stances as they work and what this means concretely for their practice and the relationships with the witnesses.

The Czech and Slovak interpreter Michael Benesch is able to exploit the level of institutional trust he has developed after taking over interpreting duties at a moment of crisis. Alongside Kapkajew, Benesch is the interpreter who seems best able to balance the competing demands of trust from the court and the witness. He does this by ensuring that everything the witness says is heard, conducting quiet negotiations with the witness over meaning, and employing metalinguistic strategies to explain his actions to the court where necessary.

A small example illustrates Benesch's sense of responsibility for the way the witness expresses certain things. When Ota Fabián (November 6, 1964, 105') is describing an appalling incident in which the defendant Schlage murders a family, Benesch corrects judge Hofmeyer on a seemingly tiny point:

1. Hofmeyer:	Das war also ein Mann + eine Frau und ein
2. Hofmeyer:	Kind
Fabián:	Ein Kind
Benesch:	Ein Mann, ein Kind und eine Frau + in der Reihenfolge hat der Zeuge ausgesagt.

1. Hofmeyer:	So that was a man + a woman and a
2. Hofmeyer:	child
Fabián:	A child
Benesch:	A man, a child and a woman + that's the order that the witness made his statement in.

Benesch does not attempt to imitate the voice or intonation of the witness, but his ethical concern here is with precision in rendering Fabián's priorities, whether or not they are relevant for the case, and he shifts to the third person in order to provide a commentary on the witness for the court. In practice this means that Benesch makes a judgment, not just about the meaning that is to be conveyed but also about what is significant from the witness's perspective and adopts a strategy based on this judgment. Here, it entails a metacommentary on the witness, but in other cases the intervention occurs earlier.

The witness Karel Klein (January 28, 1965, 7') clearly develops a relationship of trust with Benesch quite quickly: he uses Benesch as an informal source of support and information and relies on him to challenge the court when he is unhappy about how the proceedings are conducted. For example, when Hofmeyer interrupts Benesch before he has finished translating a narrative about how Klein's brother was selected for a transport, causing audible upset in the witness, Benesch intervenes to act on his behalf: "Darf ich die Aussage des Zeugen erst übersetzen, die er vorher gemacht hat?" (May I first translate the statement of the witness that he made before?).

This sequence comes very early in the testimony, and it appears to be a moment that establishes the relationship between witness and interpreter in terms of "thick" trust: the interpreter has ensured that Klein's brother is mentioned in court, and so Klein subsequently relies on him for support. From now on, we regularly hear Klein whispering to Benesch in response to what is happening (9') or looking to him for permission to say things when he is uncertain (23').

Benesch develops this kind of relationship with other witnesses, too: Ota Fabián, for example, whispers to him at a moment when the defendant Schlage is clearly lying (Fabián, November 6, 1964, 115').

These details illustrate the ambivalence of the interpreter's role here: having established the trust of the witness, he finds himself coping with a complex series of demands, ensuring that the questioning operates effectively in the court's terms while also acting as intermediary for the witness and making his own choices about what is important enough to translate for the official record. Because of the institutional trust that Benesch has earned, Hofmeyer allows the private conversations to take place without challenge so that the communication runs smoothly from the court's perspective. Benesch's positioning in relation to the witness is quite different from Grünblatt's, but it still makes clear that even an ethical decision to take up a supportive position towards the witness brings with it power imbalances in the distribution of roles in the courtroom.

Switching to a third-person stance is not unusual when the interpreter wishes to explain the witness's feelings and, possibly, protect them. These moments occur when witnesses are talking about their feelings in the moment of articulation rather than how they felt in the past, for example, when witnessing atrocities in the camp. Interpreters appear to want to shift their stance in moments like this as if there was a danger of confusing the voices at that moment. This is not so much a case of distancing but rather of shifting the terms of performance to a different form of representation that displays the interpreter's understanding of the situation and the feelings expressed by the witness while also ensuring that there can be no confusion about exactly who is confused or upset. These moments also often require the interpreter to perform acts of mediation in order to bring the interaction back on track: the shift back into first-person consecutive interpreting marks the moment when the issue has been resolved.

The Dutch interpreter Erika Diedrich frequently resorts to shifts into the third person as a way of dealing with witnesses' moments of emotional anxiety. The witness Abraham de la Penha (March 26, 1956, 1') expresses mistrust in the courtroom procedures and anxiety about whether testifying is worth the emotional risk, and Diedrich has to mediate a potential trust crisis right at the beginning, during the standard interaction establishing the witness's permission for the testimony to be recorded.

1. Hofmeyer:	Sind Sie damit einverstanden, dass ich Ihre Aussage auf ein Tonband] nehme zum Zweck der Stützung des Gedächtnisses des Gerichts?
2. Diedrich:	=eh= bent u akkoord indien we uw getuigenis op een magnetofonband opnemen?
3. de la Penha:	Ja, maar niet voor sensatie.
4. Diedrich:	=eh= der Zeuge =eh= ist einverstanden, aber nicht =eh= zu er sagt zu sensationellen Zwecken, nicht zur Veröffentlichung.
5. de la Penha:	[quiet, while Hofmeyer is speaking in background to someone else]: Want voor sensatie kom ik hier niet.
6. Hofmeyer:	[whispered conversation] (...) Bitte schön, wollen Sie es noch einmal sagen?
7. Diedrich:	Ja =eh= der Zeuge würde sich =eh= einverstanden erklären, wenn es nicht für =eh= später =eh= für publizike Zwecke.
8. Diedrich: Hofmeyer:	auch Nein, es ist nur zur Stützung des Gedächtnisses des Gerichts.
9. Diedrich:	Ja
10. de la Penha:	Niet voor sensation?
11. Diedrich:	Nee, het is alleen maar voor het recht.
12. de la Penha:	Dass sie ein Spiel davon machen, dat will ich nicht.
13. Diedrich:	=mhm=
14. de la Penha:	Het is werkelijkheid.
15. Hofmeyer:	Ist er einverstanden?
16. Diedrich:	U bent akkoord? [it seems that the witness nods here]
17. Hofmeyer:	Ja

1. Hofmeyer:	[German] Do you consent to me recording your statement on tape in order to support the court's memory?
2. Diedrich:	[Dutch] =eh= do you consent to us recording your testimony on tape?
3. de la Penha:	[Dutch] Yes, but not for sensation.
4. Diedrich:	[German] =eh= the witness =eh= consents, but not =eh= for he says for sensational reasons, not for publication.
5. de la Penha:	[Dutch, quiet, while Hofmeyer is speaking in background to someone else]: Because I have not come here for sensation.
6. Hofmeyer:	[German] Would you say that again, please?
7. Diedrich:	[German] Yes =eh= the witness would =eh= consent if it is not =eh= later =eh= for reasons of publicity
8. Diedrich: Hofmeyer:	also [German] No, it is only to support the court's memory.

9. Diedrich:	Yes.
10. de la Penha:	[Dutch] Not for sensation?
11. Diedrich:	[Dutch] No, it's only for the law.
12. de la Penha:	[German] I don't want them to play games with it.
13. Diedrich:	=mhm=
14. de la Penha:	[Dutch] It's reality.
15. Hofmeyer:	[German] Does he consent?
16. Diedrich:	[Dutch] Do you consent? [it seems that the witness nods here]
17. Hofmeyer:	Yes.

Diedrich has to clarify what de la Penha is saying and assuage his anxiety while also ensuring that the court's procedures are upheld. The exchange between de la Penha and Diedrich is very quiet, indicating perhaps that the witness is seeking reassurance through her: this is hard to interpret on the tape, though. The witness's switch to German in step 12 shows a desire to speak directly to the court and anxiety about being heard properly: his expressed fear of sensationalism shows that he regards the act of testifying as face-threatening and potentially traumatic. Here, I have made an interpretive choice since it is not absolutely clear whether the witness is addressing the court directly ("Dass Sie ein Spiel davon machen," that *you* play games with it) or speaking through the interpreter ("Dass sie ein Spiel davon machen," that *they* play games with it). This would be clear from visual cues in context. I find that the tone of voice implies a quiet conversation in the third person between the witness and interpreter about the court, but the transcribers working for the Fritz Bauer Institute make the other choice, perfectly legitimately. This is a vital moment, as it sets up the relationships for this emotional testimony, and the choice between a direct, confrontational address to the court and quiet exchange between interpreter and witness makes a fundamental difference to how we read this testimony. This moment demonstrates the limits of the information provided by the tapes and the necessity of contextualizing interpretation.

Hofmeyer switches from second-person direct address through the interpreter to third person ("Does he agree?"), characteristic of moments when he needs to restore discursive order and the established patterns of the questioning. Diedrich here has the responsibility of transmitting the judge's authority and providing an opinion about the witness; she chooses to do this by turning to address the witness directly rather than responding to the judge, which we can read as an ethical decision not to engage in a conversation *about* the witness without including him.

The emotional intensity of de la Penha's testimony seems to make this stance hard to maintain, and Diedrich frequently shifts to third-person interpreting: she appears not to have internalized the interpreter's required professional discipline and resorts to the third person at moments when the witness talks about his distress in the present. Thus, the act of representing the witness's voice becomes an act of explaining the witness.

Diedrich continues to work in this way even when de la Penha speaks German, the rhythms of the exchange ensuring that she continues to "translate" automatically. At one point, he describes how he saw the defendant Dr. Lucas on television, which prompted him to come forward to testify, even though he had spent years avoiding all mention of his experiences. Judge Hofmeyer asks whether he had heard about the trial before this moment, and the witness replies directly in German (16'):

1. de la Penha:	Ich will Ihnen sagen, ich will das nicht lesen. Ich habe so viel Elend mitgemacht, ich will das nicht lesen.
2. Diedrich:	Er will es nicht lesen. Er sagt, er hat so viel Elend mitgemacht, dass er es nicht liest.
3. de la Penha:	Das interessiert mich nicht.
4. Hofmeyer:	Ja, das ist verständlich.

1. de la Penha:	[German] I want to say to you, I don't want to read that. I have gone through so much misery, I don't want to read it.
2. Diedrich:	[German] He doesn't want to read it. He says, he has been through so much misery, that he doesn't read it.
3. de la Penha:	[German] That doesn't interest me.
4. Hofmeyer:	[German] Yes, that's understandable.

De la Penha's shift to German here is significant: he uses German when talking about the most difficult emotional issues in his testimony, which questions any easy assumptions about witnesses "falling back" into their first language(s) when under stress. He wishes to communicate these feelings directly to the court and may not have developed sufficient trust in the interpreter to transmit them properly. Diedrich is effectively reduced to conducting a parallel conversation with the judge.

When trust is absent, the relationship can degenerate to the extent that the interpreter's work is no longer really possible. The French survivor Charles Corrin (July 27, 1964) becomes increasingly frustrated with Wilhelm Schneider-Ludorff in the course of a relationship that begins with a long negotiation while Corrin is trying to orient himself at the wall plan, a task that requires the witness to step out of the question-answer structure and return to the camp in his memory (2'). At this early stage in the testimony, Corrin appears to lose confidence in the interpreter's work, and his disorientation at his inability to establish a clear connection between his memory and the spatial discourse of the trial manifests itself in frustrated criticism. The interpreter's role here is complex: rather than simply rendering what is said by both sides in the exchange, he must organize this moment in the testimony and help to orient the witness in front of the plan on the wall.

What is negotiated here, usually at the beginning of the testimony, is complex: the relationship of past and present, between the topographical knowledge of the camp complex established by the court and the experiential memory of the witness, and different ways of speaking about the camp. The interpreter must not only have a grasp of the court's discourse but also be sensitive to how the witness may be visualizing the camp's spaces and must mediate between them, while also establishing the terms of their professional relationship, potentially for the next several hours.

Corrin and Schneider-Ludorff continue to talk between themselves, breaking the pattern and thus producing discourse that is outside the court's control: Corrin's objections to the way the communication is organized challenge the court's authority and oblige the interpreter to take a stance that makes visible his place within the power structure, namely as the individual who brings the witness back under control, so that his voice can be heard in the way the court requires.

Schneider-Ludorff finds this task difficult and has to be disciplined, in this case by the defense council Gerhardt (6'), which objects to private conversations and negotiations over meaning. The interpreter's response ("Vielen Dank, Kollege," Thank you, colleague) is revealing: as a lawyer himself, he is an insider, and his reply acknowledges this status. Corrin becomes increasingly frustrated with his work, starts to complain ("Vous n'avez pas bien expliqué," You haven't explained it well, 11'), and then resorts to talking about the interpreter in the third person (13').

It would be easy to dismiss this incident as a case of poor or unprofessional interpreting, but it is also worth considering what this reveals about the position of the interpreter within the court's power structures, about the limits of permissible speech for the witness, as well as the way that the interpreter bears the brunt of the witness's anxiety and criticism. Crises of trust like this need to be resolved by reestablishing discursive authority, visibly excluding speech that does not fit: describing the interpreter's role simply in terms of mediation plays down their active involvement and shaping of the exchange in a way that ultimately does not help witnesses like Corrin or de la Penha, who, in their different ways, find the experience challenging.

Other witnesses attempt to channel their communication through the interpreter, responding to the spatial closeness by creating a relationship of intimacy that helps them come to terms with the situation in which they are testifying. For example, Helen Goldmann, whose testimony I discussed previously, responds to the challenges of giving testimony by recruiting Regina Schmidt-Ott as an ally. Goldmann talks about her fear and disorientation on arriving at Birkenau, and it is easy to read this as a statement about the difficulty of the testimony situation, in which she is standing alone in a German courtroom trying to talk about the loss of her family: developing a relationship with the sympathetic female interpreter in this situation may well be a useful coping strategy.

She often addresses replies to the interpreter rather than through her to the court, especially at moments of stress, such as when describing the killing of a baby by Franz Lucas (20'):

1. Hofmeyer:	Es fiel auf den Boden?
2. Schmidt-Ott:	The baby fell on the floor?
3. Goldmann:	Yes, ma'am.
4. Schmidt-Ott:	Ja.

1. Hofmeyer:	[German] It fell on the floor?
2. Schmidt-Ott:	[English] The baby fell on the floor?
3. Goldmann:	[English] Yes, ma'am.
4. Schmidt-Ott:	[German] Yes.

Schmidt-Ott here makes a decision not to use the pronoun "it" to refer to the baby, which would have a dehumanizing effect that the German pronoun usage, referring to the gender of the noun, does not. Small decisions like this show us an interpreter thinking about the effect of her words on her interlocutor and are an important part of the relationship that develops between them.

Goldmann is a witness whose main aim seems to be to talk about the family she lost and to testify to her feelings and experiences: she is not always able to formulate her memories in a way that contributes evidence as the court requires it, and she occasionally insists on speaking without waiting for the interpreter to work. The prosecution counsel Christian Raabe draws attention to this problem while defending the interpreter's professionalism (10'):

> Verzeihen Sie, Herr Vorsitzender. Wenn Sie vielleicht die Zeugin drauf hinweisen würden, dass sie die Dolmetscherin doch wirklich zu Ende übersetzen lässt. Denn es stellt sich heraus, dass sie, die Dolmetscherin, korrekt übersetzt, aber sie versteht anscheinend doch Ihre Fragen nicht direkt, wenn sie sie nicht übersetzen lässt.
>
> Forgive me, Your Honour. If you could perhaps inform the witness that she should let the interpreter finish translating. It turns out that she—the interpreter—is translating correctly but she [presumably meaning the witness] doesn't understand your questions properly if she doesn't allow them to be translated.

Once Goldmann has accepted the need to speak in shorter statements to allow the consecutive interpreting to take place, she adopts a more cautious attitude: when she wishes to say something that interrupts the question-answer pattern, she carefully approaches the interpreter as her ally and conduit: "Can I say something to you, and you should tell them?" (63'). Goldmann no longer feels empowered to speak on her own terms and to interrupt the authoritative structure of the exchange: in order to speak out of turn, she now needs to turn to a figure who is closer to her position in the power structure and to whom she can entrust the responsibility for speaking on her behalf. The relationship has developed in the direction of an ambivalent form of trust: Schmidt-Ott is acting in support of Goldmann, but only once she has participated in the process of disciplining her speech. Goldmann herself has very limited choices here.

Gender may be at play as a factor here: there is no direct evidence in their interaction with each other that their status as women forced into a relationship of uncomfortable closeness in this male environment has affected how they relate to each other, but as Wadensjö points out, gender is one of the factors that can be employed by participants in a communication to establish trust as a hedge against uncertainty or anxiety (Wadensjö 1998: 191). As I will show in Chapter 11, there are other examples in this courtroom of a female witness developing a seemingly warm relationship with a female interpreter, but the relationship between Karel Klein and Michael Benesch also exhibits similar features, with Klein whispering to Benesch before speaking to the court, so it is not a question of male and female interpreters necessarily acting in different ways. Female witnesses may feel able to mobilize a shared gender identity with a female interpreter to provide reassurance in this stressful, masculine environment, but it seems more likely that the perception of a shared cultural or linguistic identity allows the survivor to see the interpreter as a trusted intermediary rather than as a representative of the court.

This trial on its own does not offer enough comparative data to be able to comment on gender as a determining factor in specific relationships, and the interpreting is so dominated by the presence and example of one female interpreter, Wera Kapkajew, whose relationships with the witnesses are all individual and distinct, that it is hard to establish a standard pattern. Nevertheless, it is clear that individuals' understanding of gender and their experience of the court's differential treatment of some of the female witnesses can lead them to employ gender strategically in securing a relationship of trust. In the case of Goldmann, the relationship with Schmidt-Ott secures a position from which she can speak at the expense of being able to speak freely in her own rhythm and foregrounding her own urgent concerns.

A fascinating contrast can be found in the testimony of George Preston (March 4, 1965, 12'), which I cited at the beginning of the introduction to this study. Preston is a confident and outspoken witness, who takes a particular interest in clarity and in emphasizing his own agency and expertise as an engineer. He also has a clear sense of how he wants to tell his stories and has a telling way of manipulating the rhythms of consecutive interpreting in order to achieve his aims: often, this makes Franz Schuh's task easier, but at other times Schuh loses control of the proceedings entirely. Their relationship is not antagonistic, but Preston uses the interpreting situation as part of his communicative strategy in his testimony.

Preston divides his statements into shorter elements, allowing space for interpreting: this controlled, explicit manipulation of rhythms lends powerful emphasis to his words at the expense of a narrative flow. He does, however, clearly have the overall structure of his statement in mind, as he does not lose his way despite the fragmentary nature of his speech:

1. Preston:	And we were told that this is a Lager of a Strafkommando.
2. Schuh:	Und man sagte uns, dass dies ein Lager eines Strafkommandos wäre
3. Preston:	Then a question arose at that time in our minds
4. Schuh:	Dann ergab sich bei uns die Frage zu der Zeit
5. Preston:	Did we pass all these examinations

6. Schuh:	Haben wir all diese Prüfungen bestanden
7. Preston:	to be punished in a Strafkommando?
8. Schuh:	um beim Strafkommando bestraft zu werden?
9. Preston:	This was to us erklärt later.
10. Schuh:	Das wurde uns später erklärt.

1. Preston:	[English] And we were told that this is a Lager of a Strafkommando.
2. Schuh:	[German] And we were told that this was a camp of a punishment battalion.
3. Preston:	[English] Then a question arose at that time in our minds
4. Schuh:	[German] Then the question arose at that time
5. Preston:	[English] Did we pass all these examinations
6. Schuh:	[German] Did we pass all these examinations
7. Preston:	[English] to be punished in a Strafkommando?
8. Schuh:	[German] to be punished in the punishment battalion?
9. Preston:	[English] This was to us erklärt later.
10. Schuh:	[German] This was explained to us later.

This excerpt also contains a good example of language interference: his word order in English and the appearance of the German word "erklärt" suggests that the interference arises from the German-language context of the testimony: this small example should remind us that language interference in these testimonies should not automatically be regarded as a traumatized falling-back into the language(s) of the camp but may well arise from the multilingual courtroom with its rhythms, rituals, and power imbalances, in interaction with the linguistic biography of the witness.

Schuh works calmly, taking the time that he is given by Preston, without imitating Preston's very emphatic speaking style, instead playing it down a little. There are moments when Preston begins to shout, and Schuh refrains from raising his voice: Preston's outbursts are intense, but not uncontrolled, and he continues to exploit the presence of the interpreter for dramatic effect (40'):

1. Preston:	He turned around, took that cane, hit me in my back.
2. Schuh:	Er drehte sich um, nahm diesen Stock, schlug mich über den Rücken.
3. Preston:	Once.

4. Schuh:	Einmal.
5. Preston:	Twice.
6. Schuh:	Zweimal.
7. Preston:	Three times.
8. Schuh:	Dreimal.
9. Preston:	I felt that I was paralysed.
10. Schuh:	Ich fühlte, dass ich gelähmt wäre.

1. Preston:	[English] He turned around, took that cane, hit me in my back.
2. Schuh:	[German] He turned around, took this cane, hit me across the back.
3. Preston:	[English] Once.
4. Schuh:	[German] Once.
5. Preston:	[English] Twice.
6. Schuh:	[German] Twice.
7. Preston:	[English] Three times.
8. Schuh:	[German] Three times.
9. Preston:	[English] I felt that I was paralysed.
10. Schuh:	[German] I felt that I was paralysed.

On occasion, the pressure of the situation gets the better of Preston, and, becoming agitated, he speaks in longer segments without regard for the interpreter: this occurs during a longer sequence (22') in which he describes the actions of the defendant Emil Bednarek. Preston does not lose control over what he is saying: he has a clear sense of how he wants to tell his story, and he simply allows this narrative necessity to take precedence over the rhythm of consecutive interpreting. When asked to pause for the interpreter, he apologizes to Schuh for not letting him do his job and says, "Do your duty," demonstratively accepting the prescribed rhythms of the questioning while maintaining an attitude of independence: he makes clear that this is his choice and that he is not a subordinate but the "main event." The relationship between the two of them is unusual in the sense that Preston establishes his wish to control the communication and expresses his impatient acceptance of the court's imposed rhythms, treating the interpreter as more than simply a means to have his words translated, but as an opportunity to make his testimony more effective.

The remainder of this chapter will explore some aspects of the work of Wera Kapkajew at the trial. Her presence and voice so dominated the parts of the proceedings in which witnesses spoke through an interpreter that we should pay greater attention to the relationships that she developed with the witnesses with whom she worked. There are good reasons for this beyond the sheer volume of work that she did for the trial: the individuality of the witnesses, the differences in their experiences and manner of narrating, and their varying attitudes toward the court present the interpreter with a variety of challenges.

In this section, I will discuss some shorter excerpts from a number of different testimonies, with no aspiration to cover anywhere near all of the Polish- and Russian-speaking witnesses with whom Kapkajew worked. My aim is to illustrate some aspects of Kapkajew's strategic self-positioning in her relationships with the witnesses in order to make comparisons with the other interpreters and to illustrate some of the complex ethical issues that arise during these sessions. In later chapters, I will discuss individual testimonies in more detail in order to show how these relationships develop through time.

I have narrowed down the discussion to a handful of aspects that help to show the role of the interpreter in displaying the witness to the court: creating the impression of a "good" or "bad" witness and helping to determine how witnesses are heard in public. Kapkajew's practice is clearly focused on creating relationships with the participants—sometimes cordial, sometimes critical and tense—rather than rendering speech word for word. She reorganizes and clarifies statements, sometimes reducing ambiguity and passing over features of speech that suggest inarticulacy and emotional difficulty while at other times introducing features that intensify the uncertainty of the witness's speech. Despite her public reputation for directly imitating the voices of the witnesses, her vocal performance indicates a more strategic sense of what needs to be emphasized in order to clarify a point or represent a witness's attitude toward the communication in the courtroom.

I suggest that she quickly makes a decision about the witness's reliability and their needs in the situation and adjusts her practice in light of this assessment. Thus, a judgment is made about the quality of the witness's account before it reaches the rest of the court. This can result in moments of extraordinary power when she collaborates with a witness in the narration of an experience, but it can also produce moments where a poor impression is created of a witness who is struggling with the emotional difficulty of the communication or the perceived inappropriateness of the questioning. At times, she goes out of her way to engage in face-saving behavior on behalf of the witness, while at others, she takes the side of the court.

Unlike the other interpreters—with the possible exception of Michael Benesch—she has accumulated sufficient trust with the court (both "thin" and "thick," based on the relationships she has developed) to engage in behaviors that are not permitted for the other interpreters, and she is rarely challenged. She feels confident enough to challenge both prosecution and defense on behalf of the witness and joins in discussions about meaning and memory without being asked. In other words, she helps to negotiate questions of testimony and truth during the proceedings. In the following, I will look at some examples of how Kapkajew organizes witnesses' speech, intervening on their behalf, and then at moments where she acts preemptively as part of the court's disciplinary apparatus.

On occasion, Kapkajew acts explicitly on behalf of the witness, challenging the authority of court officials: it is notable that she is most likely to challenge members of the defense team, indicating a certain impatience with their strategies and attitudes toward the witnesses. During his testimony on October 8, 1964, the Polish witness Józef Kret begins to narrate a story about the escape of a comrade, which led to collective punishment. As I set out in Chapter 1, the witnesses often struggled to tell their stories on their own terms: it is not so much a case of helplessly expressing their own suffering but of having a clear idea of what is important, what should be included in the narration, and how it should be shaped. For the most part, witnesses shape their speech to conform to the way they understand the requirements of the court, but there are moments when their speech has to be explicitly challenged and altered. The interpreters play a key role in this process, and in this case, Kapkajew intervenes on behalf of the witness when his chosen narration is dismissed by the defense council Hans Fertig (56'):

1. Kret:	W czerwcu z powodu ucieczki jednego z naszego komanda, ale nie z pracy, tylko on nie poszedł do pracy, został w obozie i uciekł. Ale mimo tego zaprowadzono nas do =eh= do bunkra i jedną noc siedzieliśmy w bunkrze.
2. Kapkajew:	Das war nämlich wegen der Flucht eines unserer Kameraden
3. Kapkajew: Fertig:	in einem Arbeitskommando. Der ist Herr Zeuge, den Grund möcht ich
4. Fertig:	der ist hier uninteressant.
5. Kapkajew:	Darf ich aber trotzdem bitte beenden
6. Kapkajew: Fertig:	oder muss ich aufhören? Ja, bitte schön, ja.
7. Hofmeyer:	Na bitte, dann beenden Sie,

8. Kapkajew:	Na, ich weiß es nicht, ich frage ja nur.
9. Hofmeyer:	Ja, bitte schön.

1. Kret:	[Polish] In June because of the escape of one of our kommando, but not from work, as he didn't go to work but stayed in the camp and escaped. But because of this we were taken to =eh= to the bunker and were imprisoned there for one night.
2. Kapkajew:	[German] You see, that was because of the escape of one of our comrades
3. Kapkajew: Fertig:	[German] In a work commando. He [German] Mr. witness, I don't want the reason
4. Fertig:	[German] it is not relevant here.
5. Kapkajew:	[German] May I still finish
6. Kapkajew: Fertig:	[German] or should I stop? [German[Yes, please go on, yes.
7. Hofmeyer:	[German] Fine, please, do finish.
8. Kapkajew:	[German] Well, I don't know, I'm just asking.
9. Hofmeyer:	[German] Yes, please go ahead.

Kapkajew here intervenes in order to allow the witness to be heard fully, packaging her objection as a question about correct procedure; in order to do this, she has to appeal to a higher authority than the defense council, calling on a reservoir of trust that she has accumulated with Judge Hofmeyer, which allows her to take a strong line, with a tone bordering on sarcasm.

Such questions of audibility, agency, and authority over the shape of the narrative are negotiated constantly within the complex power structure of the court: if an interpreter has sufficient status to appeal to the judge, then they can contribute significantly to the way a testimony is shaped and how the voice is heard. But this procedure confirms the discursive authority of the judge rather than challenging it.

For the most part, negotiations like this take place below the radar of the rest of the court, with the interpreter making small adjustments in order to avoid the witness appearing in a poor light: effectively, Kapkajew is making decisions about the witness and their testimony, how the testimony reflects upon the witness and vice versa. Interventions may be small, such as when Kapkajew quietly "corrects" a statement by Stanisław Głowa before translating it (June 11, 1964, 228'). At the end of his testimony, Głowa wishes to make clear that he is motivated purely by a desire for truth rather than hatred, but he uses the word "zawiść" (envy), which Kapkajew corrects to "nienawiść" (hate), reestablishing a standard formula used by many witnesses when insisting on their lack of personal bias.

Głowa is a witness who speaks slowly and methodically, leaving space for the interpreter to work and taking care of the accuracy of his account. He is also careful to be precise about what he could see and not see: a vital element of the prosecution strategy in order to secure clear evidence. Characteristic of Kapkajew's practice in these moments is to expand and clarify Głowa's often terse statements. Here, when describing what he could see of the murder of prisoners by Klehr using phenol injections, he discusses the particular case of the murder of a prisoner whom he knew. When challenged by Hofmeyer, who reminds him that he had previously claimed to have witnessed this event directly, Głowa defends himself somewhat impatiently; Kapkajew expands his statement, making it more precise while also softening the tone, although it still provokes an impatient reaction from Hofmeyer (164'):

1. Głowa:	Nie. Mogłem, nie powiedziałem, że widziałem, tylko mogłem.
2. Kapkajew:	Ich habe nicht gesagt, ich habe es gesehen. Ich habe gesagt, ich konnte es gesehen haben.
3. Hofmeyer:	Ja, was soll ich denn *damit* anfangen?

1. Głowa:	[Polish] No. I could have, I didn't say I saw, only I could have.
2. Kapkajew:	[German] I didn't say I saw it. I said I could have seen it.
3. Hofmeyer:	[German] Yes and what am I supposed to do with *that*?

Głowa's testimony is marked by some impatient reactions to questioning and his insistence on the accuracy of his memory: Kapkajew works in support of his stance, carrying out facework on his behalf where necessary. This pattern is repeated with witnesses for whom Kapkajew clearly feels some sympathy: for the most part, educated Polish former political prisoners who are able to tell their story consistently and who accept the court's authority while occasionally objecting to the strategies of the defense. For such witnesses, unless there is a specific issue, Kapkajew is willing to act in their interests while translating and making decisions about what is important and how the testimony should be heard.

Kapkajew tends to work on behalf of the witnesses when they are under pressure from cross-questioning: this occurs frequently when they are challenged on seeming discrepancies between their statements in open court and their earlier depositions. Jan Sikorski (June 19, 1964) tends to retreat into terseness when challenged on whether his memory is faulty and why there are discrepancies between his statements in court and his original interrogation (98' and 104'):

1. Sikorski:	No, pamiętam to samo, co teraz.
2. Kapkajew:	Ich erinnere mich, dass ich genau das gleiche, was ich jetzt ausgesagt habe, auch damals sagte.

1. *Sikorski:*	*[Polish] Well, I remember the same as now.*
2. *Kapkajew:*	*[German] I remember that I said exactly the same back then as I have just said now.*

1. Prosecutor Kügler:	Von den Medikamenten, die aus diesen Koffern heraussortiert wurden, kamen die zur SS-Apotheke, oder kamen sie zur Häftlingsapotheke?
2. Kapkajew:	Czy lekarstwa, które były wysortowane, wzięte z tych =eh= kufrów, czy one przychodzily do apteki więźniarskiej czy do apteki esesmanskiej?
3. Sikorski:	+ i tu i tu.
4. Kapkajew:	Sowohl in die eine als auch in die andere Apotheke.

1. Prosecutor Kügler:	The medicines that were selected from the suitcases, did they go to the SS pharmacy or did they go to the prisoners' pharmacy?
2. Kapkajew:	Did the medicines that were sorted, taken out of the =eh= trunks, did they go to the prisoners' pharmacy or to the SS pharmacy?
3. Sikorski:	+ to this one and that one.
4. Kapkajew:	Both to the one and the other pharmacy.

Sikorski clearly sees Kapkajew as an ally: when they return from a break in this long session, he shows his confidence in her by confessing tiredness in a private conversation: "Ciężko pracuję dzisiaj" (I'm working hard today, 148').

Witnesses often see the interpreter as a source of emotional support and communication channel to the court when they are finding things difficult.

Tadeusz Szymański, for example, suffers symptoms of stress during his testimony (January 11, 1965), developing a nosebleed, and Kapkajew offers support quietly in the moments before deciding what to translate and how: these pre-translation exchanges are important in developing the trust of the witness, as they offer a space for reassurance before the testimony is subject to the judgment of the court and the public. On one occasion, though, Szymański pushes back against what he seems to perceive as an attempt to get him to admit weakness or to stop him speaking. When asked to describe the gassing of a group of seven hundred typhus patients (5'), he pauses, saying to Kapkajew: "Ciężka sprawa jest" (this is a difficult issue). Kapkajew suggests to him that he should take a break—"Niech pan przerwę zrobi" (take a break)—but he refuses curtly ("Nie," no) and continues.

Henryk Porębski (August 18, 1964) struggles with his emotions when trying to orient himself on the wall plan of Birkenau, and asks Kapkajew to intervene on his behalf (116'):

1. Porębski:	Pani powie sędziemu, że nie wytrzymam.
2. Kapkajew:	Er hält das nicht mehr lange aus.

1. Porębski:	[Polish] Tell the judge that I can't bear it.
2. Kapkajew:	[German] He can't bear it for much longer.

Kapkajew's words appear to blend a translation with her own assessment of the witness's ability to continue: she shifts the force of Porębski's words, ensuring that he does continue rather than stopping straight away, which is what he appears to want.

Barbara Pozimska (March 4, 1965) loses the thread of her narrative when listing the members of her family who were killed, and Kapkajew encourages her to continue (23'):

1. Pozimska:	[very quiet] A teraz nie wiem, co ja chciałam powiedzieć + ja + [loud] wszyscy z mojej rodziny: wujkowie, ciotki, kuzyni, zostali w Oświęcimiu.
2. Kapkajew:	+ Die ganze Familie von mir, meine allen Verwandten, Onkel, Tanten, Vetter, die blieben alle in Auschwitz.
3. Pozimska:	Der eine =oh=
4. Kapkajew:	Niech pani mówi.

1. Pozimska:	[very quiet, Polish] But now I don't know what I wanted to say + I + [loud] all of my family, uncles, aunts, cousins, remained in Auschwitz.
2. Kapkajew:	[German] + The whole of my family, all my relatives, uncles, aunts, cousins, they all remained in Auschwitz.
3. Pozimska:	[German] One of the =oh=
4. Kapkajew:	[Polish] Do speak.

On occasion, the witnesses' emotional difficulties become part of a conversation between Kapkajew and other participants. During the testimony of Witold Dowgint-Nieciuński (January 29, 1965, 54'), Judge Hofmeyer sharply criticizes an audience member for lounging in their seat ("Sie sollen sich hier nicht so bequem hinsetzen. Das gehört sich nicht in einem Gerichtssaal." Don't lounge in your seat like that. That's not appropriate in a courtroom) and then asks Kapkajew to reassure the witness that he is not being criticized. Her response is striking, indicating that the witness has no ear for what is happening around him: ("Er ist vollkommen verstrickt in seine Erzählung, er hat es gar nicht bemerkt" (He is completely tied up in his account, he didn't notice it at all).

During the testimony of Leon Czekalski on May 8, 1964 (4'), Kapkajew intervenes more explicitly on behalf of the witness, whose testimony begins with an argument over whether he has colluded with other witnesses that seems to throw him into confusion for a while. The defense is trying to prove that he had colluded with another witness before testifying, and the questioning comes down to whether they arrived at the court together. The accused Willy Frank claims to have seen them arriving, while Czekalski says that he came in a taxi, whereupon the defense demands to see the receipt. Defense counsel Laternser and prosecutor Vogel argue for a while about how the witnesses' expenses are paid (do they submit receipts or receive a lump sum for travel?). Eventually, Hofmeyer dismisses the argument since it is irrelevant why the witness does not possess a receipt ("Also jedenfalls, er hat keine Quittung mehr." Anyway, he doesn't have his receipt anymore), and Kapkajew intervenes in support: "Die anderen haben sie auch nicht" (The others don't have them either). Kapkajew's intervention shows that she is well informed about the other witnesses and has been working with them outside the courtroom: she helps them with expenses and documents and here uses this information to support an argument about Czekalski's credibility.

Czekalski's testimony is characterized by arguments over the credibility and consistency of his testimony, and Kapkajew frequently intervenes in exchanges between defense, prosecution, and judge, exceeding her role in the courtroom by speaking up for the witness and providing information. On the defensive for much of his testimony, Czekalski appears to see Kapkajew as his channel of communication with the court, often addressing her directly when answering questions: "Wie pani, tego nie wiem" (You know, I don't know that, 95'). She acts as support, representative, and face-saving possibility, to the extent that he whispers to her to ask permission to speak on his own terms. Depending on the situation, Kapkajew encourages him or stops him from speaking, effectively acting for the court in enforcing its order (169' and 177'):

1. Hofmeyer:	Sind bezüglich des Bednarek noch Fragen des Gerichts?
2. Czekalski:	[quiet, to Kapkajew] Ja bym chciał powiedzieć o Höcker, Höcker, jak
3. Kapkajew:	Tak, chwileczkę, proszę pana!

1. Hofmeyer:	[German] Are there any more questions from the court concerning Bednarek?
2. Czekalski:	[quiet, to Kapkajew, Polish] I would like to ask about Höcker, Höcker, how
3. Kapkajew:	[Polish] Yes, one moment, please!

1. Czekalski:	Tak, raz był wypadek z tym księdzem, można powiedzieć?
2. Kapkajew:	No, niech pan mówi! Es war einmal ein Fall mit dem Priester.

1. Czekalski:	[Polish] Yes, there was once an incident with the priest, can I say this?
2. Kapkajew:	[Polish] Well, do speak! [German] There was once an incident with the priest.

These small incidents show the ambiguous position of the interpreter in the power hierarchy: her task is to help the witness be heard, but in order to do this she has to accept the discursive order of the court, encouraging him to speak when it is appropriate and preventing him from interrupting proceedings when it is not.

For the most part, witnesses are happy to develop a positive working relationship with Kapkajew, as she provides opportunities to intervene in their own interests. Maria Świderska-Świeratowa, who gave testimony on May 25, 1964, is clearly nervous about confronting the accused directly in court and so speaks quietly through Kapkajew when she wants to contradict their evidence. At a moment when Kaduk denies having ever been in Birkenau, she speaks under her breath to Kapkajew, using her as a mouthpiece to challenge him. She uses German here to emphasize her point, picking up on Kaduk's denial, so Kapkajew is in effect relaying a message rather than translating (93'):

1. Kaduk:	Habe in Birkenau überhaupt keinen Dienst getan.
2. Hofmeyer:	Ja.
3. Świderska-Świeratowa:	[whispers] Ich habe ihn gesehen.
4. Hofmeyer:	Würden Sie das der Frau Zeugin
5. Hofmeyer: Kapkajew:	noch mal sagen? Ja, die flüstert eben, ich habe ihn gesehen, er war dort.
6. Hofmeyer:	Er war dort
7. Hofmeyer: Świderska-Świeratowa:	Kaduk. Ja.

1. Kaduk:	[German] I was never on duty in Birkenau.
2. Hofmeyer:	[German] Yes.
3. Świderska-Świeratowa:	[whispers, German] I saw him.
4. Hofmeyer:	[German] Would you say that to the witness
5. Hofmeyer: Kapkajew:	again? [German] Yes, she's whispering, I saw him, he was there.
6. Hofmeyer:	[German] He was there
7. Hofmeyer: Świderska-Świeratowa:	Kaduk. [German] Yes.

Kapkajew at times manages the potential conflict that arises when witnesses want to speak in their own way by employing politeness forms strategically. Franciszek Znamirowski (September 10, 1964) is prevented by the judge from completing a narrative about Bednarek's treatment of prisoners: Hofmeyer wants to move the testimony on and turns to one of the defense counsels. Znamirowski tries to insist in a direct way, but Kapkajew softens his objection into a polite request, ensuring that space is made for his testimony without making a direct challenge to the court (14'):

1. Znamirowski:	[whispers] Co do bicia + jeszcze chcę coś powiedzieć, co do bicia.
2. Kapkajew:	Entschuldigen Sie bitte, Herr Rechtsanwalt. Ich möchte noch etwas über die Schläge erzählen.

1. Znamirowski:	[whispers, Polish] About the beating + I still want to say something about the beating
2. Kapkajew:	[German] Excuse me, please, defense counsel, I would like to say something else about the beating.

Kapkajew works by developing cordial relationships with some of the witnesses, in particular, Polish former political prisoners who are articulate and confident in their testimony: shared background, whether national or class-based, may play a role here since these shared factors are available as resources to build trust in an interpreted exchange. Class distinctions play an important role in the exchanges in the courtroom, in particular, with the careful use of professional and academic titles. The professor of medicine Władysław Fejkiel (May 29, 1964), who had worked as a doctor in the camp (see Stengel 2022: 201–3), is consistently addressed as "Herr Professor," and Kapkajew also uses this formal address in Polish—"panie profesorze"—even when the judges or other participants have not: she does not simply pass on the politeness formulae but demonstrates her active participation in this professional group identity across national boundaries. With Fejkiel, she is also careful to give the witness space to show that he has understood the German questions before she translates ("Pan zrozumiał, panie profesorze?" Did you understand, professor? 120') and laughs with him on occasion when he employs camp slang in a sardonic way (6'):

1. Fejkiel:	Od skrajnego muzułmaństwa, takiego poniżenia, stałem się w jednym dniu dygnitarzem obozowym.
2. Kapkajew:	[laughs] In einem Augenblick, binnen eines Tages wurde ich aus der größten Erniedrigung als Muselmann plötzlich zu einer Persönlichkeit im Lager geworden.

1. Fejkiel:	[Polish] From the most extreme state of being a muzulman, such degradation, I became in a single day a camp dignitary.
2. Kapkajew:	[laughs, German] In a single moment, within a day, from the greatest degradation as muzulman I became a personality in the camp.

A similarly cordial relationship develops with the Polish doctor Stanisław Kłodziński, who gave testimony on May 15 and 22, 1964. Their relationship here is very interesting: Kłodziński often tries to speak German, which he is encouraged to do, but his testimony is characterized by a significant degree of shifting between German and Polish, which leads to laughter between him and the interpreter. Kapkajew also on occasion intervenes to comment on his German, for example correcting his verb tenses when he confuses past and present ("nahmen" where he says "nehmen") or his syntax and lexis, even though it is clear that Hofmeyer understands (May 15, 1964, 22'):

1. Kłodziński	Und bei Schlägerei waren wir nach Block 28 durchgeführt.
2. Kapkajew:	Und unter Schlägen
3. Kapkajew: Hofmeyer:	wurden wir dann in Block 28 geführt. Ja.

1. Kłodziński:	[German] And under this brawl we were led to Block 28.
2. Kapkajew:	[German] And all the while being beaten
3. Kapkajew: Hofmeyer:	We were then led to Block 28. Yes.

Her wish to ensure that he sounds "respectable" ends up obstructing the voice of a Polish speaker with a striking way of speaking German: the word "Schlägerei" doesn't quite fit the context—it is closer in meaning to a "brawl"—but it gives a very colorful impression of the mass violence being meted out.

Kapkajew occasionally intervenes directly on the witness's behalf, engaging in behavior that is not tolerated by the court from the other interpreters. On October 16, 1964, there was an important moment when the testimonies of two witnesses, Arie Fuks and Anna Palarczyk, are tested against each other in trying to determine whether it was possible to identify precisely individual SS men on the Birkenau ramp. Though Fuks's testimony is considered by the court to be rather confusing—specifying exactly where they were standing and what they could see during the confusion and noise of the arrival of a transport was one of the most difficult tasks for a witness—Kapkajew insists throughout that he can clarify the issue, engaging in a long private dialogue with him while Hofmeyer consults with the prosecution and speaking on his behalf: "Herr Vorsitzender, darf der Zeuge das noch mal erklären? Er hat zugehört und sagt, er kann das ganz genau schildern" (Your Honour, may the witness explain it again? He has been listening, and says that he can describe it exactly, 54').

As interpreter, she plays a key role here in managing this exchange for the benefit of the witness, objecting when others claim that they cannot understand what he means: when a speaker, in a moment of frustration, says "Ja, dann ist es aber trotzdem nicht verständlich, Herr Direktor," she responds, "Doch" (Yes, but it is still not understandable, Your Honor / Yes it is, 56'). In this way, she insists on intervening in exchanges between the prosecution, defense, and the presiding judge, adapting and expanding the role of interpreter in support of the witness.

The microphone also allows us to hear Kapkajew's reactions to statements by the accused. During the testimony of Stefan Lazanowicz (September 9, 1964), we hear her gasp of disbelief, alongside many people in the audience, at a moment when Baretzki claims to have directly disobeyed orders by refusing to mistreat prisoners (47'):

> Aber einen Strick um den Hals habe ich nie einem Häftling gelegt. Wenn mir der Kommandant gesagt hat: "Tun Sie dem den Strick um den Hals," habe ich gesagt: "Das mache ich nicht" [audible gasp] Das habe ich niemals gemacht in Auschwitz.
>
> But I never put a noose around a prisoner's neck. Whenever the Commandant said, "Put the noose around his neck," I said, "I'm not doing that" [audible gasp] I never did that in Auschwitz.

The involvement of the audience here is a reminder of the embodied presence of the participants in the testimony situation: all are watching and reacting to each other, and the interpreter at this moment shifts her status to that of an implicated observer reacting along with the others, before resuming her professional role.

The complexity of the situation, and the overlapping and often conflicting interests and aims of the participants, can lead to conflicts, especially when the witnesses do not feel that they are being allowed to speak as they wish. Kapkajew has the presence of mind to deflect challenges to her onto others: Erwin Bartel (August 27, 1964), who has been following the German of the defense counsel Hans Laternser, becomes impatient with the way that Kapkajew has been summarizing his questions and demands that she translate them more accurately: "Niech pani posłucha! Niech precyzuje dokładnie pytania" (Listen to me! Ask the question right away more precisely, 193'). Kapkajew ensures that the witness's raised voice is not viewed as a criticism of her (which it is) by translating as if it is an attack on Laternser: "Wenn Sie genau die Frage präzisieren, in welchem Block ich untergebracht war zu diesem Zeitpunkt, als diese Kriegsgefangenen kamen, dann ist es wahrscheinlich der Block 25" (If you formulate the question more precisely, which block I was in at this point, when the prisoners of war arrived, then it is probably Block 25).

This subtle strategy of shifting responsibility gives us a sense of what is at stake for the interpreter's professional status in this complex situation. It is not always clear whether Kapkajew is working in support of the witness or whether her aim is to ensure that the communication runs smoothly, meaning that both she and the witness preserve face; by contrast, Moritz Grünblatt's strategies present more of a direct challenge to the court's procedures. The interpreter's interest in ensuring the smooth operation of the exchanges also means that she works at the first line of discipline on behalf of the court, anticipating and defusing conflicts and potential criticisms of the court before they are transmitted in translation.

Where a witness becomes frustrated with the court's procedures or challenges, Kapkajew will intervene to ensure that the communication does not break down, which is likely to involve enforcing discipline over the witness's speech. Where conflicts begin to arise with a witness, which cannot be resolved "under the radar," Kapkajew may shift to a more direct form of disciplinary action, characteristically involving instructions to allow her to work and to listen to the question. This tends to happen during a testimony in which the witness becomes frustrated that they are not able to make their statement in a manner of their choosing.

This becomes an issue with the handful of Soviet survivors for whom Kapkajew interprets. They come to court with a clear idea of what they want to say and react with frustration or incredulity when challenged or questioned on things that seem to be irrelevant. Dr. Aleksandr Lebedev (October 1, 1964), former Soviet POW and current Soviet delegate to the IAC (Stengel 2022: 369–70), is a witness who is unwilling to conform to the requirements of consecutive interpreting, tending to talk over Kapkajew, insisting on finishing longer statements, and often avoiding direct answers to questions.

In the following exchange, we see different conceptions of what is important at work: defense counsel Aschenauer is trying to establish whether Lebedev saw the individual killing of small children by SS men, while the witness wants to describe the industrialized mass killing at Birkenau. This is interpreted as evasiveness, and the interpreter herself eventually loses patience with him, taking on another role by insisting that he gives specific answers to questions rather than continuing with his narration (261'):

1. Aschenauer:	Ja Herr Lebedev, Sie sind Mediziner + Wie sind, sind die Kinder sofort tot gewesen?
2. Kapkajew:	Господин Лебедев, вы =eh= врач
3. Lebedev: Kapkajew:	Ja медик =eh= и что + дети сразу же были мёртвы?

4. Lebedev:	Нет. Это же это же мы видели, когда были на Биркенау когда = eh= жгли во рвах эсэсовцы. Крематории не успевали пере- пере- перемалывать.
5. Kapkajew:	На вопрос, пожалуйста, отвечайте. Das war in Birkenau, als wir gesehen haben, wie die SS-Männer in den in den Graben =eh= Gräben die =eh= Menschen =eh= verbrannten. Die Krematorien =eh= konnten ja das alles nicht erfassen.

1. Aschenauer:	[German] Yes Herr Lebedev, you are a physician + How did, were the children dead right away?
2. Kapkajew:	[Russian] Gospodin Lebedev, you are =eh= a doctor
3. Lebedev: Kapkajew:	[German] Yes [Russian] physician =eh= and what + were the children dead right away?
4. Lebedev:	[Russian] No. It was it was we saw, when we were in Birkenau when =eh= the SS men burnt them in pits. The crematoria were not capable of + grinding
5. Kapkajew:	[Russian] Answer the question, please. [German] That was in Birkenau, when we saw how the SS men =eh= burnt =eh= people in the in the pit =eh= pits. The crematoria =eh= could not contain it all.

Small exchanges like these show that it is not always possible to draw a clear distinction between support for the witness and disciplinary action: the interpreter is trying to ensure that the exchange runs smoothly, which involves negotiating with the witness in the space before translation into German. Here, she tries impatiently to move him back onto the court's line of questioning while at the same time ensuring that Lebedev's words are heard: supporting the witness means maintaining the discursive authority of the court while still creating spaces for the priorities of the witness to come through. It is an unequal relationship, however, and the witness is dependent on the way that the interpreter operates within the power discrepancy by assuming different roles in the exchange.

I will conclude this chapter with an uncomfortable moment during the testimony of Andrei Pogozhev (October 23, 1964, 53'), whose memoir I cited in the introduction to this study. Here, Kapkajew makes a point of demonstrating her secure status within the institution by making a potentially humiliating joke at the witness's expense while he is describing the experience of standing naked waiting to see who will be selected for death. Pogozhev wants to act this out for the court and asks permission: "Я могу показать, как это?" (May I show how it was?) Hofmeyer responds that it is not necessary but allows him to do it, prompting Kapkajew to comment "Nicht ausziehen" (Don't get undressed). Pogozhev wishes to act out the situation, making a physical link to the past using his body: Kapkajew's intervention puts him in his place by making this seem ridiculous. This mocking or ironic speech is rare, but it demonstrates something about Kapkajew's confidence in her own position and the lower status of the witness.

The examples discussed here are small and may seem inconsequential when we consider what the witnesses are describing and the great questions of guilt and innocence that are being negotiated, but they show how interpreters employ different strategies to create relationships that allow them to work, whether in support of the witnesses, of their own professional status or of the authority of the court. The constant, complex, moment–by-moment negotiations of trust are key to the feeling of witnesses that they are in a situation where they can make their voices heard.

These examples have all been taken out of their context and so do not give a complete picture of the relationships between witnesses and interpreters in their development through time. The final chapters in this book explore individual relationships as they develop, showing how the interpreter, the witness, and other participants interact through these often very long testimonies.

Part IV

The Work of the Interpreter Wera Kapkajew

11

The Testimony of Anna Palarczyk: Negotiating Trust

The final two chapters throw the spotlight onto the details of the relationship between interpreter and witness. It involves individuals who we have encountered before—the interpreter Wera Kapkajew, the Polish former political prisoner Anna Palarczyk, and the Polish-French-Jewish survivor Simon Gotland—but instead of picking out illustrative examples, it takes a longer view of their testimony, showing how the relationships between the participants develop through time. The chapter aims to give a sense of the dynamics of the interaction during a long testimony, whether it is one of tension or mutual support, and how the witness may take opportunities to pursue their own ends.

From the interpreter's perspective, I intend to explore different sides of the work of Kapkajew, who, as we have seen, took on the lion's share of the interpreting at the public phase of the trial. She had worked hard at accumulating a substantial reservoir of institutional trust and had developed a reputation for competence and a high public profile; the face she presents to the institution of the court stresses her professionalism, expert knowledge, and the complexity of the material. Beyond the court's internal, institutional processes, a specific view of her practice had developed that saw her as an interpreter who "voiced" the witnesses, providing access to the emotional quality of their speech as well as the content. Kapkajew herself encouraged this view of her performance in her public statements, commenting on interpreting as an emotional, embodied experience while sidestepping suggestions that she identified with the witnesses.

It is clear that she developed sympathy with some of the witnesses, as her audible exasperation with certain lines of questioning from the defense makes clear. Witnesses' apparent views of her person and work—as far as we can reconstruct it from the way they interact with her in court—vary considerably, from frustration through distance to evident sympathy. Witnesses are often monitoring her work, which may arise from the urgency of the need to have one's voice heard as much as from mistrust. We know that Kapkajew worked with some witnesses outside the courtroom, whether acting as liaison interpreter for Emmi Bonhoeffer's group of volunteers or helping witnesses with form filling and managing bureaucracy. For example, at the end of the testimony of Bartosz Oziemkowski (June 18, 1964, 81'), we hear her walking away with the witness, talking about his expenses payments. Although we know little about the relationships that developed through these contacts—and nothing about whether the other interpreters also helped in this way—it is a sign that she was working hard at developing personal trust and a positive reputation with the witnesses as well as the court.

Given the extent of Kapkajew's professional involvement with the first Frankfurt trial, it would be impossible to do justice to every witness testimony, every translation, and every facet of her work. I have endeavored in this study to devote space to the work of the other translators and interpreters in order to provide an impression of the variety of survivor voices and experiences and the range of individual approaches to the ethical problems that arose from the trial's communicative practices. This has, however, perhaps inevitably produced a distorted impression of the weight of the work carried out by this one individual and her genuinely substantial and defining contribution.

There would be many testimonies that would merit this kind of detailed attention: the highly emotionally charged testimony of Józef Kral, during which the witness comes into conflict with the interpreter, for example, contrasted with a testimony where the relationship is more harmonious and Kapkajew solves any problems "below the surface," as in the case of Tadeusz Paczuła. I particularly regret not having had space for two aspects of Kapkajew's work: interpreting for the Soviet witnesses, a remarkable group of survivors whose experiences as POWs in Auschwitz are still marginal to memory of the Holocaust, and the many Polish witnesses who described in intimate and heartbreaking detail the murder of prisoners with phenol injections. This latter complex of testimonies contains an extraordinary variety of witness voices and attitudes, with very different linguistic strategies for dealing with experiences of extreme violence described in minute detail; the interpreter is confronted with the necessity to organize these exhausting testimonies in such a way that they are usable and comprehensible to the court.

These chapters focus on the details of two witness statements, in one of which the relationship between witness and interpreter develops in a positive, supportive way, while the other is characterized by conflicts and failures of communication. I have chosen Palarczyk's and Gotland's testimonies as they are fundamentally different, even within the constraints of the court's formal discourse rules. Both survivors arrived in Auschwitz in 1942, but under very difficult circumstances—Palarczyk as a non-Jewish Pole arrested for resistance activities and Gotland as a Polish Jew deported from France. Both had spent enough time in the camp to gather significant knowledge and understanding but of fundamentally different things: Palarczyk can give detailed testimony on the mistreatment of prisoners by individual SS men in the Main Camp, while Gotland spent most of his time at Birkenau, surviving the Sonderkommando and moving through a number of spaces before ending his time at the camp in at "Canada."

Having remained in Poland after liberation, Palarczyk has a secure position to speak from as a Polish resister; this, and a naturally exuberant personality, allows her to control aspects of her testimony and speak confidently, occasionally challenging lines of questioning. She develops a relationship with Kapkajew that appears to be trusting and successfully adopts the interpreter as ally and support. Gotland has more difficulty speaking confidently and consistently, his testimony is often contradictory and confused, and the relationship with Kapkajew is tenser and more fraught. They both have a certain command of German, but their language use is very different, with Palarczyk employing her German to monitor the translation, to intervene on her own behalf, and to build the relationship with the interpreter, while Gotland speaks in a powerfully hybrid manner that the court is unable to work with. In both cases, we observe how an interpreter uses her status and the degree of trust that she has accumulated to develop a quite different relationship with each witness.

Anna Palarczyk

Anna Palarczyk (née Szyller) was born in 1918 into a middle-class professional family in Kraków. She studied law in Kraków until the university was closed after the German occupation. In her Polish testimony to the United States Holocaust Memorial Museum (USHMM), given in August 1996, she describes how she was arrested by the Gestapo in June 1942 as a member of the Związek Walki Zbrojnej (Union of Armed Struggle), the resistance organization that was the precursor of the Armia Krajowa (Home Army).[1]After interrogation, she was deported to Auschwitz on August 17, 1942, and remained there until the liberation of the camp. In the introduction, I cited Anna Palarczyk's comments, thirty years later, on her relationship with the interpreter during her testimony on October 15 and 16, 1964. Palarczyk's retrospective view of the experience of working with an interpreter is entirely positive; Kapkajew reformulated her words in a more articulate way and gave her the opportunity to exercise agency in giving herself time to think. There is also a strong emotional component to this recollection: Kapkajew is a "wonderful" woman whom Palarczyk will never forget and who helped her overcome her nerves.

Gaining trust and the confidence to speak in her own way is a feature of Palarczyk's overall experience of testifying. Katharina Stengel has noted that Palarczyk was initially unwilling to come to Frankfurt to give evidence but was persuaded by Hermann Langbein: Langbein was a vital intermediary who, though himself often critical of the Frankfurt judicial authorities, was able to persuade many survivors to set aside their mistrust of the German courts and their misgivings about attending.

In February 1963, Palarczyk had written to Langbein that many of her fellow survivors felt that giving testimony was pointless or did not want to be compelled to relive the past (Stengel 2022: 144). Yet in her oral history interview with Dagi Knellesen in 2005 (Knellesen 2007: 125), she presents the trial as a turning point in her attitude toward Germany and Germans:

> Ich habe keinen Kontakt mit Deutschen gehabt. Überhaupt keinen. Keine deutsche Sprache, kein deutsches Wort. Ich hatte genug! No ja, aber wir wussten über Hermann, dass das ist eine ernste Sache. Also habe ich gesagt: "Ja, ich werde fahren."
>
> I had had no contact with Germans. None at all. No German language, not a single German word. I'd had enough! Well yes, but we knew from Hermann that this is a serious business. So I said, "Yes, I'll go."

Things could potentially have gone very wrong, due to neglectful organization on the part of the judicial authorities: Palarczyk recalls how she encountered the accused, Pery Broad, in the corridor of the court building (Stengel 2022: 435). Despite this terrifying experience, the experience of meeting friendly people in Frankfurt changed her attitude toward Germany; in particular, she mentions the women who organized volunteer support services for the witnesses (Knellesen 2007: 134; Stengel 2022: 553). Palarczyk's narration about how her attitude toward Germany was transformed through personal friendships (she also mentions that her son's best friend is German) gives us an insight into the importance she places on "thick," interpersonal trust as a means of navigating through the potentially hostile or frightening environment of the trial. It helps us also to understand the way her relationship with the interpreter Kapkajew develops during her testimony: as I will show, Palarczyk appears to value the quality of their interaction as a foundation for the telling of her story. She sees the interpreter as a collaborator, going well beyond the prescribed role of linguistic conduit or mediator and beyond even the potential role of advocate for the witness. She is able to employ this trust as a resource in making her voice heard.

The relationship that develops between Palarczyk and the interpreter Wera Kapkajew during the former's testimony gives us a sense of how a witness can develop strategies that deploy "thick," interpersonal trust in order to counter institutional challenges to her perceived trustworthiness. Palarczyk presents Kapkajew with a choice between different stances: does she maintain the professional "objectivity" required by the court, or does she operate as the witness's ally? The interpreter is required to perform a balancing act throughout this testimony; one could argue that she has accumulated institutional trust in her extensive work for the court, which she can "spend" in building a relationship with the witness.

Other shared—or perceived shared—identities that Palarczyk may be able to mobilize in developing a tactical relationship between them are gender (two women speaking together before male defendants and almost entirely male court personnel); age (both born in 1918); class and professional background (both studied Polish law, Palarczyk in Kraków, Kapkajew in Vilnius); and perceived nationality (Palarczyk may perceive Kapkajew as Polish, though the latter's family were anti-Bolshevik Russian émigrés). It is also possible that the two of them had met previously since Kapkajew worked with the volunteers who looked after many of the witnesses who came to Frankfurt: there is no direct evidence for this, however.

Palarczyk negotiates trust in order to be able to exercise agency and to be heard as she wants to be. She does not enter into open conflict with Kapkajew but constantly monitors the translation and intervenes to make linguistic corrections or adjustments when it is important to her. This allows her to steer aspects of the exchange and act in her own interests, even within the overarching structure of an exchange that is determined by the judge and the court's practices. She is also able to use her relationship with Kapkajew to negotiate a potentially tricky situation when she is called back later to be confronted with challenging testimony by another survivor, Arie Fuks, as I discussed in the previous chapter. Taking my cue from the witnesses' commentaries on interpreting that I cited at the beginning, I will explore Palarczyk's testimony and the relationship that develops with her interpreter in terms of trust, agency, and language choice.

From the beginning, Palarczyk is keen to show that she understands enough German to be often able to follow the questioning. This shows that a simple conduit model of interpreting is inadequate for a trial such as this, where knowledge of German (and other languages) is shared to varying degrees by many of the participants: meaning is always leaking past the interpreter, and other parties in the exchange are able to negotiate understanding or believe that they understand what is being said. They try, in other words, to bypass both the linguistic and coordinating roles of the interpreter. This is in addition to the elements of meaning that always pass the interpreter—intonation, tone of voice, hesitations, and gesture—and can affect how the exchanges are perceived by the different parties.

Witnesses' language use is therefore never neutral or value-free, and Palarczyk's desire to participate in the German communication may represent a complex combination of factors: to be seen as a competent and helpful witness, to "get to the point" quickly, to lay claim to German as a language of the victims as well as the perpetrators, and to communicate directly with Germans beyond the courtroom who are paying attention to the trial.

At the very beginning of her testimony (October 15, 1964, 3'), Palarczyk establishes herself as someone who can understand Presiding Judge Hans Hofmeyer's questions. She interrupts the interpreter's turn, disrupting the established pattern of consecutive interpreting:

1. Hofmeyer:	Im Frühjahr 43 =eh= bekamen Sie welche Arbeit?
2. Kapkajew: Palarczyk:	Na wiosnę 43 roku Rozumiem
3. Hofmeyer:	na wiosnę 43 roku został zorganizowany u nas tak zwany Musterblock.

1. Hofmeyer:	[German] In spring 43 what work did you receive?
2. Kapkajew: Palarczyk:	[Polish] In spring 43 [Polish] I understand
3. Palarczyk:	[Polish] in spring 43 the so-called Musterblock was set up where we were.

Kapkajew is by now used to this kind of interaction with witnesses who understand German, and so she steps aside to let Palarczyk speak. Palarczyk gains in confidence, at 7' taking the unusual step of intervening to suggest a possible translation for a Polish word: where Kapkajew momentarily struggles to find the German translation for the Polish "studnia" (a well), Palarczyk steps in with the correct translation "Brunnen."

Palarczyk continues to monitor the interpreting, taking the opportunity to insist on being heard in the way she wants to be. On two occasions, she intervenes to intensify a translation of the Polish word "nagi" (naked): her motivation for this is not clear, but the fact that she repeats the intervention shows that it is important. The words she chooses in German are intensified in comparison to the Polish, stressing the prisoners' extreme vulnerability. This is about the effect in the courtroom rather than a more accurate description of what happened at the time (13'):

1. Palarczyk:	Zostałam przyjęta na rewir, w ten sposób, że po zmierzeniu gorączki kazano nam nagim stać na słońcu przez trzy godziny, aż przejechał SS-Arzt, Lagerarzt Oświęcimia. To był chyba doktor Kitt, wysoki szczupły w okularach.
2. Kapkajew:	=eh= Ich bin auf folgende Weise ins Revier gekommen, also als Kranke. Man hat mir Fieber gemessen, und dann ließ man uns uns ausziehen und wir standen nackt
3. Palarczyk:	Ganz nackt
4. Kapkajew:	ganz nackt, in prallender Sonne, stundenlang, bis ein + Lagerarzt, also SS-Arzt, aus Auschwitz kam, ich glaube, sein Name war Kitt + das war ein dunkler großer schlanker mit Brille.

1. Palarczyk:	[Polish] This is the way I was admitted to the hospital block, after taking our temperature we were ordered to stand naked in the sun for three hours, until the SS doctor came, the Oświęcim Lagerarzt. This was perhaps doctor Kitt, tall slim with glasses.
2. Kapkajew:	[German] =eh= I came to the hospital block in the following way, that is I was sick. my temperature was taken, and then we were made to undress and we stood naked
3. Palarczyk:	[German] completely naked
4. Kapkajew:	[German] completely naked, in blazing sun, for hours, until a + Lagerarzt, that is SS doctor, came from Auschwitz, I believe his name was Kitt + he was a dark tall slim man with glasses.

The later occasion is very similar (35'):

1. Palarczyk:	Był wielki transport kobiet, który widziałyśmy nago na autach więzione do krematorium
2. Kapkajew:	Es gab einen großen Frauentransport, und den haben wir gesehen, wie sie nackt

3. Palarczyk:	ganz nackt
4. Kapkajew:	ganz nackt ins Krematorium gebracht wurden

1. Palarczyk:	[Polish] There was a large transport + of women, that we saw naked imprisoned in cars to the crematorium
2. Kapkajew:	[German] There was a large women's transport, and we saw them naked
3. Palarczyk:	[German] completely naked
4. Kapkajew:	[German] =eh= completely naked being taken to the crematorium

Palarczyk's interventions in her own interest do not always come off. When talking about the arrival of the Hungarian transports in the spring of 1944, she points out that many of her fellow inmates had relatives on these transports, and she begins to recite a list of names (27'). Judge Hofmeyer interrupts and shifts focus onto the defendants: "Ja, also jetzt wollen wir nicht die Einzelheiten insofern wissen. Uns interessiert mehr die Beteiligung der einzelnen Angeklagten an diesen Selektionen auf der Rampe" (Yes, so we don't want to know the details now. We are more interested in the individual defendants' participation in these selections on the ramp). When she pushes at the limits of what the court permits, Judge Hofmeyer brings the exchange back to what he considers relevant: simply ensuring that the names of fellow victims are heard disrupts the court's focus on the perpetrators. In this case, Palarczyk is not able to be heard as she wishes.

In cases like these, the judge's actions may silence the witness and erase the names, but the act of silencing is visible; interventions like Palarczyk's expose the limits of the court's discourse and force it to exercise power visibly. If they are careful not to go too far, witnesses like Palarczyk can exploit this feature to talk about experiences, facts, subjects, or people in their own way; an interpreter can either help or hinder this exercise of agency.

Moments of open exclusion are rare in Palarczyk's testimony: it seems that she has worked out the limits of the discursive freedom available to her and operates within them in order to ensure that she is heard. This means that she feels entitled to correct the interpreter but not to challenge the judge. In this exchange, she intervenes to produce a more precise visual image of prisoners being forced to carry snow and ice in their jackets; she clearly indicates the correct image using a gesture that the tape cannot capture. Monitoring the translation is about maintaining control of the testimony in this complex situation, but it also implies an unwillingness to trust the interpreter unquestioningly (42'):

1.	Palarczyk:	[Polish] Znaczy Stiwitz i blockführerzy
2.	Kapkajew:	[German] Stiwitz and the Blockführers
3.	Palarczyk:	i z okrzykami Fröhliche Weihnachten, chyba tak Fröhliche Weihnachten, bito ich, kopano aż kazano im biegiem nosić śnieg i grudę w tych + w marynarkach.
4.	Kapkajew:	=eh= damals brachten Stiwitz und andere =eh=
5.	Palarczyk:	Blockführer
6.	Kapkajew:	Blockführer, diese Männer =eh= zu uns ins Lager, und sie riefen dabei fröhliche Weihnachten, traten nach ihnen und schlugen sie, und zwangen sie in ihren Taschen =eh= Sch
7.	Palarczyk:	Nicht in den Taschen. So
8.	Kapkajew:	Ach so, nur + in der Jacke
9.	Palarczyk:	in der Jacke (…)
10.	Kapkajew:	In der + Schnee
	Palarczyk:	śnieg i grudę (…)
11.	Kapkajew:	Schnee und =eh= Eisblöckchen =eh= reinzu =eh= also hin und herzuschleppen.

1.	Palarczyk:	[Polish] that is Stiwitz and the Blockführers
2.	Kapkajew:	Stiwitz und die Blockführer
3.	Palarczyk:	[Polish] and with cries of Happy Christmas [German in the original], probably like this Happy Christmas, they were beaten, kicked until they were ordered to run carrying snow and clods in these + in their jackets.
4.	Kapkajew:	[German] =eh= then Stiwitz and other =eh=
5.	Palarczyk:	Blockführers
6.	Kapkajew:	[German] Blockführers, brought these men =eh= to us into the camp, and they were shouting as they did it Happy Christmas, kicking them and beating them, and forced them in their pockets =eh= sn
7.	Palarczyk:	[German] <u>Not</u> in their pockets. Like this
8.	Kapkajew:	[German] Aha, just + in the jacket
9.	Palarczyk:	[German] in the jacket (…)
10.	Kapkajew:	[German] In the + snow
	Palarczyk:	[Polish] snow and clods (…)
11.	Kapkajew:	[German] to carry in =eh= that is back and forth =eh= snow and =eh= small blocks of ice.

In a situation in which the witness wants to ensure that her testimony is heard properly, the interpreter is close enough to be able to challenge, but the judge is out of reach: the potential risk and loss of face are bearable here because of the relationship that has been built up with the interpreter. That is, the witness can make herself heard by challenging the interpreter but not by challenging the judge.

When interacting with the prosecutor Joachim Kügler, she feels less confident in insisting on her own way of narrating than with the interpreter but more than with the judge. Here, Palarczyk is relating how she had to witness small babies being neglected until they died (39'):

1. Palarczyk:	Tak to widziałam na własne oczy
2. Kapkajew:	Das habe ich mit meinen eigenen Augen gesehen
3. Kügler: Palarczyk:	Danke sehr, Frau Zeugin a +
4. Kügler: Kapkajew:	Bitte? Bitte?
5. Palarczyk:	Wystarczy danke
6. Kügler:	Wollte die Zeugin noch etwas sagen?
7. Kapkajew: Palarczyk:	Chciała pani No nie
8. Palarczyk:	Wiadomo było w 42 roku jeżeli kobieta była w ciąży + nie wracała już z rewiru nigdy
9. Palarczyk: Kapkajew:	ani ona ani dzieci Es war ja bekannt im Jahre 1942
10. Kapkajew:	dass eine Frau die ein Kind erwartete + dass weder sie noch ein Kind lebend aus dem Revier zurückgekommen ist.
11. Palarczyk:	Tak

1. Palarczyk:	[Polish] Yes I saw that with my own eyes
2. Kapkajew:	[German] I saw that with my own eyes
3. Kügler: Palarczyk:	[German] Thank you madam. [Polish] but +
4. Kügler: Kapkajew:	[German] Pardon? [German] Pardon?
5. Palarczyk:	[Polish] That's enough [German] thank you
6. Kügler:	[German] Did the witness want to say something else?
7. Kapkajew: Palarczyk:	[Polish] Did you want [Polish] Well no
8. Palarczyk:	[Polish] it was known in 42 if a woman was pregnant + she never came back from the hospital block.

9. Palarczyk:	[Polish] neither she nor the children
Kapkajew:	[German] It was known in 1942
10. Kapkajew:	that a woman expecting a child + that neither she nor the child came back alive from the hospital block.
11. Palarczyk:	[Polish] Yes

Even though Kügler is supporting her testimony in the interests of gaining a conviction, she has to be encouraged to speak when she clearly has something else to say. But given the opportunity, she takes it and overrides the interpreter's turn in her desire to be heard. The false start in her response ("No nie," Well no) is telling: she is not denying that she has something to say, but the apparent denial is a face-saving strategy to avoid appearing too insistent in disrupting the prosecutor's turn. Interpreters tend not to translate such false starts: a translated version (such as "na, nein") might carry more weight than the original and convey a negative impression of the witness' competence (Wadensjö 1998: 222). But it is still an ethical choice that the interpreter has to make here.

In the latter part of the testimony, the relationship between Palarczyk and Kapkajew has developed to the extent that they laugh together about a translation issue (49'):

1. Palarczyk:	W 44 roku wtedy kiedy ja mogłam widzieć Baretzkiego, nie było jeszcze tej + ta sauna jeszcze nie była gotowa
2. Kapkajew:	44 roku
3. Kapkajew:	Im Jahre 19
Palarczyk:	Na początku 44
4. Kapkajew:	Anfang 44 als ich den Baretzki gesehen habe da war =eh= das Sauna-Gebäude noch nicht +
5. Palarczyk:	Fertig
Kapkajew:	fertig
6. Palarczyk	*Frühling* 44, nicht *Anfang*, nur *Frühling* 44.
7. Kapkajew:	Frühling *ist* Anfang [laughs]
8. Palarczyk:	Frühling *ist* Anfang [laughs]

1. Palarczyk:	[Polish] in 44 when I was able to see Baretzki, there wasn't yet that + that sauna wasn't ready yet.
2. Kapkajew:	[Polish] in 44
3. Kapkajew:	[German] In 19
Palarczyk:	[Polish] at the beginning of 44

4. Kapkajew:	[German] at the beginning of 44 when I saw Baretzki =eh= the sauna building wasn't yet +
5. Palarczyk: Kapkajew:	[German] finished [German] finished
6. Palarczyk	[German] *Spring* 44, not *beginning*, just *spring* 44.
7. Kapkajew:	[German] Spring is the beginning [laughs]
8. Palarczyk:	[German] Spring is the beginning [laughs]

Here, the relationship between them seems to be more important than the precise chronology (after all, spring is not necessarily the beginning of the year). The court may well need more precise information about the time of year when Palarczyk saw Baretzki; it will need to test her claims against Baretzki's account of when he was present in the camp. But Kapkajew and Palarczyk seem here less interested in clarifying meaning for the court than in maintaining their relationship. Palarczyk suggests a German word ("fertig") when Kapkajew hesitates, and their exchange about the season is in German rather than Polish, demonstrating a level of comfort with each other and that Palarczyk is now confident in performing in German in front of the court. In this latter part of the testimony, the voices of witness and interpreter overlap more frequently; the turn-taking implies collaboration rather than interruption, indicating that a significant degree of trust has developed between them.

In the next extract, Palarczyk responds to a challenge to the clarity of her testimony about Baretzki's role on the Birkenau "ramp": did Baretzki lead prisoners away from the selection on the ramp, knowing that they were to be gassed? Palarczyk here insists that the prisoners who were selected for work had already been led away, so Baretzki must have known that the rest were destined for death (52'):

1. Palarczyk:	Byli przeznaczeni na spalenie, ci do obozu wchodzili, od razu do obozu, bo przecież Sortierung odbywał się niemal przed wejściem do obozu.
2. Kapkajew:	Diese Leute, die dahin geführt wurden, waren fürs Krematorium, also zur Vergasung vorgesehen.
3. Hofmeyer: Kapkajew: Palarczyk:	Ja + waren das waren das diejenigen mit Kindern und Die <u>anderen</u> (…)
4. Kaplajew:	Entschuldigen Sie bitte
5. Hofmeyer:	Bitte schön ja

6. Kapkajew:	Entschuldigen Sie vielmals, aber die Zeugin hat noch nicht beendet den Satz. Und die *anderen*, die ins *Lager* bestimmt wurden, die gingen ja *sofort* raus, weil die Selektion direkt dort in der Nähe des Tors stattgefunden hat.
7. Palarczyk:	Ja

1. Palarczyk:	[Polish] They were intended for burning, those who went to the camp, straight to the camp as the Sortierung took place almost in front of the entrance to the camp.
2. Kapkajew:	[German] These people who were led there were intended for the crematorium, that is for gassing.
3. Hofmeyer: Kapkajew: Palarczyk:	[German] Yes + were they were they the ones with children and [German] The *others* (…)
4. Kapkajew:	[German] Excuse me please
5. Hofmeyer:	[German] Of course, yes.
6. Kapkajew:	[German] Please do excuse me, but the witness has not finished the sentence. And the *others*, who were chosen for the *camp*, they went out *straight away*, because the selection took place right there near the gate.
7. Palarczyk:	[German] Yes.

Kapkajew now openly supports Palarczyk's testimony, ensuring that everything is heard correctly: this is of course part of her professional task, but it still requires a challenge to Judge Hofmeyer's authority that interpreters do not always feel confident enough to perform. Palarczyk's words are not possible to decipher on the tape, but it is clear that she and Kapkajew are collaborating in this action: she is talking more quietly and maybe addressing her words to Kapkajew rather than the judge, using her as a conduit for her challenge to the judge's power to determine who can speak and when.

Judge Hofmeyer repeats the beginning of his question ("waren das waren das"), attempting to assert himself over the cross talk, and so Kapkajew has to make a direct challenge to him; the elaborate politeness forms she employs indicate the degree of perceived risk in this action after she and Palarczyk have talked over the judge's question. The strong emphasis she places on specific words in the final statement and the way she expands, strengthens, and clarifies in translation Palarczyk's shorter and somewhat ambiguous explanation demonstrate a wish to ensure that the witness's words are heard effectively in a potentially critical situation.

This sense is strengthened by Kapkajew's words: "entschuldigen Sie vielmals, aber die Zeugin hat noch nicht beendet den Satz" (Please do excuse me, but the witness has not finished the sentence). Of course, she means that she herself has not finished speaking, as the witness had finished her sentence before translation, but she equates the translated speech with the witness's words; the witness has not had the opportunity to make herself heard.

Palarczyk's language choice is fascinating when responding to challenges to her testimony by the defense: on several occasions, she chooses to hit back in German, speaking directly rather than through the interpreter. The action of bypassing the interpreter and disrupting the rhythms of consecutive interpreting gives this extra emphasis by drawing attention to the "rule break"; she may also be speaking to the defense as the embodiment of Germans who doubt her testimony rather than in his institutional role. There is no sign here of her using the interpreting to give herself time to think, as she claims in her interview with Dagi Knellesen.

Palarczyk feels confident enough to respond cheekily in German to the defense. The defense counsel Hans Laternser is trying to probe the accuracy of her recollection of the topography of the camp and whether there were roads on either side of the track on which trains arrived at Birkenau: "Frau Zeugin, war das eine Straße?" (Madam, was that a road?) To which Palarczyk replies: "Ja, ich habe sie gebaut" (Yes, I built it, 60').

Kapkajew and Palarczyk have now begun to collaborate in the face of skeptical questioning from the defense. For example, Kapkajew pointedly does not translate part of a challenge to Palarczyk's memory from defense counsel Gerhardt, even though she has been asked specifically to translate it (67'):

1. Gerhardt:	Ich mache der Zeugin ja keinen Vorwurf + vielleicht würden Sie es bitte mal übersetzen + wenn sie es heute nicht mehr weiß. Ich wollte nur festgestellt haben dass sie gesagt hat vor Kanada fanden Selektionen statt, sie aber *nicht weiß* welchen Weg die Häftlinge dorthin gegangen sind.
2. Kapkajew:	Ale nie zna pani *drogi*, jaką prowadzono tych ludzi do Kanady
3. Hofmeyer: Kapkajew:	Waren sonst noch Fragen zu stellen? Herr Doktor Eggert? na tą selekcję. jaką drogą oni szli.
4. Palarczyk:	Oni byli wyładowywani chyba trochę wyżej.

1. Gerhardt:	[German] I'm not accusing the witness of anything + perhaps you could translate this please + if she can't remember it today. I just wanted to establish that she said there had been selections in front of Canada but she *does not know* which path the prisoners took to get there.
2. Kapkajew:	[Polish] But you don't know the *path* that these people were taken to Canada
3. Hofmeyer:	[German] were there any further questions to ask? Dr. Eggert?
Kapkajew:	[Polish] to the selection, which path they took.
4. Palarczyk:	[Polish] They were unloaded probably a little higher up.

Kapkajew translates the factual question that Gerhardt is interested in but not the performed expression of concern that the witness may be offended at the challenge. This is an interesting choice: Kapkajew seems to have interpreted Gerhardt's words as an undermining or face-threatening gesture of fake sympathy for Palarczyk's faulty memory and is not willing to convey this to the witness. She also shifts the emphasis from Gerhardt's challenge to Palarczyk's memory ("but she *does not know*") to the object of the memory (the path), moderately reducing the face-threatening potential of the question. As before, Kapkajew and Palarczyk collaborate to prevent the judge from switching to a new topic before Palarczyk has finished her statement: Kapkajew here insists on completing her turn even though the judge has begun speaking. Toward the end of this 85-minute testimony, Palarczyk feels confident enough in her collaboration with Kapkajew to intervene and interrupt the other participants in order to be heard as she wishes.

Anna Palarczyk's testimony to the Frankfurt Trial shows how a witness can develop and employ trust in her relationship with an interpreter as a resource to support the aim of being heard in a way that she defines. The interaction with the interpreter allows her at times to override the judge's attempts to assert discursive authority and move things along, though she at times comes up against the limits of these tactical opportunities, as in the moment when she simply wants to relate the names of her fellow prisoners: this small action of paying tribute to dead comrades falls too far outside the limits set by the court and has to be sanctioned. Nevertheless, those in court hear the sanction taking place, which draws attention to processes of inclusion and exclusion and the exercise of power. We can say that Palarczyk is able to be heard *in* the courtroom, even where she is not heard *by* the court.

12

The Testimony of Simon Gotland: A Terrible Spectacle?

Simon Gotland, a survivor of the Birkenau *Sonderkommando*, gave public testimony to the First Frankfurt Auschwitz Trial on July 27, 1964. His testimony has attracted some commentary but not for its potential usefulness as a historical source or as legal evidence. Rather, it has been interpreted as an exemplar of traumatized speech, as an incoherent mishmash of languages and as a demonstration of the impossibility of bearing witness to such extreme experiences. In his history of the trial, Devin Pendas describes Gotland's speech as a "chaotic mix of the broken French he had picked up since his post-war emigration mingled with his childhood Polish and a bit of Yiddish," meaning that he "struggled to make himself understood" (Pendas 2006: 162). We should note first of all that Gotland had emigrated from Poland to France in 1929 and had been rounded up and deported from Drancy to Auschwitz in July 1942: his migration journey will be discussed further below. Pendas interprets Gotland's difficulty in terms of an argument about the impossibility of representing the Holocaust in language and the clash between the needs of the court for a specific kind of evidence and the survivors' wish to testify to the "experiential reality" of Auschwitz (Pendas 2006: 142). The questioning elicits from the witnesses moments of pain and emotional truth that have to be interpreted according to the court's strict rules of evidence. A "profound emotional truth" becomes "simply a factual truth claim" (Pendas 2006: 166).

Hermann Langbein also notes the "linguistic mishmash of Polish, French, and Yiddish" in which Gotland gives his testimony (Langbein 1995: 80); however, he does not connect this with an inability to communicate as he is interested in establishing the validity of the evidence against the accused rather than reflecting on the difficulties of testifying. The same goes for Bernd Naumann, who cites Gotland's testimony extensively in his reporting from the trial, especially his account of the cruelty of the accused Stefan Baretzki (Naumann 2013: 162).

I cited these comments and others on Gotland's speech in more detail in Chapter 7, but we can sum it up by saying that there are two ways in which Gotland's testimony has been interpreted. First, a view that focuses on the person of the witness and interprets the supposed confusion and incoherence of his words in terms of a larger argument about the representability of the Holocaust and the inadequacy of language to convey the victims' experiences. Contrasting with this is an approach that focuses attention on the crimes of the perpetrators, citing the witness's words as direct eyewitness evidence: drawing attention to the incoherence of the testimony would create doubt about its validity. In these accounts, therefore, Gotland's words are transcribed in standard German, using the words of the interpreter, who, as I discuss below, has tidied up and organized his statements as well as translate them.

Both of these approaches are justified, but neither of them allows Gotland to speak in his own terms and voice and neither listens to his testimony as it emerges from the specific communicative situation in which he finds himself. There is a certain condescension in the view that he is unable to express himself effectively and that his words are little more than the uncontrollable product of trauma: "As the terrible spectacle of Simon Gotland's testimony reminds us, the will to communicate in many ways mattered more than the facts communicated" (Pendas 2006: 168). Chare and Williams take a critical view of Pendas's interpretation: "Here a practical difficulty—finding a language which was mutually intelligible—and what might be called identity claims or desires (Gotland claiming French citizenship, claiming also to be able to speak German) are confused with (or blend into) the overarching claim of the Shoah's unspeakability" (Chare and Williams 2019: 123).

My aim here is to give an account of Gotland's testimony to the trial that takes a different approach: I will read it neither in terms of a theory of trauma nor as a historical source. I take Gotland seriously as a witness exercising agency in shaping his testimony rather than treating him as a problem to be solved or as inarticulate and passive. This is a specific choice that I have made to treat his communicative strategies as a matter of choice rather than confusion: I give him the benefit of the doubt and take seriously what he says and how he says it. I have chosen to treat his language use not as confusion but as hybridity. This means not working with a deficit theory of language, which assumes either that he is not an adequate speaker of any of the languages he uses (Polish, Yiddish, French, and German) or that his language is affected by trauma. Instead, I shift responsibility for the problem to the court, arguing that the court does not have the resources to deal with a speaker whose language use is hybrid and who does not command the registers of legal discourse in any of his languages. Gotland's language use tells us as much about his migration biography as his experiences in Auschwitz, but with careful listening we also find powerful evidence for the way that groups of victims communicated with each other.

Born in December 1898 in Warsaw, Simon Gotland immigrated to France in 1929, becoming a French citizen only after the War in 1947. He was arrested by the Gestapo on August 7, 1941 and was deported to Auschwitz via Drancy in July 1942. He was assigned to the Birkenau *Sonderkommando* for a number of weeks but managed to avoid the mass killing of this group in December, having been transferred to other forced labor details. From the end of 1942, he was transferred between Monowitz and the main camp in various labor details before finally in April 1944 being selected for work in the "Canada Kommando" sorting the possessions of the Hungarian Jews arriving at Birkenau. In October 1944, he was transferred to the camp complex at Kaufering, Bavaria, which was liberated in April 1945 by the US Army, after which he returned to France, keeping in touch with other former prisoners through the Union Nationale des Associations de Déportés, Internés et Familles de Disparus. His testimony at the trial focused on two aspects of his work that were most relevant for the case being made against the defendants: the work of the *Sonderkommando* in digging and filling mass graves and the selection of arriving prisoners on the Ramp at Birkenau.

Sociolinguistic accounts of migrants' language use have moved away from deficit models of communication toward approaches that stress diversity, creativity, and collaboration. Jan Blommaert and Dong Jie have drawn attention to how communication is characterized by "complex multilingual repertoires, in which often several (fragments of) migrant languages and of lingua franca are combined" (Blommaert and Dong 2010: 4). They conceptualize language use in terms of the linguistic resources available to a particular speaker and the communicative repertoires that they develop for dealing with specific situations: "The repertoires of new migrants often appear to be 'truncated': highly specific bits of language and varieties of literacy combine in a repertoire that reflects the fragmented and highly diverse life trajectories and environments of such people" (5).

The truncated repertoires compel individuals to collaborate and share linguistic resources: this becomes a normal way of interacting and getting on in a situation of linguistic diversity. People very often pool their linguistic competences when they have to accomplish demanding communication tasks: this calls into question notions of "fluency" that focus on *individual* competences and thus assume that migrants' language use is characterized by deficit or inadequacy.

While the situation of survivor-witnesses is not the same as that of migrants in an era of "globalization and superdiversity" (Blommaert and Backus 2011), thinking about the witnesses as migrants, as well as survivors, allows us to rethink attitudes toward their language use. Multilingual witnesses, who had been through experiences of migration, expulsion, or exile *and* the extremity of the camp experience, were living, working, and bearing witness in countries with a strong political impetus toward postwar national integration, which included emphasizing a single national language with a prestigious "standard" variant.

In his discussion of publication practices for Holocaust testimonies in the immediate postwar period, David Gramling describes a grim irony: "Resocializing inmates' use of language to the status quo ante effectively annulled the radical linguistic resubjectification they experienced over their years in a given camp" (Gramling 2012: 182). Gramling's focus is on the *Lagerszpracha* itself, but Gotland's migration experience goes beyond this. As a Polish and Yiddish-speaking migrant to France, Gotland would likely have interacted with people of a similar background within the French majority context, developing the linguistic repertoires that he needed in order to work and to deal with bureaucracy where necessary. The source of his understanding of German is not clear, but it may have been a language of schooling in Poland, which he was able to support with his knowledge of Yiddish.

In the camp, his linguistic resources were vital for survival rather than a disadvantage, with an ephemeral, shifting hybrid of Polish, Yiddish, and German emerging as a lingua franca among the Jewish prisoners: Gotland is an active, competent speaker of this *Lagerszpracha*. Hannah Pollin-Galay (2024: 171) has referred to Gotland as a speaker of "Khurbn Yiddish" (Yiddish of the Holocaust), namely the dynamically shifting and hybridizing idiolect of Yiddish that developed in ghettoes and camps. This is a useful reflection, but we should also acknowledge that his language use reflects his pre- and post-Holocaust migration biography and is influenced by the concrete linguistic situation in the courtroom. Rather than assuming that he is simply an inadequate speaker, we should instead consider that the community of survivors that provided him with support and opportunities to talk about his experiences after liberation was likely similarly multilingual within a majority French context. Survivors' solidarity networks allow testimony to be formulated in ways that are different from those used in communication with broader society.

For this reason, I make an assumption that will structure my analysis: Gotland is a powerful speaker of the hybrid language of the prisoners, and his experiences of bearing witness after liberation were within a collaborative communicative context among people with similar—or more likely complementary—linguistic resources. The slippage between languages that characterizes his Frankfurt testimony is therefore not a result of confusion, trauma, or chaos but is a meaningful feature of how he has learned to speak about his experiences. Thus, for Gotland, this hybrid language use is not only the medium of testimony but also the testimony itself.

This idea helps us to understand Gotland's language use in the court. The court has to operate with a specific standard national language, offering interpreting between one such language and another. As I will show, the interpreters perform a vital role in mediating between witness and court (going far beyond simply translating from one language to another), but they also help to create the gap between supposedly separate languages that they then "bridge" with their expertise. They pin Gotland to one or other of these languages, with more or less success. Where things go wrong, the fault is seen to lie with the witness: many witnesses are not able to operate within languages as national, ideological constructs, so their "competence" is judged by the wrong standards.

For Gotland's testimony, I argue that the interpreters are not making a fundamentally incoherent and incomprehensible testimony coherent and comprehensible, but they are in fact mediating between two different forms of coherence, both of which have their legitimacy, one of which possesses far more institutional power than the other: Gotland's testimony is entirely coherent if we read it in a way that takes into account his history rather than starting from the court's reading of it. The powerful discourse does not recognize the legitimacy of the less powerful one, and so the interpreters' task, as far as the court is concerned, is to make the testimony useful in its terms. Languages are not natural barriers: barriers are erected, maintained, and policed by power.

Bearing this in mind, I will concentrate on the following aspects of Gotland's testimony in the context of his interactions with the other participants: questions of power, authority, and discipline; facework; and the extent to which Gotland's voice and intentions are heard by the court.

In Chapter 6, I cited correspondence between Gotland and Judge Heinz Düx in which Gotland states that he does not require an interpreter for his questioning on September 4, 1962; this letter is formulated in correct, formal German. During his questioning at the pretrial investigation, which was led by Düx, he sets out his experiences at the camp in detail and gives specific incriminating testimony about Baretzki and Kaduk. As is the normal practice for this stage of the identification, the testimony is summarized in standard German as a consistent first-person narrative: this is not a record of Gotland's voice, but the protocol of his statement shifted into a discourse that the court can use and authenticated by the first person and the witness's signature.

The testimony about Baretzki will become the target of intense challenge by the defense at the main proceedings, as Gotland appears to become entangled in contradictions. He discusses a memory of a transport of Hungarian Jews that included a woman who had given birth on the journey; Gotland describes how he had tried to help but was driven away by Baretzki, leaving the woman to be thrown onto a truck with other prisoners who were unable to walk. At the trial itself, Gotland describes this scene differently, stating that the woman gave birth as she arrived and that Baretzki had killed both her and the child himself.

Gotland also talks about the accused Wilhelm Boger, who had tortured prisoners to death as a member of the Auschwitz "Political Department," although he doesn't have direct eyewitness evidence of his activities. During this questioning, Baretzki is led into the room for Gotland to identify and is confronted with the allegations. He states that he was present on the ramp but was not responsible for selections or violent actions, and when Gotland identifies him on a photograph, he denies that the image is of him.

There is a short confrontation here that is key for understanding the linguistic context of Gotland's testimony. Baretzki is confronted with Gotland's statement that he was actively involved in selections on the Ramp. Apparently under the impression that Gotland can only speak French, Baretzki tries to argue that they cannot have been at the Ramp at the same time, as the prisoners all spoke German:

> Die Häftlinge, die auf der Rampe tätig waren, sprachen durchweg Deutsch. Der Zeuge [i.e., Gotland] erklärte hierzu: Ich spreche auch Deutsch. Ich bin im jiddischen Sprachkreis aufgewachsen. In dem Kommando, das mit mir auf der Rampe gearbeitet hat, waren aber auch Häftlinge, die weder Deutsch noch Jiddisch konnten, sondern nur Französisch sprachen. (37638/73, 13438)
>
> The prisoners who were working on the ramp all spoke German. The witness [i.e., Gotland] made the following declaration: I also speak German. I grew up in a Yiddish-speaking environment. But the commando that worked on the ramp with me also contained prisoners who spoke neither German nor Yiddish, but only French.

We should note here that the original stenographer wrote "jüdisch" (Jewish) for "jiddisch" on both occasions; this has been corrected with a pen later. Gotland here insists on his ability to understand and communicate in German, the language of the perpetrators and of the court. His ability to speak German is thus also vital for his claim to be able to identify Baretzki from the Ramp.

Baretzki himself was a Romanian-German *Volksdeutscher* for whom German was not his first language. He tries to use this fact as an excuse when, a little later in the session (37638/73, 13439), he responds to a challenge to his evidence with an outburst: "Hier ist es schlimmer als bei der Politischen Abteilung" (It's worse than the [Auschwitz] Political Department here). On being informed that this is an insult to the court which is potentially punishable by a fine of DM 300, he tries to excuse himself by saying he finds the proceedings difficult to follow: "Ich kann nicht ganz hunderprozentig Deutsch … Ich sehe nicht ein, warum meine Erklärung eine Beleidigung sein sollte" (I don't speak German 100 percent … I don't see why my statement should be insulting). For Gotland, it is vital to employ his imperfect German as a means to understand and communicate, while Baretzki uses his competence in German as a way of evading responsibility for his words.

Gotland's two-hour testimony to the main phase of the trial (July 27, 1964) is remarkable for many reasons: the story of his survival and the extent of his experiences in the Auschwitz complex are extraordinary, as is the direct confrontation with Baretzki that comes at the end. I will give a brief overview here before concentrating on specific details in the second half of this section. The questioning is led by the Presiding Judge Hans Hofmeyer, and Gotland's testimony is supported by two interpreters: the French interpreter Wilhelm Schneider-Ludorff followed by the Polish interpreter Wera Kapkajew. The session begins with standard questions on the witness's personal details, followed by questions intended to establish the chronology of his time in Auschwitz, his movements through the camp complex, and the work he was required to do at each stage. Although Schneider-Ludorff interprets the judge's questions into French, it is clear that Gotland understands them and very quickly insists on replying in German ("Ich will Deutsch sprechen." I want to speak German).

The questions at this stage concern details of locations and identifying them on the bird's eye overview plan of the camp complex hanging on the wall. Gotland's language here shifts between German and Yiddish, meaning that the interpreter cannot work, and there is confusion about what he is trying to say. He is asked to provide precise dimensions of the huts in which he slept in Birkenau and their location in relation to the gas chambers, but he does not have this kind of technical information at his disposal, and his replies are confusing. There is real tension here between the court's insistence on these objective, spatial descriptions and Gotland's desire to move the conversation on to his experiences.

Gotland's frustration at this line of questioning boils over when he is asked to define the precise dimensions of the mass graves that the Sonderkommandos had to dig (9'):

1. Gotland:	Zehn Meter + Dix mètres de longueur, sept mètres de largeur et dix mètres de + profondeur. C'est tout.
2. Schneider-Ludorff:	Zehn mal sieben mal zehn
3. Gotland:	Vielleicht ist da aber ein Irrtum mit einem halben Meter, ich habe nicht gemessen + Moi, j'ai même pas regardé spécialement + seulement je suis travaillé dedans (...)
4. Hofmeyer:	Was sagt er jetzt noch?
5. Schneider-Ludorff:	Er hat die genauen Maße natürlich nicht genommen.

1. Gotland:	[German] Ten meters + [French] Ten meters long, seven meters wide and ten meters + deep. That's all.
2. Schneider-Ludorff:	[German] Ten by seven by ten
3. Gotland:	[German] Perhaps there is an error by half a meter, I didn't measure + [French] I didn't pay special attention + I just worked in it (...)
4. Hofmeyer:	[German] What is he saying now?
5. Schneider-Ludorff:	[German] Of course, he didn't take exact measurements.

Gotland addresses the court directly in German when he admits that he may have made a mistake: this is a face-threatening act, which could potentially be understood as an admission that his memory is not reliable. Gotland has difficulty with questions that ask for precise descriptions of spaces or buildings.

He quickly shifts back to French in an attempt to save face, explaining that there was no reason to take exact measurements under the circumstances. His intonation on the recording shows that he is irritated by the line of questioning and that we should not take his word to be an apology: Judge Hofmeyer's sharp remark shows that he has noticed this challenge, and his shift to the third person, addressing the interpreter rather than the witness, is a move to reassert authority. Schneider-Ludorff defuses the situation with his short summary reply, but this exchange in the third person shows the interpreter talking about the witness with the judge rather than making his voice heard. This tense exchange sets the tone for the rest of the testimony.

The questioning circles around, shifting between three languages, with Judge Hofmeyer insisting in vain that Gotland should speak French and allow the interpreter to work. Gotland has thus developed a reputation here as a "difficult" witness who has to be managed rather than simply allowed to speak.

After twelve minutes, it has become clear that the current arrangements are no longer appropriate for Gotland's specific linguistic needs, and he requests a Polish interpreter instead. After a break, the questioning continues with the interpreter Wera Kapkajew. This works better at first, with Gotland able to respond more clearly to the questions about the mass graves: he has also accepted the structure of the court's questioning and does not try to shift the discussion onto his own territory. In other words, he has accepted the power structure for the moment and submits to discipline.

This is an important moment: the overall authority of the court in the person of the judge is affirmed, but Kapkajew ensures in a professional manner that Gotland's testimony is heard without further interrupting the flow of proceedings. But "professionalism" in this case effectively means taking up a position on the side of the court and participating in the disciplining of Gotland's speech: from this point on it is Kapkajew who ensures that Gotland sticks to Polish, repeating the phrase "Niech pan mówi po polsku" (Please speak Polish) as soon as he begins to shift to Yiddish, German, or French. Thus, she ensures that the judge no longer has to directly discipline the witness for his language use but takes on this labor herself. These shifting power constellations at the micro level of interaction are vital for understanding Gotland's possibilities for taking control of his testimony as well as for understanding how the difficulties of this testimony come to be evaluated as arising from his inadequacy as a speaker.

Gotland continues to talk about his time in the *Sonderkommando*, with further discussion of the precise dimensions of the pits that they had to dig. The questioning then moves on to Gotland's work in "Canada." He states laconically that a group of about 200 men were transferred to the Main Camp from the Birkenau *Sonderkommando*: this is the move that saved him from the fate of other SK members, but there is no further discussion of the exact circumstances of how he avoided the fate of many others, and Gotland does not make much of it. Difficulties with communication arise when Gotland is asked to be precise about the length of time he spent in "Canada" (17').

---

1. Hofmeyer:	Und wie lange blieben Sie dort?
2. Kapkajew:	Jak długo pan tam został?

3. Gotland:	In »Kanada« var ikh arayn
4. Kapkajew:	Niech pan mówi proszę po polsku
5. Gotland:	Ja wszedłem może w + September, Oktober + czternastego Dezember 1942.
6. Kapkajew:	Als ich da hinkam, da war es September, Oktober etwa. Und ich blieb bis zum 14. Dezember 1942.

1. Hofmeyer:	[German] And how long did you stay there?
2. Kapkajew:	[Polish] How long did you stay there?
3. Gotland:	[Yiddish] I arrived at Canada
4. Kapkajew:	[Polish] Would you please speak Polish
5. Gotland:	[Polish] I arrived maybe in + [German/Yiddish] September October + [Polish, with German or Yiddish month name] 14th December 1942.
6. Kapkajew:	[German] When I arrived there, it was perhaps September, October. And I stayed until 14th December 1942.

In this moment of uncertainty, Gotland starts to slip into Yiddish again after a long passage in which he had submitted to the discipline of speaking Polish. Interpreting this language shift is not easy, but it is a key aspect of this testimony. In this case, it seems to have been triggered by the camp slang term "Canada," indicating that he is used to working with this vocabulary in Yiddish, perhaps in conversation with other survivors or as a memory of how the prisoners communicated. This is complicated by his use of the Yiddish or German names for months at the end of this extract: is he shifting to Yiddish here or making an effort to communicate with the court directly in German, as he did at the beginning?

How we read these small moments is very important for our view of Gotland as a witness. Is he incoherent, shifting between languages as the past intrudes into the present? Is he perhaps making an active effort to speak in the language of the court but not succeeding as he does not have the appropriate linguistic resources and command of the correct register in any of his languages? Or has he developed specific linguistic repertoires in each language, meaning that he is more used to talking about these issues in Yiddish than Polish, or perhaps in a hybrid form that is understandable for his fellow survivors? Isolated from this collaborative context, he becomes a lone witness who is unable to express himself adequately.

Kapkajew is making an effort to create a new form of coherence from this testimony that the court will find useful, but she struggles and asks for more time ("Momentchen bitte," Just a moment, please). At this point, the questioning is interrupted by the defense counsel Eggert, who addresses the issue of what he sees as the witness's linguistic confusion, in the process revealing more about his own attitudes toward Yiddish and language mixing in general (19'):

1. Eggert:	Herr Vorsitzender, nur um einen weiteren Zeitverlust zu ersparen: Ich kann nicht Polnisch, aber um mit Salcia Landmann zu sprechen, hier scheint es sich doch um das "Abenteuer einer Sprache" zu handeln.
2. Kapkajew:	Nein, nein, es ist verständlich durchaus
3. Eggert:	Der Tonfall ist also derselbe wie vorhin. Das Deutsch haben wir ja auch verstanden, wenn man zugehört hat, aber
4. Kapkajew:	Es tut mir leid, ich verstehe es.
5. Eggert:	Ist denn Polnisch die Muttersprache des Zeugen? Entschuldigung.
6. Hofmeyer:	Genau so. Deshalb haben wir
7. Hofmeyer: Kapkajew:	die Dolmetscherin holen lassen. Polnisch ist die Muttersprache des Zeugen.
8. Eggert:	Er hat ja selbst um die polnische Dolmetscherin
9. Gotland:	Tak, bo dlatego ja już 29, 35
10. Kapkajew:	Aber dadurch, dass er vorher Deutsch gesprochen hat, kommt er noch nicht so richtig in die Sprache hinein. Ich kann ihn aber vollkommen verstehen.
11. Eggert:	Ah ja, gut. Danke schön.

1. Eggert:	Your Honour, just to save us wasting more time. I can't speak Polish but, to quote Salcia Landmann, I think we are dealing here with the Adventures of a Language.
2. Kapkajew:	No, no it's entirely understandable
3. Eggert:	The tone of voice is the same as before. We understood the German if we listened but
4. Kapkajew:	I'm sorry, I understand it.
5. Eggert:	Is Polish the witness's mother language then? Apologies.
6. Hofmeyer:	Exactly. That's why
7. Hofmeyer: Kapkajew:	we sent for the interpreter. Polish is the witness's mother tongue
8. Eggert:	He asked himself for the Polish interpreter
9. Gotland:	[Polish] Yes, because I already in 29, 35

10. Kapkajew:	But because he was speaking German before he finds it difficult to feel his way back into the language. But I can understand him completely.
11. Eggert:	Ah yes, fine. Thank you.

Eggert jokingly refers to a popular collection of Yiddish anecdotes that had recently been published by Salcia Landmann (1962): Yiddish is clearly not taken seriously as a language but as a more or less comprehensible version of German. Kapkajew takes Gotland's part, doing facework on his behalf by insisting on the coherence of his speech, but at the same time speaking over him when he tries to talk about the date of his emigration: Gotland's linguistic biography is of no interest to the court. It is notable also that Kapkajew "corrects" Gotland's German when he imitates the voices of SS men giving orders: "Sämtliche Juden antreten" becomes "Alle Juden austreten" (21'). The shift from "sämtliche" to "alle" is really a stylistic correction to a form more likely to be used in an order, but "austreten" (come out or exit) describes a different action to "antreten" (line up), so we have a different impression of what is happening here. Performing facework on behalf of the witness can lead to distortions at this level.

The questioning moves on to the time that Gotland spent cutting wood at the Kobier sub-camp; he says that the prisoners were aware that some of the wood would go to the crematoria while the better-quality material would be used for making furniture. He talks briefly about the next stage in his odyssey through the Auschwitz complex—a number of months in the Buna complex hauling bricks for construction work—before a few words about his stay in the Auschwitz I infirmary in December 1943. Gotland speaks matter-of-factly, in short sentences, in other words in a rhythm determined by the need for interpreting.

There is a key moment at this stage when Gotland begins to anticipate the disciplinary action when he begins to speak Yiddish. At a moment when he wants to bring the focus onto what he knows about experiments being conducted on female prisoners, his language takes on a high degree of hybridity: "kaygeniber di =eh= frauenblock =eh= tseyn di experiensen vos zey hobn gemokht" (opposite the =eh= women's block =eh= ten the experiments that they were doing, 23'). The form of his statement suggests that he assumes this knowledge on the part of his listeners; this is perhaps a way of softening the attempt to change the subject against the flow of the questioning. The word "experiensen" suggests a hybrid of French ("expérience" for "experiment") and German or Yiddish.

Shortly afterward, Gotland tries to raise the subject again: "Block zehn to było gdzie =eh= to zrobili experiensy avec des gens avec des kobiety" (Block ten that was where =eh= they did experiments on the people on the women). This statement shifts between German, French, and Polish, with another hybrid form for "experiments," this time with a Polish plural ending on the French word. This dynamic blend of Gotland's four languages within a few sentences is remarkable and tricky to interpret with any certainty. Given the presence of French here, it seems likely that this moment gives us insight into the ways he has talked about his experiences after liberation. Also, this is a moment of pressure in which he is trying to shift the questioning onto territory that is important to him, meaning that he is momentarily not able to sustain the effort to maintain the artificial monolingualism required of him. In this case, the interpreter has to do the skilled work of making his testimony monolingual in translation, conveying the content but not the form.

Gotland finds this particular passage of questioning difficult, and his agitation is clear when describing the selection that brought him to "Canada" in Birkenau. Whether this is because of the emotional pressure of the memory or frustration because Judge Hofmeyer does not follow up his statement about the women's block is not clear. Kapkajew makes an effort to produce coherent translations, but there is a real tension here between Gotland's urgent, compressed speech and Kapkajew's expanded syntactically smoother versions. As the questioning moves on from this topic, which has caused Gotland some anxiety, he begins to "correct" his own language use, anticipating the disciplinary measures and switching from Yiddish to Polish without being told: "i m'hot gemokht + iz nas zrobili Kanada-Kommanda" (And they put + they put together the Canada commando from us, 24').

Gotland now gives a brief account of the time he spent on the Birkenau "ramp" in spring 1944 unloading the possessions of the Jews arriving from Hungary, followed by a return to "Canada" in September and evacuation via Oranienburg, Sachsenhausen, and Kaufering, where he was liberated. In total this initial section has taken thirty minutes, not including the break in the middle. In the final section, rather than giving a detailed account of the rest of the testimony, I will concentrate on a few telling moments that help us to understand the success or failure of Gotland's attempt to communicate his testimony.

The presiding judge now moves to questions on the specific areas of interest for the crimes being investigated, concentrating on Gotland's testimony against Baretzki. When answering questions about his work on the "ramp," Gotland makes an important statement that shows how he sees his task in court: he is there to bear witness to what he saw: "Ja obserwowałem wszystko co się stało" (I observed everything that happened, 29').

It is notable that Kapkajew emphasizes the "I" in her translation, where Gotland only uses infinitive verbs to describe what he did: opening the wagon doors, driving the people out, piling up the baggage, and lining the new arrivals up in ranks of five. Her interpreted version stresses personal involvement and obligation, while Gotland's words are more distanced (29').

1. Hofmeyer:	Wo waren Sie, und was hatten Sie dort zu tun?
2. Kapkajew:	Gzie pan był i co pan miał robić?
3. Gotland:	Otwierać wagony, którymi ludzie przyjechali.
4. Kapkajew:	Ich musste die Wagen öffnen, wenn die Menschen angekommen sind.
5. Gotland:	I tych ludzi wygnać z tych wagonów.
6. Kapkajew:	Und ich musste die Menschen aus diesen Waggons rausjagen.

1. Hofmeyer:	[German] Where were you and what were your tasks there?
2. Kapkajew:	[Polish] Where were you and what were your tasks there?
3. Gotland:	[Polish] Open the wagons that the people had come in.
4. Kapkajew:	[German] I had to open the wagons when the people arrived.
5. Gotland:	[Polish] And drive these people out of these wagons.
6. Kapkajew:	[German] And I had to chase these people out of these wagons.

In general, Gotland is much more interested in talking about the things that he saw, in particular, mentioning specific situations and victims that he remembers, than in describing precisely the actions of the accused. When asked who gave the orders while the trains were being unloaded—a question that is vital for identifying concrete perpetrators—he is unable to give a name: "Ja nie chciałem nawet wiedzieć od niego nazwiska" (I didn't even want to know his name, 31').

Perpetrators are here a collective of interchangeable individuals whom Gotland has no inclination to identify separately (with the exception of Baretzki, later in his testimony). He is so unforthcoming on this issue that it causes some frustration in the court, and Kapkajew shifts to siding with the court, sharing her frustration that he will not answer a specific question: "Ich habe noch mal gefragt: Wer aber, wer hat den Befehl gegeben?" (I asked again: But who, who gave the order?, 35') This strategy presents Gotland as unreliable or incompetent as a witness and ensures that the interpreter cannot be blamed for any communication problems. Under the power imbalance of the court, facework may become a zero-sum game: Kapkajew's aim to deflect blame contributes to the court's negative view of Gotland as witness.

He also finds it difficult to answer questions that imply an overview of numbers arriving and how many people on average were selected for work from each transport. Instead, he prefers to focus on the suffering of the victims, describing what he saw in a highly compressed, paratactic style, which Kapkajew expands on in translation, inserting temporal and causal connectors in order to add coherence to the statements (37'):

1. Gotland:	Es gibt =eh= było takie takie takie + transporty, to przyszli, wszystkie cały transport było + nieżywy.
2. Gotland: Kapkajew:	Raz było tak Es gab einmal auch ein Transport, das kam an, und =eh= alle waren tot, die drin waren
3. Gotland:	Oni byli dwanaście dni byli oni przyszli z Ukrainy, z Białorusji. Dziesięć dni byli w drodze. Cały transport, myśmy robili dwa + trzy dni + wyrzucaliśmy ludzi
4. Kapkajew:	Es gab einen Transport, der kam aus Weißruthenien oder der Ukraine, die waren zehn bis zwölf Tage unterwegs, und alle waren tot. Wir haben drei Tage gearbeitet, bis wir sie alle herausgeworfen haben, also die Leichen aus dem Transport.

1. Gotland:	[German] There was [Polish] a kind a kind a kind of transport, that arrives, all the whole transport was + dead.
2. Gotland: Kapkajew:	Once there was [German] There was once a transport that arrived and everyone in it was dead
3. Gotland:	[Polish] They had been for twelve days, they had been had come from Ukraine, from Belarus. ten days they were on the way. The whole transport, we worked for two + three days + we threw out the people
4. Kapkajew:	[German] There was a transport that came from White Ruthenia or Ukraine, they were travelling for ten or twelve days, and they were all dead. We worked for three days until we had thrown them all out, that is the corpses from the transport.

Gotland's testimony shifts between individual cases and a general overview: for him, these cases are representative of the whole. He goes on to say (38') that one small girl survived this transport and was killed by *Unterscharführer* Moll on arrival: he did not see this himself but was told by members of the

Sonderkommando. For Gotland, the prisoner networks were and are a reliable source of truthful information to help make sense of what was happening and to bring this knowledge to the world: a chain of testimony that also pays tribute to those who did not survive but whose words and experiences are sources of truth.

The court cannot use hearsay evidence like this and passes over it without comment. It will have no effect on the final judgment, except that it potentially adds to the impression that Gotland's evidence is of little value, but he has still been able to say it, and it has been translated and heard. These small shifts within the testimony do not necessarily show Gotland's inability to express himself but that he is trying on a small scale to shift the conversation around to the subjects that are important to him. Not only that, he is introducing a different knowledge paradigm to the one that the court has to work with: the prisoners' solidarity networks as a source of collective truth and trust, as opposed to the court's requirement for direct eyewitness evidence from a trustworthy individual.

Gotland's style here is fragmentary and quite hesitant when he is talking about precise numbers. Judge Hofmeyer insists on a line of questioning about the proportion of Jews who were selected for work from each transport and whether this changed through time, but Gotland is not in a position to answer this. He becomes quite defensive at this line of questioning and pushes back against it: "Tam nikt nie mógł być mądrym, co się tam dzieje" (Nobody could make any sense of what was happening there, 44').

This statement is telling but tricky to interpret. On the surface, it is clearly a statement about the inability of a prisoner in Gotland's position to understand any system behind what was happening: the perspective of a prisoner having to carry out repetitive tasks in a situation of seeming chaos, noise, and violence would give little opportunity for reflection. However, Gotland had been in the camp since 1942 and had moved around between the main camp and Birkenau several times, so had been able to gather a significant amount of knowledge: this is one of the reasons why he was invited to testify. It became clear in his description of the pits dug by the Sonderkommando, his observational gifts did not extend to numbers, structures, and patterns but to striking individual memory images, which may explain the appearance of disorder in his testimony.

We should note here that Gotland describes his task on the Ramp in terms of trying to create order: sorting the baggage, lining up the prisoners. His testimony betrays a desire to create order in retrospect, but without imposing meaning on a situation that lacks one. This leads us to a deeper possibility in his words: even in retrospect, there is still no sense that can be made of it, and rather than submitting his memory to the structures offered by the court, Gotland just wants to report on what he and his comrades saw.

We must also consider the concrete linguistic context of this statement. It is a form of objection to a line of questioning that Gotland feels uncomfortable about. A direct challenge is a potentially face-threatening action, which may bring sanction for the lower status individual in this situation, so Gotland formulates his challenge in an indirect way so as not to confront the judge directly: so what appears to the court to be an admission of ignorance can also be read as a challenge to the form that the questioning is taking, which leads away from the kinds of knowledge that are important to Gotland.

Finally in this section of the testimony, Gotland insists on telling the court about a woman he knows who survived a selection as a small child because Dr. Mengele picked her and her mother out and led them away: the child survived and is still alive. This story is important enough to him that he interrupts the flow of questions and turns to Kapkajew for support: "Proszę pani, niech pani powie to …" (Please tell this story, madam …, 44') He clearly sees her as an ally here, as his closest interlocutor and as an individual who will both bridge the distance between him and the court and soften any potential conflict: he invests his trust in her as a way of gaining support in shifting the ground onto his own terms.

Judge Hofmeyer leaves this story uncommented and moves on to issues that are of relevance to the court, asking Gotland to identify individual SS men by name. Gotland is reluctant to do this: it is very striking how he will only speak about individual SS men when asked directly by Hofmeyer, while he is willing to take face-threatening action to talk about individual victims. When pressed to give evidence on individuals in the next part of the testimony, his evidence is vague in the court's terms, but we gain a strong impression of how the prisoners talked about certain SS men.

Hofmeyer's questioning focuses on Baretzki, asking him how well Gotland knew him. The witness replies, "Ja go znam jak moje serce. Bo ja jego widziałem codziennie" (I know him like my heart. Because I saw him every day, 46'). Gotland does not wait for the translation of the question before answering, indicating some urgency in what he wants to say and a willingness to challenge the discipline of the questioning. His answer that he knew him as well as his own heart is breathtaking, indicating an intimate, embodied knowledge of the effects of power and violence. This is a moment where Gotland overcomes his diffidence about speaking about the SS: it is as if he has now decided to confront the issue directly, now that the court insists, but to set his own terms.

His responses to questions about Baretzki's actions give us an impression of how the prisoners spoke about him but cause frustration because they do not provide any useful evidence. Here, Kapkajew's role has shifted again from ally to enforcer of discipline (49'):

1. Hofmeyer:	Nun =eh= wie ist er denn auf die Rampe gekommen? Ist er da mit dem Fahrrad gekommen oder zu Fuß?
2. Gotland: Kapkajew: 3. Gotland:	Er komme er komme Niech pan słucha On przyszedł jak *tiger*.
4. Gotland: Kapkajew:	(…) przyszedł *Niech pan słucha pytanie!* Jak on przychodził przyjeżdżał na rampę? Rowerem czy na piechotę?
5. Gotland:	Nie + piechotą widziałem
6. Kapkajew:	Er ging zu Fuß, wie ich gesehen habe, wie ein Tiger.

1. Hofmeyer: 2. Gotland: Kapkajew:	[German] Now =eh= how did he come to the ramp? Did he come by bike or on foot? [German] He came he came [Polish] Listen to
3. Gotland:	[Polish] He came like a [Yiddish/German] *tiger*.
4. Gotland: Kapkajew:	[Polish] (…) he came [Polish] *Listen to the question*! How did he come to the ramp? By bike or on foot?
5. Gotland:	[Polish] No, on foot I saw
6. Kapkajew:	[German] He came on foot, as I saw it, like a tiger.

Having expressed her irritation and brought Gotland back onto the territory required by the court, she then ensures that Gotland's comparison of Baretzki with a tiger is heard at the end. His use of the Yiddish or German "tiger" instead of the Polish "tygrys" is also significant here.

Hofmeyer's questions focus on Baretzki's personal responsibility and his active role in giving orders on the "Ramp," but Gotland shows little interest in giving precise details, seemingly misunderstanding the aim of the questioning. Hofmeyer formulates his questions very carefully, framing them in order to elicit statements about Baretzki's motivation or ownership of the criminal activity ("Und hatte er ein Interesse daran, dass die Arbeiten beschleunigt wurden, dass die Leute beschleunigt aus den Waggons herausgetrieben wurden?" And was it important to him to speed up the work, that the people were driven out of the wagons faster?, 50'). This is vital for the legal distinction between murder and accessory to murder under the legal code of the time, but Gotland is unwilling or unable to formulate his responses according to this distinction. For example, when Judge Hofmeyer asks whether Baretzki took an active role in the selections, Gotland replies, "On dwa razy był czynny. On od swojej ręki był czynny. Ja (…) powiedzieć czy on był czynny, on sobie sam zrobił czynny" (He was active twice over. He was active with his own hands. I (…) say that he was active, he made himself active, 51'). Gotland's colorful manipulation of language, which, although confusing, gives a striking impression of Baretzki as a whirlwind of activity, is a sign of the difficulty he has been having with responding to the court's line of questioning: it is less a description of Baretzki than an expression of exasperation at the court's unwillingness to accept what he is saying at face value.

Hofmeyer tries to resolve the problem, as he sees it, by asking Gotland whether he can remember anything specific beyond what he has said so far. This open question leads to a remarkable section in which Gotland varies something that he reported on during his pretrial questioning. He talks about a transport containing a woman who was giving birth at the moment of arrival; in his pretrial testimony he had mentioned this but said that the baby had been born during the journey.

Gotland here varies the story, putting himself at the center. Narrating in a clear and direct way, he describes how he saw the woman in labor, approached her, and assisted with the birth. He describes it laconically, "Ja wszedłem do tego wagonu. Ja to dziecko wyjąłem z tej kobiety" (I went up to the carriage. I took the child out of the woman, 54'). He says that he wrapped the child in clothing and helped the mother to sit down with it on a parcel from the transport. Baretzki saw this and threatened him: "Dlaczego ja się bawię z tym gnojem?" (why am I playing around with this filth? 56'). Baretzki takes the child and kicks it away; Gotland switches to French to describe this: "comme un football." He then orders Gotland to bring the child back, but it is already dead. When Gotland returns to the scene later, he finds that the woman is also dead and claims that Baretzki had killed her.

Following the standard procedures, Hofmeyer draws the witness's attention to the discrepancy between this narrative and his previous statement, asking whether he stands by what he has just said, and Gotland turns to Kapkajew for support: "To z mojego serca przysięgam. To jest dziesięć procent, ja mówię, jeszcze było sto procent więcej … Proszę pani, ja wiem co ja mówię" (I swear it on my heart. That is ten percent, what I say, that was one hundred percent more … Please madam, I know what I am saying, 61'). Gotland again addresses

Kapkajew directly as an ally in this final statement, characteristically asking her to align with him at a moment when he is being challenged.

It is not possible to make a judgment about the accuracy of Gotland's account here, and his allegation against Baretzki is too contradictory to meet the legal standard of proof. But what it does show is Gotland's need to place himself in the center of the narration; he has talked before about his role as observer and witness, and his re-narration of this episode in a way that shows him as active helper rather than passive observer is perhaps a way of coping with a sense of shame and helplessness. It also allows him to show he has agency in a courtroom situation in which he has very little.

His explanation for the discrepancies between his statements is somewhat obscure; again, he tries to cope with a face-threatening situation with an indirect challenge to authority, which Kapkajew softens and expands (59'):

1. Gotland:	No, mało rozumieli po polsku.
2. Kapkajew:	Vielleicht hat man mich wenig verstanden. Jetzt, wo ich ja polnisch reden kann, ist es leichter, besser.

1. Gotland:	[Polish] Well, they didn't understand much Polish.
2. Kapkajew:	[German] Perhaps they didn't understand me well. Now that I can speak Polish it's easier, better.

Gotland's statement suggests that he was speaking Polish during his initial questioning and was poorly understood: this contradicts the evidence from the transcript, in which Gotland confirms that he is able to follow German and requires no interpreter. He pushes back against the idea that problems with understanding are down to his incoherence, attempting to lay the blame on his interrogators. Kapkajew's translation picks this up, changes the sense, giving a different impression of what language Gotland had been speaking (not Polish), and gives it a more positive conclusion, supporting the coherence of his testimony now. She is trying to support Gotland while also blunting his criticism of the court.

Gotland finds it rather difficult to confront the accused directly, expressing anxiety about how he will be perceived when making this allegation against Baretzki: the face threatening challenge to his changed story puts him in a complicated situation which he can only get out of by backing down and putting himself in a less powerful position by weakening his account of Baretzki's inhumanity. He may also worry about being perceived as vengeful after so many years. This moving statement tells us a lot about the witness's feelings of helplessness and shame:

1. Gotland:	Ja nie jestem łobuzem, ja nie jestem, ja nie życzę nikomu, może on chory, on jak się upił, nie wiem. To jest chorzy ludzie, co oni tak zrobili, ja nie wiem, dlaczego tego oni zrobili z ludźmi.
2. Kapkajew:	Ich bin ja kein schlechter Mensch, und ich wünsche ihm auch nichts. Vielleicht wenn er betrunken war, da war er krank. Ich weiß nicht, vielleicht waren sie krank, als sie dieses mit den Menschen taten.

1. Gotland:	[Polish] I'm not a bad person, I am not, I don't wish anything on anyone, perhaps he is sick, he was drunk, I don't know. These are sick people, that did this, I don't know why they did this to people.
2. Kapkajew:	[German] I am not a bad person and I don't wish him anything. Perhaps he was sick when he was drunk. I don't know, perhaps they were sick when they did this to the people.

Kapkajew's version here shifts the sense a little: while Gotland suggests that the sickness is a permanent condition, using the present tense, she locates it in the past as something that came over them back then.

Gotland goes on to talk about the Theresienstadt Family Camp and the "Gipsy Camp": there is no space here to talk about these sections in any detail, except to say that he continues to find it difficult to identify individuals directly. But rather than considering this testimony useless, we should instead let Gotland speak in his own voice as he describes the end of the "Gipsy Camp" in August 1944. He claims to have observed what happened on the evening of August 2, when the SS began to clear the camp.

The discussion revolves around what it was possible to see in the dark, and Gotland, finding it hard to explain this, gives us a spectral image of SS men moving in groups "like tigers" around the barracks carrying small lanterns. Hofmeyer here displays some irritation by addressing his challenge question to the interpreter rather than, as the convention demands, directly to the witness (67'):

1. Hofmeyer:	Nun, wenn es dunkel gewesen wäre, hätte er ja trotzdem nichts sehen können.
2. Kapkajew:	Ale kiedy ciemno, jeśliby było ciemno, to pan mimo to nie mógł widzieć.

3. Gotland:	Oni lecieli, jak te tygrysy z lampkami, jak to powiedzieć? Z małymi lampkami co się świecą.
4. Kapkajew:	Die liefen überall her wie Tiger mit den Taschenlampen.

1. Hofmeyer:	[German] Now, if it had been dark he wouldn't have been able to see anything anyway.
2. Kapkajew:	[Polish] But if it is dark, if it had been dark, you would nevertheless not have been able to see.
3. Gotland:	[Polish] They flew, like tigers with lanterns, how to say this? With little lanterns that shone.
4. Kapkajew:	[German] They ran around everywhere like tigers with the flashlights.

Gotland is here trying to describe a scene, imbued with drama and emotion, while Hofmeyer wants to get at details of who he could see and how. This causes frustration on both sides because Gotland's testimony arises from collective knowledge shared by many witnesses at the time rather than his individual observation ("Tam ludzie widzieli, ludzie, ludzie," People saw it there, people, people, 67'). When pressed, he does eventually claim to have seen these events directly, but it is clear that this is not the most important thing ("Ja też słyszałem, widziałem. Ja też." I heard it, saw it too. Me too). Collective knowledge is the key to testimony, as one individual cannot see everything, and the victims are a single, trusted collective. On being challenged about how he could identify faces in the dark, Gotland claims that he knew Baretzki was there as the prisoners all shouted his name: "Cygańskie wszystkie, Baretzki, Baretzki, wszystko Baretzki było" (The gypsies, all of them, Baretzki, Baretzki, it was all Baretzki, 68').

Throughout this section, Gotland responds defensively to challenges to his testimony: he is trying to save face by recruiting other voices to secure his version of events, as he finds the logic of the legal questioning hard to follow and, perhaps, insulting. As a result, the victims who were on the point of being killed are also called upon as witnesses: in Gotland's narrative, the voices of the victims join in a chorus of denunciation against Baretzki. Two conceptions of testimony clash here irreconcilably.

At the end of this sequence, Hofmeyer warns Gotland of the consequences of giving false evidence against a guard who had beaten him; Gotland denies that he intends this ("Nie, nie. Bóg niech mnie skaże! Ja nie, nie chcę. Nie, nie." No, no. May God condemn me! Not me, I don't want to. No, no, 69'). Hofmeyer then concludes his questioning by asking Gotland whether he can say anything about Oswald Kaduk. Gotland has little to say about Kaduk that is not hearsay, but this section is notable for more language shifts than the previous one. Several times in this section, Gotland needs to be reminded to speak Polish as he has shifted to Yiddish at moments of uncertainty or challenge or when he can't answer a question. This may simply be a consequence of tiredness at this stage in an intense session, though the language slippage tends to occur at moments of pressure and confusion, for example, when he takes a moment to recall Kaduk's precise rank and function in the camp and becomes flustered when apologizing for his memory, mixing German, Yiddish and French: "Ja, di funktie + schon 22 Jahre + leider + badoyren + bon + =eh eh= Kaduk war =eh= Rapportführer." ([Yiddish] Yes, the function + [German] 22 years already + unfortunately + [Yiddish] apologies + [French] fine + [German] Kaduk was Rapportführer, 70').

The testimony concludes with questions from the prosecution, the *Nebenklage*, and the defense. In terms of the content of Gotland's testimony there is little of substance here, but some vital issues are negotiated to do with language, power, and the conditions under which testimony can be heard. When challenged and asked to repeat or justify aspects of his testimony—in particular over discrepancies with his testimony in the pretrial questioning—he finds it difficult to understand the sense of the questioning and to respond in the terms the court requires.

This is a deliberate strategy on the part of the defense in order to cast doubt on his testimony, but even supportive questioning from the prosecution causes problems. There is discussion between defense and prosecution over the conduct of the pretrial investigation, with the defense claiming that Gotland was guided illegitimately to identify Baretzki by the prosecution and that contrary to the transcript there was in fact an interpreter present: Gotland's grasp of German is not seen as good enough for him to have given a statement without one.

Without legal expertise, Gotland finds the sense of these questions hard to understand and feels himself under attack. He explains that he had turned down the offer of an interpreter as he wanted to speak directly and from the heart (83'):

1. Gotland:	Przepraszam pani (...) Gericht to mnie powiedział, czy ja chcę wziąść Dolmetscher. Ja powiedziałem: Mnie lepiej powiedzieć samemu. Dlatego ja mówię sercem sprawiedliwości. Ja nie chcę
2. Kapkajew:	Der Untersuchungsrichter hat mich gefragt, ob ich einen Dolmetscher haben möchte. Und ich habe gesagt: Nein, ich möchte selbst sprechen, weil ich so aus dem Herzen heraus rede, und da ist es mir so leichter.

1. Gotland:	[Polish] Excuse me madam (...) [German] court [Polish] asked me if I wanted to take a [German] interpreter. [Polish] I said I prefer to speak for myself. Because I speak with the heart of justice. I don't want
2. Kapkajew:	[German] The investigating judge asked me if I wanted to have an interpreter, and I said: No, I would like to speak myself, because I speak from my heart, and that is easier for me.

The association of uninterpreted speech with direct testimony with the "heart of justice," which Kapkajew finds hard to translate, is important for Gotland's testimony here: it is why he began by attempting to speak German. The interpreter is always a barrier, but he needs to be able to trust her in order to be heard. This may also explain why he so often addresses her directly, as he does here: he needs to work on the relationship with her throughout the testimony.

Gotland denies there is any discrepancy between his words in his pretrial testimony and what he has just said about helping the mother give birth and Baretzki killing the child, speaking German to emphasize his point ("Niemand hat anderes gesagt. Ich sage immer dasselbe." Nobody said anything different. I always say the same, 97'). He is on dangerous ground here, as his story is clearly different now, and the allegation against Baretzki that he killed the child is new. The prosecution councils Vogel and Ormond try to support him, and Ormond and the defense council Gerhardt get into a dramatic confrontation and have to be called to order by Judge Hofmeyer, which adds to Gotland's agitation, as he cannot follow what is happening. Defense counsel Gerhardt makes a short speech in which he casts doubt on Gotland's identification of Baretzki, arguing that he must have heard the prosecution talking to the accused and addressing him by name before he was brought into the room.

The judge cuts this speech off, but Gotland is upset and offended by this challenge to his authority as witness; the more the defense challenges him, and the more he has to repeat the point, the more confused and agitated he becomes. He resorts to an outburst in Polish against Baretzki, calling him a bandit, and shifts to German and Yiddish one final time for a statement about recognizing Baretzki from his eyes: "Ja go w oczy poznałem (...) + Tiere oygn da, ja + z oczu go poznałem." ([Polish] I recognized him from his eyes + [Yiddish] beasts' eyes there, yes + [Polish] from his eyes I recognized him, 100').

There are also protests in the audience at the defense's line of questioning, which Judge Hofmeyer silences instantly, but it shows with what intensity and sympathy some of the audience members are following Gotland's testimony.

Finally, Gotland is asked to identify Baretzki on a picture taken during his time in Auschwitz, as he had in the pretrial questioning, which he does. Baretzki steps up to deny that the SS man in the photograph is him, as he had previously, and Gotland's testimony concludes with him swearing the formal oath that he has told the truth.

The conclusion of a session of testimony always seems unsatisfactory from the perspective of the witness: instead of a big closing statement or gesture of gratitude, the witness has to go through potentially confusing or upsetting questioning and challenges, as well as elements of legal procedure that need tying up. Unless the witness is familiar with the country's legal procedures and discourse, the sense of these elements may not be obvious. This is especially true in an interpreted testimony, which may be disorienting enough even where the defense is not trying to sow doubt and confusion.

The cross-questioning and ritualized elements are about confirming the legitimacy of the proceedings, but they make clear to witnesses that they themselves are ultimately not the central concern of the trial. Their testimony is of vital importance, but it is also an object of suspicion and challenge. Many witnesses at the trial accept this and are prepared for it, but Gotland finds this troubling, and his frustration becomes increasingly clear as the questioning develops; his manner also demonstrates anxiety about how he is perceived by the court, his attempts to cope with face-threatening events, and an unwillingness to confront the defendants directly unless pressed.

However, if we look at the testimony as a whole, it is clear that any view that reduces it to "confusion" or "incoherence" does it no justice. Gotland seems not to possess the linguistic resources in any language to cope with the specific discourse of the courtroom, whether to understand it fully or to intervene in it effectively and finds it hard to give precise statistical details or measurements that he has no access to. He also finds the cross-questioning difficult and at times insulting. But Gotland is not an incompetent witness: he is able to answer all questions if he can see the sense behind them and is more than capable of making himself understood in clear Polish when he feels comfortable and in control. He is frustrated at not being believed, at having to prove things that he regards as obvious, or at having to be absolutely consistent in his language: he has come to speak but finds he cannot speak on his own terms.

We should therefore avoid the temptation to judge Gotland's testimony in terms of whether he is a "good witness" or not and instead assess the qualities of this unique survivor voice. He has an extraordinary story, told in a powerful language that needs to be listened to on its own terms. His language use, in particular its creativity, compression, and hybridity, gives us insights into the linguistic situation of the camp, but it also cannot be understood without acknowledging this survivor as a migrant with a telling linguistic biography. His language use is therefore meaningful, not chaotic, characterized by richness, not deficit; just as much as the content of his narrative, his language use is his testimony.

Gotland takes the opportunity to push back against questioning, which challenges him in an unequal power situation but is constrained by the limits to the kinds of speech that are allowable in court. The language situation of the court is an expression of the institutional power imbalance: the witness is pinned to a specific language, with artificial barriers constructed between languages that are not absolutely distinct in his speech. Shifts or hybridity encounter disciplinary action or condescension. A form of language use that powerfully reflects Gotland's experiences and the way he is used to communicating his experiences is devalued and dismissed.

If we assume that Gotland has been used to giving testimony in a sympathetic, collaborative, and multilingual environment, then he does not possess the linguistic repertoires necessary to give individual testimony in the courtroom situation. He has not learned how to do it or to occupy this social role with its specific behavioral and linguistic demands. His attempts to speak on behalf of others or to give evidence that he gained from trusted sources in the camp are invalid here. The court requires him to speak with a lone voice rather than a collective one, and this produces defensiveness and a feeling of isolation.

In this situation, it is natural for the witness to seek allies in the courtroom, and the interpreter is the individual with the most intimate relationship with the witness. We see on a number of occasions how Gotland appeals to Kapkajew for support, often addressing her directly. In terms of the economy of trust in the courtroom, Kapkajew plays a complex and ambiguous role, making moment-by-moment decisions about how to respond to the situation, whether to side with the court in terms of disciplining Gotland or to respond to his need for alliances and to what extent face work is necessary, whether on Gotland's behalf or her own. At times she supports him by tidying up his words and reducing uncertainty or ambiguity, for example, by expanding his syntax, putting statements in an order that seems more coherent, ensuring that certain things are heard by emphasizing them, raising the register of his speech, or translating in a way that refers to legal discourse. She also often ignores things that might potentially weaken his testimony, such as verbal habits like "Jak to powiedzieć?" (how to say this?) that convey Gotland's anxiety.

On the other hand, she also plays a role in bringing Gotland into line, ensuring that he stays on the subject and answers the questions that are asked. She participates in discussions about the witness and his supposed incoherence during which the court is coming to a view on his competence. She also takes on the key role of defining him as a monolingual witness. In all these cases, she transmits the authority of the court to the witness.

Both behaviors—supportive and disciplining—are two sides of the same coin. They add up to a role that entails assessing Gotland's "value" as a witness in the terms set by the court, defining him as problematic, and making him available and useable for procedures that operate with specific legal truth criteria. In these terms, his testimony is for the most part too contradictory to be of use: the indictment against Baretzki had quoted Gotland's account of Baretzki's behavior at the "Ramp," including the story about the women who had given birth on the transport (Gross et al. 2013: 435), but after questioning had exposed his account as unreliable, there is no mention of it in the verdict.

So, in whose terms is this testimony "chaotic" or a "terrible spectacle"? Simply interpreting Gotland's words through a lens of incoherence or trauma, we miss aspects of his linguistic biography and of the communicative situation of the court and do not acknowledge the complex issues of agency and power in how he expresses himself. No monolingual communicative situation for giving testimony, however sympathetic, would do justice to the power of Gotland's speech and the insights it gives us. The value of this testimony lies exactly in its hybridity and in the visibility of linguistic issues that are all too often hidden or dismissed. We hear a unique voice with a unique history struggling to make itself heard in a specific communicative context: with sympathetic listening and an eye for the specifics of language, context, interaction, and power, these trial testimonies reveal extraordinary riches.

Concluding Remarks

The year 2023 saw the premiere of a German miniseries, *Deutsches Haus* (available with English subtitles at the time of writing on Disney+ as *The Interpreter of Silence*). This drama and the bestselling novel by Annette Hess on which it is based (Hess 2018) are as far as I can see the only works of art dealing directly with this book's theme, the interpreters and translators at the Frankfurt trial. There have been numerous artistic responses to the trial, the best known being Peter Weiss's play *Die Ermittlung* (*The Investigation*). Like Weiss, many artists responded at the time to the dramatic exchange of voices in the courtroom, often citing them directly, or at least from the stenographic notes taken by Langbein and his collaborators: for example, Hinnerk Einhorn, "Klär, Sanitäter in Auschwitz," Armin Müller "Auschwitz-Prozess," or Uwe Berger, "Der KZ-Arzt" (Grasnick 1988: 94, 100, 102).

The public availability of the recordings has led to renewed interest in the quality of the voices, prompting aesthetic responses in different genres, such as a documentary radio play by Ronald Steckel that edits together extracts from the statements of perpetrators and survivors in order to contrast, analyze or expose aspects of their language use; a fifteen-minute audio installation by Sigrid Sigurdsson and Gunnar Brandt-Sigurdsson that concentrates on the pauses and silences between the words (Steckel 2006; Sigurdsson and Brand-Sigurdsson 2014); and a theatre production at the Schauspiel Frankfurt (*Gegen alle Widerstände*, 2018, dir. Marie Schwesinger) that employed live actors and recordings in a set dominated by strings of audio tape. All these artistic responses exploited the startling sense of immediacy that the Frankfurt tapes seem to offer while also responding in interesting ways to the materiality of the tape recordings and the paradoxes of a form of mediation that produces a feeling of intimacy in the listener.

Despite the considerable press interest at the time in the work of the interpreters and their defining presence on so many of the recordings, none of these artistic works have dealt with the issue of interpreting: they are keenly interested in language in multifaceted and critical ways, but the material they employ is taken from witnesses who spoke German or moments in which non-German speaking witnesses shifted to the language of the court. Earlier works like Peter Weiss's *Die Ermittlung* (*The Investigation*) bypassed the issue of interpreting by citing the German transcript of the proceedings taken by Langbein and his collaborators. So the artistic works that interrogate the language of testimony and memory of the Holocaust avoid dealing with questions of translation, perhaps because it is too undramatic and repetitive, is perceived as a barrier to the authentic experience of the witnesses' voices, or is simply too complicated. It can be seen as a bureaucratic feature of the proceedings rather than as a complex of human relationships through which meaning and memory are negotiated.

The one exception is *Deutsches Haus* (*The Interpreter of Silence*), with its lead character an interpreter clearly inspired by Wera Kapkajew, though with an entirely different biographical background and attitude to professional conduct. The novel and drama take a hard look at the interpreter's ideal of neutrality in the West German 1960s, a time when neutrality was impossible to claim. They also, unusually, stage the courtroom exchanges between witness and interpreter, though they concentrate on the effects of the work on the interpreter rather than the detail of the interactions.

Deutsches Haus draws attention to an aspect that is absent from almost all historical, artistic, or political studies, namely that the trial is a translation moment, a moment in which translation becomes visible as a defining contributor to memory and understanding of the Holocaust. The voices of witnesses from across the world, speaking different languages and hybrid forms or speaking different forms of German, made visible the international scale of the genocide, the variety of victim groups at Auschwitz, and the multiple contexts from which Jews were deported. An encounter with survivors and their voices becomes a key contributor to understanding and social change.

Interpreting and translating are more than just vital auxiliary activities, without which a trial such as this could not operate at all, but add an extra quality to the proceedings, affecting how witnesses give testimony and how listeners encounter their words. This is the case in any trial in which interpreters work, but the tension between the attempted normality and regularity of the proceedings and the number of witnesses, the variety of their speech, and the extremity of the material is what gives this trial its particular intensity and interest. This is a multilingual courtroom in which multiple issues of language and identity, loss and survival, history, and power are constantly under dispute.

To use a non-scholarly word, the "sound" of the trial arises from the tense negotiation between an authoritative standard legal German and the variety and hybridity of survivors' voices. There is more at stake here than questions of justice: it is about who can speak, how they are heard, and under what conditions it is possible to become a witness. Interpreters and translators made—and continue to make—a defining contribution to this process, responding to and sometimes struggling with the complex ethical, not to mention physical and psychological, demands of the work.

This study has been framed as a contribution to a number of different histories in which the First Frankfurt Auschwitz Trial plays a role. Firstly, as a different angle on the historical discussion about the trial as a "turning point" in West German history after the Holocaust, showing how the scale and international nature of the trial relied on the work of many translators and interpreters, drawing attention to vital questions of language, mediation, and communication: knowledge about and understanding of the Holocaust is inconceivable without the work of interpreters and translators. Secondly, to establish the trial as a key moment in the history of translating and, especially, interpreting in the post-Nuremberg era. And thirdly, to show that the ethical dilemmas of both witnessing and interpreting are negotiated moment by moment in the detail of interaction between the participants in a communication. The task of scholarship should be to make this work and the people who do it visible, whether they are professionals working for an institution or survivors supporting each other; it is impossible to count the individuals who made this trial possible by working for the court, for other organizations, or in ad hoc, informal settings. The named interpreters whose work is preserved in the archive are the tip of the iceberg.

Most importantly perhaps, this study is an account of and tribute to the agency and commitment of survivor-witnesses, their languages and ways of speaking, their willingness to contribute to the pursuit of justice, and their wish to communicate directly with their German listeners, even under these complex and trying circumstances. Despite the dilemmas, frustration, and power struggles that ensue, this is how we should understand Simon Gotland's insistence: "Ich will Deutsch sprechen."

Notes

Introduction

1 By "author" ("Autor" in her German), she refers humorously to herself, the original speaker.

Chapter 3

1 My thanks go to the editors for permission to reproduce portions of this publication here.

2 I have used the German transliteration of Russian names, as used in the trial archive.

3 His matriculation record can be found here: https://is.cuni.cz/webapps/archiv/public/?lang=en (accessed June 7, 2023).

4 See also a local history blog by Jan Mareš: https://www.kohoutikriz.org/autor.html?id=stego (accessed June 7, 2023).

5 Since the *Kostenbände* do not give individual item numbers for documents, I have here and in the following pages exceptionally referred to the page number of the digitized versions of pieces 37638/190–211 to allow them to be located.

Chapter 5

1 The interpreter is careful here to use two Polish words for "come/arrive," distinguishing between arriving on foot and by transport: this is to make the intention of the question as clear as possible for Gotland.

Chapter 7

1 Moll's breathtakingly cynical words ("Es ist möglich, sich satt zu essen," in Jarolim's rendering of Müller's rendering of Moll's speech) are hard to translate since Naumann's piece gives no context; on the recording of Müller's testimony there is

also no real explanation. Does he mean that killing the children means there are no extra mouths to feed, or does he mean that he can now eat well as he has fulfilled his duty? I have assumed the second as more likely, but the sentence is obscure, and it involved inserting an “I” in the first phrase instead of the more ambiguous impersonal expression in the original.

Chapter 8

1 Addressing the interpreter by her title like this is not usual in English as a term of respect, but I have translated it this way as it gives a sense of the court’s linguistic rituals of politeness and formality. I use the phrase Mr. or Madam Witness for similar reasons, though it is not natural English.

Chapter 9

1 Prokop uses two different words for “separate” here, indicating the importance of being precise about what he means.

Chapter 10

1 I am not sure here whether this word reflects direct interference from the English “before” or whether he is searching for a German word like “früher” and ends up with the word “bevor”, which sounds similar to the English but would be incorrect here. He pronounces the word in his US-English accent.

Chapter 11

1 Anna Palarczyk testimony: https://collections.ushmm.org/search/catalog/irn504869 (last accessed November 29, 2022).

References

Recorded Testimonies

The recordings, along with full transcripts, are freely available here: https://www.auschw itz-prozess.de/.

Archives

The majority of the material used in this study is found in the Hessen Main State Archive, Wiesbaden (Hessisches Hauptstaatsarchiv Wiesbaden, abbr. HHStAW). The trial archive itself is digitized and is freely available online: https://landesarchiv.hessen. de/mow/chapters.

Trial Archive:

HHStAW, Abt. 461 (Staatsanwaltschaft bei dem Landgericht Frankfurt am Main), 4 Ks 2/63, Mulka, Robert u.a. (1. Auschwitz-Prozess), 37638, Bd. 1-456

Other Archives:

Fritz-Bauer-Institut, Frankfurt a.M.: Sammlung Auschwitz-Prozess
Landgericht Limburg an der Lahn (HHStAW, Abt. 462)
Landgericht Hanau (HHStAW, Abt, 470)
Justizministerium des Landes Hessen (HHStAW, Abt. 505)
Wirtschaftsministerium des Landes Hessen (HHStAW, Abt. 507)
Amt für Lehrerbildung Frankfurt am Main (HHStAW, Abt. 801)

Audio-Visual Material

Achter Het Nieuws (1965), [tv documentary] Dir. LouisWage, Netherlands: VARA.
Auschwitz.Stimmen (2006), [radio play] Dir. Ronald Steckel, FRG: WDR / SWR / radiobremen.

Auschwitz: Topographie eines Vernichtungslagers. Überlebende berichten (1961), [radio feature] Dir. H. G. Adler and Hermann Langbein, FRG: Westdeutscher Rundfunk.

Der Auschwitz-Prozess: Tonbandmitschnitte, Protokolle, Dokumente (2007), [DVD-ROM], 3rd ed. Berlin: Fritz-Bauer-Institut and State Museum Auschwitz-Birkenau.

Golik, Ignacy (2005), Interview, *Das Interview-Archiv "Zwangsarbeit 1939–1945."* Available online: https://archiv.zwangsarbeit-archiv.de/de/interviews/za400 (accessed March 4, 2021).

Krausz, Adrienne (1996), Interview 12555. Interview by Francene Rotenberg. *Visual History Archive*, USC Shoah Foundation, February 29. Available online: https://vha.usc.edu/testimony/12555 (Accessed November 29, 2022).

Palarczyk, Anna (2005), Interview, *Das Interview-Archiv "Zwangsarbeit 1939–1945."* Available online: https://archiv.zwangsarbeit-archiv.de/de/interviews/za401 (accessed March 4, 2021).

Redepausen (2014), [video], dir. Sigrid Sigurdsson and Gunnar Brand-Sigurdsson. Available online: https://sigrid-sigurdsson.de/redepausen/ (accessed April 3, 2024).

Strafsache 4 Ks 2/63: Auschwitz vor dem Frankfurter Schwurgericht (1993), [tv documentary], dir. Rolf Bickel and Dietrich Wagner, FRG: Hessischer Rundfunk.

Secondary Sources

Altano, William (1990), "The Intricate Witness-Interpreter Relationship," in David Bowen and Margareta Bowen (eds.), *Interpreting: Yesterday, Today, and Tomorrow*, 96–100, Binghamton: SUNY.

Arendes, Cord (2009), "Teilnehmende Beobachter. Prozessberichterstatter als Vermittler von NS-Täterbildern," in Georg Wamhof (ed.), *Das Gericht als Tribunal oder: Wie der NS-Vergangenheit der Prozess gemacht wurde*, 78–100, Göttingen: Wallstein.

"Auschwitz: Finale" (1965), *Christ und Welt*, May 14, 1965.

Balaei, Hafez (2004), *Notwendigkeit der Professionalisierung von Dolmetschern im Justizwesen*, Frankfurt am Main: Verlag Dr. Kovac.

Beermann-Schön, Johannes (2020), "Archiv und Zufall: Entstehung und Überlieferung der Tonbandmittschnitte von Zeugenaussagen," in Sybille Steinbacher and Katharina Rauschenberger (eds.), *Der Auschwitz-Prozess auf Tonband: Akteure, Zwischentöne, Überlieferung*, 87–108, Göttingen: Wallstein.

Behr, Martina, and Maike Corpataux (2006), *Die Nürnberger Prozesse: Zur Bedeutung der Dolmetscher für die Prozesse und der Prozesse für die Dolmetscher*, München: Meidenbauer.

Benz, Wolfgang (2004), "Entnazifizierung und Strafjustiz. Zur Aufarbeitung der nationalsozialistischen Vergangenheit," in Irmtrud Wojak (ed.), *Auschwitz-Prozess 4 Ks 2/65 Frankfurt Am Main*, 111–21, Frankfurt am Main: Snoeck.

Berk-Seligson, Susan (2002), *The Bilingual Courtroom: Court Interpreters in the Judicial Process*, Chicago: University of Chicago Press.

Beyda, Oleg, and Igor Petrov (2017). "Свержение коммунизма возможно только с немцами …: письмо и интервью Фарида Капкаева," in A. Martynov (ed.), *История Отечественной Коллаборации*, 181–220, Moscow: Staraya Basmannaya.

Blommaert, Jan, and Ad Backus (2011), "Repertoires Revisited: Knowing Languages in Superdiversity," *Working Papers 67 in Urban Languages*. Available online: https://www.academia.edu/1416183/WP67_Blommaert_Backus_2011_Repertoires_revisited (accessed December 23, 2024).

Blommaert, Jan, and Jie Dong (2010), "Language and Movement in Space," in Nikolas Coupland (ed.), *The Handbook of Language and Globalization*, 366–85, Chichester: John Wiley & Sons.

Brinker, Klaus, and Sven F.Sager (2010), *Linguistische Gesprächsanalyse: Eine Einführung*, Berlin: Erich Schmidt Verlag.

Bruder, Franziska (2003), "'Der Gerechtigkeit zu dienen': Die ukrainischen Nationalisten als Zeugen im Auschwitz-Prozess," in Irmtrud Wojak and Susanne Meinl (eds.), *Im Labyrinth der Schuld: Täter, Opfer, Ankläger*, 133–62, Frankfurt: Campus Verlag.

Buchheim, Hans, Martin Broszat, Hans-Adolf Jacobsen, and Helmut Krausnick (1965), *Anatomie des SS-Staates*, Olten: Walter.

Buck, Tobias (2024), *Final Verdict: A Holocaust Trial in the Twenty-First Century*, London: Weidenfeld & Nicolson.

Chare, Nicholas, and Dominic Williams (2019), *The Auschwitz Sonderkommando: Testimonies, Histories, Representations*, Cham: Springer International.

"Das ist der polnische Haß gegen uns!" (1964), *Frankfurter Rundschau*, May 26.

Davies, Peter (2021), "Translation and the Language of Testimony: Filip Müller's Testimony at the Frankfurt Auschwitz Trial," *Holocaust Studies* 27 (1): 118–30.

Davies, Peter (2022), "'The Interpreter of Horrors': The Interpreter Wera Kapkajew at the First Frankfurt Auschwitz Trial (1963–1965)," *Interpreting and Society* 2 (1): 32–54.

Dean, Robyn, and Robert Pollard (2011), "Context-Based Ethical Reasoning in Interpreting," *Interpreter and Translator Trainer* 5 (1): 155–82.

Degen, Sylvia (2008). *Das Problem der Perspektive: Die Übersetzung von Shoah-Überlebendenberichten ins Deutsche. Am Beispiel von Diana Wangs 'Los Niños Escondidos: Del Holocausto a Buenos Aires'*, Frankfurt am Main: Lang.

Demme, Heike (2017), "Dolmetschen bei Gericht: Ein Beispiel aus der Praxis in Schleswig-Holstein," in Roland Hoffmann, Denise Mallon and Norma Kessler (eds.), *Sprache und Recht: Übersetzer und Dolmetscher als Mittler zwischen Sprachen und Rechtssystemen*, 19–27, Berlin: BDÜ Fachverlag.

"Der Knall war der Startschuß für den nächsten Todeskandidaten" (1964), *Die Welt*, May 15, 1964.

Deutschkron, Inge (2018), *Auschwitz war nur ein Wort: Berichte über den Frankfurter Auschwitz-Prozess, 1963–1965*, trans. Beata Kosmala, Berlin: Metropol-Verlag.

"Der Zeuge Seweryn kennt keinen Haß. Gespräche am Rande des Auschwitzprozesses. Kontakte nehmen zu" (1964), *Frankfurter Rundschau*, May 16.

"Die Sprache, die niemand versteht" (1964), *Frankfurter Neue Presse*, July 28.

Dobrawa, Ralph (2013), *Der Auschwitz-Prozess: Ein Lehrstück deutscher Geschichte*, Berlin: Das Neue Berlin.

Domagała-Pereira, Katarzyna, and Bartosz Dudek (2019), "Auschwitz przed sądem: 'To było zadanie mojego życia' (Interview with Gerhard Wiese)," *Deutsche Welle*, November 23. Available online: https://www.dw.com/pl/auschwitz-przed-s%C4%85dem-to-by%C5%82o-zadanie-mojego-%C5%BCycia/a-51359633.

Driesen, Christiane (2018), *Gerichtsdolmetschen Grundwissen und -fertigkeiten*, Tubingen: L Narr Francke Attempto.

Düx, Heinz (2013), *Justiz und Demokratie: Anspruch und Realität in Westdeutschland nach 1945: Gesammelte Schriften 1948–2013*, Bonn: Pahl-Rugenstein.

Elias-Bursać, Ellen (2015), *Translating Evidence and Interpreting Testimony at a War Crimes Tribunal: Working in a Tug-of-War*, Basingstoke: Palgrave Macmillan.

Elias-Bursać, Ellen (2019), "Translation Institutions: War Crimes Tribunals," in Michael Kelly, Hilary Footitt and Myriam Salama-Carr (eds.), *The Palgrave Handbook of Languages and Conflict*, 331–51, Cham: Springer International.

"Entlastungszeugen werfen Bednarek mehrere Morde vor" (1965), *Neue Presse*, March 5.

"Erlass vom 1.6.1955," *Amtsblatt des hessischen Kultusministeriums* 1955: 166.

Frei, Norbert (1997), "Der Frankfurter Auschwitz-Prozess und die deutsche Zeitgeschichtsforschung," in Hanno Loewy (ed.), *Auschwitz. Geschichte, Rezeption und Wirkung. Jahrbuch 1996 zur Geschichte und Wirkung des Holocaust*, 123–38, Frankfurt am Main: Fritz-Bauer-Institut.

Freudiger, Kerstin (2002), *Die juristische Aufarbeitung von NS-Verbrechen*, Tübingen: Mohr-Siebeck.

Gaiba, Francesca (1998), *The Origins of Simultaneous Interpreting: The Nuremberg Trial*, Ottawa: University of Ottawa Press.

Gańczak, Filip (2022), *Jan Sehn und die Ahndung der Verbrechen von Auschwitz: Eine Biografie*, trans. Lothar Quinkenstein, Göttingen: Wallstein.

Głowacka, Dorota (2012), *Disappearing Traces: Holocaust Testimonials, Ethics, and Aesthetics*, Seattle: University of Washington Press.

Gramling, David (2012), "An Other Unspeakability: Levi and Lagerszpracha," *New German Critique* 39 (3): 165–87.

Grasnick, Ulrich, ed. (1988), *Zwei Ufer hat der Strom: Deutsch-polnische Beziehungen im Spiegel deutschsprachiger Dichtung aus 150 Jahren*, Berlin: Verlag der Nation.

Gross, Raphael, Werner Renz, Sybille Steinbacher, Devin Pendas, and Johannes Schmidt, eds. (2013), *Der Frankfurter Auschwitz-Prozess (1963–1965): Kommentierte Quellenedition*, Frankfurt am Main: Campus.

Hájková, Anna (2020), "What Kind of Narrative Is Legal Testimony? Terezín Witnesses before Czechoslovak, Austrian, and German Courts," in Norman J. W. Goda (ed.), *Rethinking Holocaust Justice: Essays across Disciplines*, 71–99, New York: Berghahn Books.

Hale, Sandra (2007), "The Challenges of Court Interpreting: Intricacies, Responsibilities and Ramifications," *Alternative Law Journal* 32 (4): 198–202.

Hale, Sandra Beatriz, and Jemina Napier (2016), "We're Just Kind of There: Working Conditions and Perceptions of Appreciation and Status in Court Interpreting," *Target: International Journal of Translation Studies* 28 (3): 351–71.

Hammel, Andrea (2004), "The Destabilisation of Personal Histories: Rewriting and Translating Autobiographical Texts by German-Jewish Survivors." *Comparative Critical Studies* 1 (3): 295–308.

Henne, Thomas (2007), "Zeugenschaft vor Gericht," in Michael Elm and Gottfried Kössler (eds.), *Zeugenschaft des Holocaust: Zwischen Trauma, Tradierung und Ermittlung*, 79–91, Frankfurt am Main: Campus.

Hess, Annette (2018), *Deutsches Haus*, Berlin: Ullstein Verlag.

Hirsch, Rudolf (2001), *Um die Endlösung: Prozessberichte*, Berlin: Dietz.

Hofmann, Kerstin (2018), *'Ein Versuch nur – immerhin ein Versuch: Die Zentrale Stelle in Ludwigsburg unter der Leitung von Erwin Schüle und Adalbert Rückerl (1958–1984)*, Berlin: Metropol.

Horn, Sabine (2009a), "Der Gerichtssaal als Geschichtsunterricht. Pädagogische Sinngebungspraktiken in der medialen Repräsentation von NS-Prozessen," in Georg Wamhof (ed.), *Das Gericht als Tribunal oder: Wie der NS-Vergangenheit der Prozess gemacht wurde*, 101–23, Göttingen: Wallstein.

Horn, Sabine (2009b), *Erinnerungsbilder: Auschwitz-Prozess und Majdanek-Prozess im westdeutschen Fernsehen*, Essen: Klartext.

Hutchby, Ian, and Robin Wooffitt (2008), *Conversation Analysis*, Cambridge Malden: Polity.

Inghilleri, Moira (2012), *Interpreting Justice: Ethics, Politics and Language*, New York: Routledge.

Insana, Lina (2009), *Arduous Tasks: Primo Levi, Translation, and the Transmission of Holocaust Testimony*, Toronto: University of Toronto Press.

Jasch, Hans-Christian (2021), "NS-Verbrechen vor bundesdeutschen Gerichten: Zu Täterschaft und Täterbegriff," in Magnus Brechtken (ed.), *Aufarbeitung des Nationalsozialismus: Ein Kompendium*, 210–47, Göttingen: Wallstein Verlag.

Jasch, Hans-Christian, and Wolf Kaiser (2017), *Der Holocaust vor deutschen Gerichten: Amnestieren, Verdrängen, Bestrafen*, Ditzingen: Reclam.

Kalz, Eva-Lotte (2020), "Stimmen und Stimmungen: Zum Auftreten der Strafverteidiger im Prozess," in Sybille Steinbacher and Katharina Rauschenberger (eds.), *Der Auschwitz-Prozess auf Tonband: Akteure, Zwischentöne, Überlieferung*, 63–86, Göttingen: Wallstein.

Kamiński, Alina (1984), "Todesanzeige Wera Kapkajew," *Frankfurter Allgemeine Zeitung*, July 7.

Kapkajew, Georgij (1984). "Todesanzeige Wera Kapkajew," *Frankfurter Allgemeine Zeitung*, July 7.

Kelsall, Tim (2009), *Culture under Cross-Examination: International Justice and the Special Court for Sierra Leone*, Cambridge: Cambridge University Press.

Knellesen, Dagi (2007), "Momentaufnahmen der Erinnerung: Juristische Zeugenschaft im ersten Frankfurter Auschwitz-Prozess. Ein Interview-Projekt," in Michael Elm and Gottfried Kößler (eds.), *Zeugenschaft des Holocaust: Zwischen Trauma, Tradierung und Ermittlung*, 116–39. Frankfurt am Main: Campus Verlag.

Korotin, Ilse (2016), "Firtel, Hilde," in *BiographiA: Lexikon Österreichischer Frauen*, 1 A–H: 824–25, Vienna: Böhlau.

Landmann, Salcia (1962), *Jiddisch: Abenteuer einer Sprache*, Munich: dtv.

Langbein, Hermann (1972), *Menschen in Auschwitz*, Wien: Europaverlag.

Langbein, Hermann, ed. (1995), *Der Auschwitz-Prozess: Eine Dokumentation*, Frankfurt am Main: Verlag Neue Kritik.

Langbein, Hermann (2004), *People in Auschwitz*. Chapel Hill: University of North Carolina Press.

Marder, Irving (1964), *New York Times International Edition*, November 19.

Mason, Ian, (2001), *Triadic Exchanges: Studies in Dialogue Interpreting*. Manchester: St. Jerome.

Mason, Ian (2006), "On Mutual Accessibility of Contextual Assumptions in Dialogue Interpreting," *Journal of Pragmatics* 38 (3): 359–73.

Mason, Ian, and Miranda Stewart (2001), "Interactional Pragmatics, Face and the Dialogue Interpreter," in Ian Mason (ed.), *Triadic Exchanges: Studies in Dialogue Interpreting*, 51–70. Manchester: St. Jerome.

Mason, Ian, and Wen Ren (2012), "Power in Face-to-Face Interpreting Events," *Translation and Interpreting Studies* 7 (2): 233–52.

Miquel, Marc von (2001), "Aufklärung, Distanzierung, Apologie. Die Debatte über die Strafverfolgung von NS-Verbrechen in den sechziger Jahren," in Norbert Frei and Sybille Steinbacher (eds.), *Beschweigen und Bekennen: Die deutsche Nachkriegsgesellschaft und der Holocaust*, 51–70, Göttingen: Wallstein.

Miska, Peter (1964), "Den Kindern schlug das Herz noch," *Frankfurter Rundschau*, October 9.

Moeketsi, Rosemary (1999), "Discourse Structure in a Criminal Trial of a Magistrate's Court," *South African Journal of African Languages* 19 (1): 30–8.

Naumann, Bernd (1964), "25000 Ermordete in 24 Stunden," *Frankfurter Allgemeine Zeitung*, October 9.

Naumann, Bernd (2013), *Der Auschwitz-Prozess. Bericht über die Strafsache gegen Mulka u. a. vor dem Schwurgericht Frankfurt am Main 1963–1965. Aktualisierte Neuausgabe mit einem Vorwort von Werner Renz*, Hamburg: CEP Europäische Verlagsanstalt.

Pendas, Devin (2006), *The Frankfurt Auschwitz Trial, 1963–1965: Genocide, History, and the Limits of the Law*, Cambridge: Cambridge University Press.

Pendas, Devin (2009), "Seeking Justice, Finding Law: Nazi Trials in Postwar Europe," *Journal of Modern History* 81 (2): 347–68.

Pendas, Devin (2013), "Der 1. Frankfurter Auschwitz-Prozess 1963–1965: Eine historische Einführung," in Raphael Gross, Werner Renz, Sybille Steinbacher and Johannes Schmidt (eds.), *Der Frankfurter Auschwitz-Prozess (1963–1965): Kommentierte Quellenedition*, vol. 1, 55–88, Frankfurt am Main: Campus.

Petersen, Uwe-Jens (1965), "Dolmetscherin des Grauens," *Frankfurter Rundschau*, January 12.

Pfuhl, Walter (1964), "Der Tod beherrschte die Arbeit im 'Standesamt' von Auschwitz," *Die Welt*, August 1.

Pfuhl, Walter (1965), "Zeugen aus neunzehn Ländern sagten aus," *Die Welt*, May 6.

Plato, Alice von (2001), "Vom Zeugen zum Zeitzeugen: Die Zeugen der Anklage im ersten Frankfurter Auschwitz-Prozess (1963–1965)," in Irmtrud Wojak (ed.), *"Gerichtstag halten über uns selbst …" Geschichte und Wirkung des ersten Frankfurter Auschwitz-Prozesses*, 193–216, Frankfurt am Main: Campus Verlag.

Pöchhacker, Franz (2004), *Introducing Interpreting Studies*, London: Routledge.

Pogozhev, Andrei, and Pavel Sten'kin (2005), "Смерть стояла у нас за спиной," in *Побег из Освенцима. Остаться в живых*, Moscow: Yauza / Eksmo.

Pogozhev, Andrei (2007), *Escape from Auschwitz*, trans. Vladimir Krupnik and John Armstrong, Barnsley: Pen & Sword Military.

Pollin-Galay, Hannah (2018), *Ecologies of Witnessing: Language, Place, and Holocaust Testimony*, New Haven, CT: Yale University Press.

Pollin-Galay, Hannah (2024), *Occupied Words: What the Holocaust Did to Yiddish*, Philadelphia: University of Pennsylvania Press.

Pym, Anthony (1999), "'Nicole Slapped Michelle': Interpreters and Theories of Interpreting at the O. J. Simpson Trial," *The Translator* 5 (2): 265–83.

Renz, Werner (2009), "Tonbandmitschnitte von NS-Prozessen als historische Quelle," in Jürgen Finger, Sven Keller, and Andreas Wirsching (eds.), *Vom Recht zur Geschichte: Akten aus NS-Prozessen als Quellen der Zeitgeschichte*, 142–66, Göttingen: Vandenhoeck & Ruprecht.

Renz, Werner (2015a), *Fritz Bauer und das Versagen der Justiz: Nazi-Prozesse und ihre "Tragödie"*, Hamburg: CEP Europäische Verlagsanstalt.

Renz, Werner, ed. (2015b), *"Von Gott und der Welt verlassen": Fritz Bauers Briefe an Thomas Harlan*, Frankfurt: Campus Verlag.

Rexhausen, Felix (1964), "'Es ist doch so lange her …', Zeugen kämpfen mit der Erinnerung," *Kölner Stadt-Anzeiger*, August 8.

Rizzi, Andrea, Birgit Lang, and Anthony Pym (2019), *What Is Translation History? A Trust-Based Approach*, Cham: Springer International.

RK (1964), "Die erstaunliche Frau Kapkajew," *Frankfurter Rundschau*, December 5.

Rumprecht, Katrin (2014), "Die Nürnberger Prozesse und ihre Bedeutung für die Entwicklung des modernen Konferenzdolmetschens," in Hartwig Kalverkämper and Larisa Schippel (eds.), *Simultandolmetschen in Erstbewährung: der Nürnberger Prozess 1945*, 151–336, Berlin: Frank & Timme.

Russell, Debra, and Kayoko Takeda (2015), "Consecutive Interpreting," in Holly Mikkelson and Renée Jourdenais (eds.), *The Routledge Handbook of Interpreting*, 96–109, London: Routledge.

Schlie, Heike, Aurélia Kalisky, Matthias Däumer, Burkhard Liebsch, Sybille Krämer, Claudia Blümle, and Günter Thomas (2017), *Über Zeugen: Szenarien von Zeugenschaft und ihre Akteure*, Paderborn: Brill | Fink.

Skinner, William, and Thomas F. Carson (1990), "Working Conditions at the Nuremberg Trials," in David Bowen and Margareta Bowen (eds.), *Interpreting: Yesterday, Today, and Tomorrow*, 14–22, Binghamton: SUNY.

Steinbach, Peter (2015), *Nach Auschwitz: Die Konfrontation der Deutschen mit der Judenvernichtung*, Bonn: Dietz Verlag.

Steinbacher, Sybille (2001), "'Protokoll von der Schwarzen Wand': Die Ortsbesichtigung des Frankfurter Schwurgerichts in Auschwitz," in Irmtrud Wojak (ed.), *Gerichtstag halten über uns selbst ...', Geschichte und Wirkung des ersten Frankfurter Auschwitz-Prozesses*, 61–96, Frankfurt am Main: Campus Verlag.

Steinbacher, Sybille (2005), *Auschwitz: A History*, trans. Shaun Whiteside, London: Penguin.

Steinbacher, Sybille (2020), *Auschwitz: Geschichte und Nachgeschichte*, Munich: Beck.

Steinke, Ronen (2013), *Fritz Bauer, oder Auschwitz vor Gericht*, München: Piper.

Stengel, Katharina (2012), *Hermann Langbein: Ein Auschwitz-Überlebender in den erinnerungspolitischen Konflikten der Nachkriegszeit*, Frankfurt: Campus Verlag.

Stengel, Katharina (2022), *Die Überlebenden vor Gericht: Auschwitz-Häftlinge als Zeugen in NS-Prozessen (1950–1976)*, Göttingen: Vandenhoeck & Ruprecht.

Strothmann, Dietrich (1964), "Das Tribunal der Advokaten," *Die Zeit*, May 8.

Takeda, Kayoko (2010), *Interpreting the Tokyo War Crimes Trial: A Sociopolitical Analysis*, Ottawa: University of Ottawa Press.

Thorne, Benjamin (2021), "Remembering Atrocities: Legal Archives and the Discursive Conditions of Witnessing," *International Journal of Human Rights* 25 (3): 467–90.

Tryuk, Małgorzata (2015), *On Ethics and Interpreters*, Frankfurt am Main: Peter Lang.

Turner, Matthew (2018), *Historians at the Frankfurt Auschwitz Trial: Their Role as Expert Witnesses*, London: I.B Tauris.

Vismann, Cornelia (2019), *Medien der Rechtsprechung*, Frankfurt am Main: Fischer.

Wadensjö, Cecilia (1998), *Interpreting as Interaction*, London: Longman.

Wagner, Julia (2010), "The Truth about Auschwitz: Prosecuting Auschwitz Crimes with the Help of Survivor Testimony," *German History* 28 (3): 343–57.

Wagnerová, Alena, ed. (1993), *Odsunuté Vzpomínky: Z Vyprávění Mých Sudetoněmeckých Generačních Vrstevníků*, Prague: Prostor.

Wamhof, Georg (2009), "Gerichtskultur und NS-Vergangenheit. Performativität – Narrativität—Medialität," in Georg Wamhof (ed.), *Das Gericht als Tribunal oder: Wie der NS-Vergangenheit der Prozess gemacht wurde*, 9–40, Göttingen: Wallstein.

Weinke, Annette (2002), *Die Verfolgung von NS-Tätern im geteilten Deutschland: Vergangenheitsbewältigungen 1949–1969*, Paderborn: Schöningh.

Weinke, Annette (2008), *Eine Gesellschaft ermittelt gegen sich selbst: Die Geschichte der Zentralen Stelle Ludwigsburg 1958–2008*, Darmstadt: Wissenschaftliche Buchgesellschaft.

Weinke, Annette (2009), "Täter, Opfer, Mitläufer. Vermittlungs- und Bewältigungsstrategien in westdeutschen NS-Prozessen," in Georg Wamhof (ed.), *Das Gericht als Tribunal oder: Wie der NS-Vergangenheit der Prozess gemacht wurde*, 55–77, Göttingen: Wallstein.

Wilke, Jürgen, Birgit Schenk, Akiba A. Cohen, and Tamar Zemach (1995), *Holocaust und NS-Prozesse: Die Presseberichterstattung in Israel und Deutschland zwischen Aneignung und Abwehr*, Cologne: Böhlau.

Wilss, Wolfram (1999), *Translation and Interpreting in the 20th Century: Focus on German*, Amsterdam: Benjamins.

Wittmann, Rebecca (2002), "The Wheels of Justice Turn Slowly: The Pretrial Investigations of the Frankfurt Auschwitz Trial 1963–65," *Central European History* 35 (3): 345–78.

Wittmann, Rebecca (2005), *Beyond Justice: The Auschwitz Trial*. Cambridge, MA: Harvard University Press.

Wojak, Irmtrud (1999), "Herrschaft der Sachverständigen? Zum ersten Frankfurter Auschwitz-Prozess," *Kritische Justiz* 32 (4): 605–16.

Wojak, Irmtrud, ed. (2001), *"Gerichtstag halten über uns selbst ..." Geschichte und Wirkung des ersten Frankfurter Auschwitz-Prozesses*, Frankfurt am Main: Campus Verlag.

Wojak, Irmtrud, and Susanne Meinl, eds. (2003), *Im Labyrinth der Schuld: Täter, Opfer, Ankläger*, Frankfurt: Campus Verlag.

Wolf, Michaela, ed. (2016), *Interpreting in Nazi Concentration Camps*, London: Bloomsbury Academic.

Index

www.ingramcontent.com/pod-product-compliance
Ingram Content Group UK Ltd.
Pitfield, Milton Keynes, MK11 3LW, UK
UKHW020220041026
15470UKWH00012B/686

9 781350 469648